Performance
Monitoring

Performance Monitoring

Theodore H. Poister
The Pennsylvania State
University

LexingtonBooks
D.C. Heath and Company
Lexington, Massachusetts
Toronto

Library of Congress Cataloging in Publication Data

Poister, Theodore H.
  Performance monitoring.

  Includes index.
  1. Evaluation research (Social action programs). 2. Administrative agencies—Evaluation. 3. Transportation and state—Evaluation. I. Title.
H62.P574   1982   388.4'068   81–47574
ISBN 0–669–04683–3

Published simultaneously in Canada

Printed in the United States of America

International Standard Book Number: 0–669–04683–3

Library of Congress Catalog Card Number: 81–47574

For my mother (and best fan),
Dorothy B. Poister

Contents

Figures

Tables

Preface and Acknowledgments

This book is an outgrowth of roughly three years of work in developing and refining performance-monitoring tools for the Pennsylvania Department of Transportation, or PennDOT, under Secretary Thomas D. Larson. Monitoring has been around for some time, particularly in the form of purely administrative monitoring as a control mechanism, but the use of true performance monitoring aimed at improving effectiveness and efficiency has not begun to reach its potential in the public sector. The dynamic circumstances surrounding the Department, in which a new administration has been very successfully revitalizing a laggardly and sometimes corrupt organization to improve performance and "do more with less" in the face of tight financial constraints, have provided a rare opportunity to experiment with monitoring tools in a large public-service agency.

Dr. Larson became secretary of PennDOT in January 1979, charged with the responsibility of reversing the continuing deterioration in the Department's operations and the notorious decline in the condition of the state's 45,000-mile highway system. Through a professional engineer's understanding of the technical aspects of transportation problems coupled with strong executive leadership and an unswerving commitment to providing the best possible service to the public, he has effectively met this challenge by improving PennDOT's performance and restoring its credibility. The major accomplishments of Larson's top management team include significant cost savings through reducing the total work force and increasing managerial efficiencies, the elimination of the patronage system in the county highway-maintenance organizations and the corresponding increased professionalization of personnel at various levels, the allocation of more of PennDOT's resources to highway maintenance along with the increased productivity of the maintenance work forces, generally improved highway conditions, the securing of a predictable funding base for the Department, and a dramatic increase in the leveraging of federal funds flowing into Pennsylvania. While the state still faces substantial transportation problems involving highways and other modes, given the resources available along with the legal, economic, and intergovernmental environment within which it operates, the Department has become a very productive organization. In short, PennDOT is now generally recognized as one of the best managed state agencies in Pennsylvania and a leader among state DOTs nationally.

In his previous positions as director of the Pennsylvania Transportation

Institute and chairman of the state's Transportation Advisory Committee, Dr. Larson led a comprehensive review of the Department's fiscal affairs. This review produced recommendations for substantial changes in capital program funding, revenue sources, and the relative priority of highway maintenance as opposed to new construction. In addition, the fiscal-review task force recommended several management strategies including the development of performance indicators and a Department "report card." When Larson became secretary, PennDOT moved quickly to develop and implement performance-monitoring tools in order to support new management initiatives and help gain executive direction over organizational units and programs.

Both the style and substance of the set of management and policy initiatives mentioned above reflect a more general performance ethic that has been instilled in the Department by the current administration for the first time in recent years. This overall performance orientation and the commitment to improving service greatly facilitated the undertaking of this particular project by university researchers working closely with departmental personnel in various positions. In addition to the support of Secretary Larson, the author would like to acknowledge the help of several other individuals from the Department in completing the research project that became the basis for much of this book. These include Kant Rao, former associate deputy secretary for fiscal and systems management; Lou O'Brien, former director of the Bureau of Maintenance; Cal Heinl of the Bureau of Maintenance; Bill Moyer, chief of the Operations Review Group; Ron Helwig of the Operations Review Group; Tom May, former director of the Bureau of Transportation Planning Statistics; George Wass of the Bureau of Planning Statistics; Lou Schultz of the Bureau of Traffic Engineering; and Doug Tobin, director of the Bureau of Motor Vehicles and Licensing.

Several research assistants at Penn State's Institute of Public Administration and the Pennsylvania Transportation Institute contributed significantly to the development of performance indicators and analysis of preliminary data as reported in this book. These include Scott Huebner, Gary Gittings, Kathy Phillips, Cindy Parsons, Nancy Slaybaugh, Jody Lyons and Paul Zvonkovic. Beyond the data-analysis stage, the author is particularly indebted to Nancy Slaybaugh for her insightful critique of draft chapters and suggestions for revisions and to Paul Zvonkovic and Jody Lyons for their careful proofreading and attention to detail. Finally, the author appreciates the competent typing services of Joanne Treaster in quickly turning out draft chapters and a final manuscript. As always, the responsibility for any inaccuracies, omissions, or intemperate judgments rests solely with the author.

1   Introduction

This book concerns the development and use of performance-monitoring systems in government agencies. *Performance monitoring* means the periodic measurement of progress toward explicit short- and long-run objectives and the reporting of the results to decision makers in an attempt to improve program performance. While generally taking an advocacy position on performance monitoring, the book offers a balanced approach, focusing not only on how monitoring systems can help managers make better decisions but also on the kinds of problems that arise in developing and implementing them. In addition, the costs of implementing monitoring systems are discussed as well as the benefits.

This book presents a general approach to developing a performance-monitoring system (PMS) that is applicable to any program area and then illustrates its application in one major transportation agency, the Pennsylvania Department of Transportation (PennDOT). Most of the book deals directly with the development and utility of various monitoring elements used to track the performance of highway and other transportation programs. However, the approach—involving the specification of evaluative criteria and data sources ranging from internal program-operation data to citizen surveys—has a high degree of transferability to other program areas, including human services.

The process of establishing the purposes of a PMS, specifying program objectives and the underlying program logic, developing performance indicators, evaluating existing data bases, initiating new data-collection procedures, and designing data-processing and reporting systems would be remarkably similar for most programs or agencies. In particular, the systems approach to program-performance specification—sorting out inputs and process measures from outcomes, identifying program components and their intended interactions, and specifying the set of means/ends relationships that comprise the program logic—is a generic process that is a necessary step toward improved management and evaluation in most program areas. Similarly, the kinds of problems encountered in this particular effort, involving such disparate factors as incompatibilities among data bases, wariness of possible negative feedback from citizen surveys, organizational resistance to monitoring, and concern over the costs of additional data

1

collection are common to most departments or agencies interested in developing a formal PMS.

This book makes use of many concepts that are common to the design of program evaluations and management-information systems. In addition to explaining how monitoring systems are designed, however, the book emphasizes data analysis and results from the PennDOT illustration in order to show how performance monitoring can be helpful to management at various levels. Presenting real data is critical for conveying an understanding of how a PMS can help management make programs more effective and efficient. Thus the book shows both transportation officials and public administrators in other areas that carefully constructed performance-monitoring systems can be very worthwhile, and it also illustrates how to go about designing and implementing such systems.

Background: Performance Monitoring

Although the professional literature is still fairly sparse, increasing attention is centering on performance monitoring within the field of public administration. Given the difficulties and high costs of conducting intensive program evaluations along with the desire to increase executive control over program administration, there has been a move in practice toward routinizing the tracking and evaluation of program performance, usually at a highly aggregated level. This concept fits well with the general thrust of the management-science approach, including program budgeting, management by objectives, management-information systems, and productivity improvement, all of which are of greater concern given the current context of shrinking resources and cutback management. As indicated by the title of a recent book by Steiss and Daneke, the term "performance administration" is used to characterize this general orientation to public-sector management, and performance monitoring is a core component of this approach.[1]

Monitoring activity is quite prevalent in government agencies and has been for years; almost all large agencies have program-monitoring or financial-monitoring systems in place. Yet the literature on monitoring in the public sector as either a general management function or an evaluation function is by no means abundant. In part, this shortage may be due to confusion over different types of monitoring that go on in public agencies, creating the illusion that performance monitoring is much more prevalent in government than is actually the case. To cut through this confusion, we need to make a distinction between (the more common) *monitoring* or *administrative monitoring* as opposed to true *performance monitoring*. For the purposes of this discussion, *monitoring* refers to reporting systems focusing on descriptive measures of program activities and costs, while *performance monitoring* pertains to those systems that emphasize evaluative measures, especially those related to the program's outcomes.

While the line between the two is sometimes hard to draw, administrative monitoring is concerned first and foremost with the implementation and ongoing administration of programs, and thus falls primarily into the province of management control and management-information systems. On the other hand, performance monitoring focuses on the effectiveness and efficiency of programs (and to a lesser extent on equity and responsiveness), and as such belongs in the realm of evaluation—that is, providing performance feedback to decision makers. Traditionally, much of the monitoring activity in government has *not* been performance oriented. This is particularly true of programs administered with decentralized delivery systems or through the intergovernmental system, with funding agencies or central offices that require grantees or field offices to routinely report data on expenditures, program activities, and numbers and characteristics of program participants.[2] However, with the increasing emphasis on performance and evaluation over the past ten or fifteen years, much of this monitoring activity is evolving into true performance monitoring as effectiveness and efficiency indicators are becoming required.

Current Literature

As evidenced by one of the few contemporary books devoted to the topic, a volume edited by Donald L. Grant, which looks at both public- and private-sector applications but sometimes confuses "monitoring" and "evaluation," the literature on performance monitoring is fairly shallow.[3] There are general texts on management control with chapters on monitoring performance, but these tend to have a narrow accounting orientation and are aimed primarily at business applications.[4] Somewhat more useful are books in the implementation literature or the evaluation literature that focus in part on implementation.[5] However, these treatments are concerned solely with the implementation stage and thus deal with process monitoring but not with outcomes monitoring.

Probably the best overviews of comprehensive performance monitoring are found in *Monitoring for Government Agencies* by Waller et al. and more recently in *Evaluation: Promise and Performance* by Joseph Wholey, both based on extensive work conducted by the Urban Institute.[6] The Wholey book, in particular, is useful here because its treatment of performance monitoring is purposefully set within the context of the overall evaluation process. In fact, the Urban Institute has been on the forefront in producing materials concerning the development of performance-monitoring systems and has published a number of reports on monitoring both the efficiency and effectiveness of the general array of local government programs,[7] as well as monitoring in selected policy areas at the state level.[8] Collectively, these works provide indepth treatment of the development of performance measures. They also discuss the various potential uses of performance-monitoring systems as well as problems and strategies in implementing such systems.[9]

Prevalence and Uses of Performance Monitoring

Outcomes-oriented performance-monitoring systems are possibly most prevalent in local government, particularly in large urban jurisdictions with responsibility for actual service delivery in a whole set of program areas. The District of Columbia, for example, has had a comprehensive performance-monitoring system in operation for several years, which covers administrative functions as well as line agencies. This system incorporates both effectiveness and efficiency indicators, measures progress in all program areas, and as a result of past and current performance, produces recommendations for improving service delivery and general fiscal status.[10] Prodded by the Urban Institute, the National Science Foundation and the International City Managers Association, many local jurisdictions apparently are maintaining some type of performance-monitoring system. Dayton, Ohio, and Dallas, Texas, are two prime examples of cities using a mix of data including citizen surveys to track program performance.[11] Results of a survey taken a few years ago showed that roughly two-thirds or more of all cities responding reported using measures of workload, unit cost or efficiency, or effectiveness measures. Presumably, some of these cities obtain these measures from at least skeletal versions of performance-monitoring systems.[12]

Formal performance-monitoring systems appear to be less prevalent at the state level, although states using budgeting systems such as Planning Programming and Budgeting (PPB) and Zero-Based Budgeting (ZBB) would be using workload and impact measures in a very macro level of performance monitoring. Where states are the direct providers of service, monitoring might be expected to be more established; this is apparently true with respect to mental-health programs[13] but is less true with respect to transportation.[14] Federal agencies support numerous monitoring systems designed to track the implementation and ongoing operation of programs that they fund, many of which are conducted at lower levels of government. While traditionally these reporting systems have focused primarily on process rather than outcome measures, in some cases they include indicators taken to represent the effectiveness of the local program.[15] Within the Department of Health and Human Services (DHHS), there was a movement underway in the Carter administration to develop "program measures" for all programs as the beginning of a comprehensive performance-monitoring effort, but under the Reagan administration that approach has stalled. The demonstration/study of Total Performance Management (TPM) mounted by the General Accounting Office and other federal agencies relied heavily on continuous performance monitoring from a variety of perspectives.[16]

PMS and Program Evaluation

While monitoring systems based on routinely collected and updated indicators of performance serve a number of immediate management functions such as programming and management control, they result in accumulated data bases that can both facilitate specific intensive evaluations and support the evaluation process in general. A distinction between *monitoring* and *evaluation* is in order here. *Performance monitoring* is the periodic observation of effectiveness and efficiency indicators in order to track the progress that a program or system of programs is making in light of specified objectives. As an evaluative function, it is likely to focus on aggregate impact and net effect without tying effects to individual elements or taking environmental shifts into account. The emphasis tends to be on tracking outcomes but not to measure linkages and draw conclusions about cause and effect. *Program evaluation,* on the other hand, focuses first on the program and tries to measure the effects that it is directly producing. As distinguished by Wholey, while performance monitoring tracks indicators to compare actual performance with prior or expected values, an *intensive* evaluation uses more rigorous methodology to determine the extent of causal connection between program activities and apparent results.[17]

Performance monitoring can be an important part of the evaluation process, because it directly provides evaluative findings in a relatively cost-effective way and contributes to other evaluation activities. While performance-monitoring data generated by periodic observation of the same subjects naturally lend themselves to longitudinal approaches to evaluation, particularly time-series analyses, the same data bases actually facilitate evaluations employing a wide range of research designs.[18] These range from simple correlational designs, through quasi-experimental comparison group designs, to the classic experimental pretest-posttest control-group design, depending on the program features under study and the mode of implementation.[19] Moreover, performance monitoring provides support to the overall evaluation process through macro "state-of-the-system" monitoring, the identification of problem areas for further study, the tracking of "environmental" variables that may help interpret evaluation results, exploring linkages among various monitoring data sets, and checking on the plausibility of underlying program logics.

Thus performance monitoring can contribute to the overall evaluation process in a number of ways, from (1) top management's state-of-the-system monitoring, through (2) the provision of accumulating data bases that may meet the needs of set-piece intensive evaluations utilizing a variety of research designs, to (3) providing underlying support for the development of a program of evaluation in terms of thinking through program designs and identifying the need for intensive evaluations. In a period of shrinking resources and cutback management, evaluation can and does become suspect as a relatively superfluous activity that could be reduced or eliminated in the course of "cutting out the fat." On the other hand, it is precisely during such periods when evaluation, if done well, can potentially be most useful, aiding in important decisions about which programs to cut, which to keep, which to de-emphasize, and so on.

Within this context, it is important that the evaluation process itself be cost effective, keying on the most suitable issues, and producing results with practical significance on a timely basis. Performance monitoring can be a useful tool in this regard, both as an evaluative mechanism itself and as an approach to developing more effective evaluation programs. Along these lines, it has been promoted as one stage in a "sequential-purchase-of-information" strategy aimed at maximixing the payoff from resources devoted to the evaluation process.[20]

While conclusions about program performance drawn directly from macro-monitoring data are necessarily somewhat loose in terms of methodological rigor and depend heavily on management's view of the overall institutional and programmatic context, that kind of judgmental interpretation matures with accumulating experience with performance monitoring. More importantly, monitoring can have great utility in this context because it is comprehensive and promotes a global view of performance with the capability of then moving into disaggregate analysis. It can therefore lead to a more effective evaluation process by helping to better target evaluation resources.

PMS and Management Functions

While performance monitoring is primarily an evaluative function, performance-monitoring systems may potentially serve many managerial functions ranging from resource allocation through employee motivation and management control.[21] The city of Dayton, Ohio, for example, uses results from its periodic citizen survey and other monitoring data as a partial basis for managers' promotions and salary increases. The performance indicators developed for PennDOT were initiated as a macro-monitoring tool for the purpose of tracking progress over time, but they serve other specific functions, and new uses evolve as the system matures. For example, data on highway conditions improving or worsening over time serves not only to evaluate past performance but also to assess needs for routine maintenance and betterments programs and as an aid in programming maintenance activities. Used in conjunction with output and efficiency measures collected routinely on maintenance activities—another part of the monitoring system—these data further contribute to the budgeting process. Moreover, the performance indicators serve a management-control function. The entire Department operates on a Management by Objectives (MBO) system, and the monitoring system is used both as a basis for establishing objectives and for determining whether those objectives have been met. In addition, through the use of a "report card," which highlights key performance indicators over time in a format that communicates clearly with external audiences, such as the legislature and the press, the monitoring system plays a role in the Department's public relations. Beyond these functions, the performance-monitoring system does directly serve a program-evaluation function.

Performance monitoring is integral to such representative approaches to modern public-sector management as Planning Programming and Budgeting Systems (PPB), Management by Objectives (MBO) and the Program Evaluation Review Technique (PERT). PPB and other performance-oriented budgeting systems use the financial-management process to gain direction and control over government agencies by allocating funds and controlling expenditures according to programs rather than organizational units.[22] Priorities among programs and activities are derived by establishing objectives and analyzing the amount of output and impact that various programs can be expected to produce at alternative funding levels. PPB is necessarily an accumulative process, with budget allocations in subsequent cycles based on estimates of changing levels of needs for programs, as well as past performance in generating outputs and impacts. This may pertain to allocations within agencies, as well as allocations among major programs and agencies from the viewpoint of the central executive. In any case, a macro-level-monitoring system is clearly necessary to track needs and accomplishments so that financial decision making may be sensitive to past and prospective program performance.

While PPB is very definitely a "top-down" approach to guiding resource allocation, MBO is a participative-management system aimed at directing and controlling an organization by holding managers responsible for the attainment of worthwhile program objectives.[23] Unlike PPB, it encompasses little cumbersome administrative machinery, but it should be viewed as complementary to PPB rather than as a competing alternative management system. Most important for our purposes is that MBO "ensures a control mechanism by providing for feedback and measurement of accomplishment."[24]

By contrast to PPB and MBO, PERT is not an overarching strategy designed to manage organizations through control over programs, but instead is an approach to implementing programs and projects. PERT uses a critical-path methodology based on the establishment of intermediate objectives (milestones) and the time and resource requirements needed to achieve them in an attempt to complete projects or reach the routine operating stage of programs as quickly and efficiently as possible.[25] As implied by its name—Program Evaluation Review Technique—PERT monitors progress toward objectives. Indicators used in the more formative stages of program development and implementation then may be used more regularly to monitor the performance of the ongoing program. Similarly, the term "productivity improvement programs" refers to a rubric of efforts to achieve productivity increases through a variety of technological, managerial, and incentive-type strategies.[26] Invariably, agencies undertaking concerted productivity-improvement programs need some kind of performance monitoring to determine the success of these efforts.

Performance Monitoring and Transportation

A major theme emerging in the literature of the last few years regarding state-highway programs and policy issues concerns the shifting fiscal environment surrounding these programs.[27] Reductions in the flow of money into several states' highway programs, coupled with rising costs and tighter constraints on allocation, have required cutbacks and changes in these programs and, in general, have made programming and budgeting a more critical process. In Pennsylvania, for example, a decrease in real purchasing power and the obligation to fund a growing debt service resulted in inadequate funding for necessary maintenance activities. This forced the temporary curtailment of new construction with first priority being accorded to the maintenance program.[28]

Continued cost inflation and the uncertain effects of the energy crisis on liquid-fuel-tax revenues, along with heightened citizen awareness of transportation costs and services in general, have made state transportation officials more concerned than ever about accountability and the effective use of the resources at their disposal. In earlier periods when funding was plentiful, the major objective was to get new highways built. In these new and still changing circumstances, focus must be on the allocation of scarce resources to maximize the effectiveness of state-highway programs.

Along with programmatic changes, these tighter environmental constraints have prompted greater recognition of the need for strong management tools. Thus maintenance-management, pavement-management, and project-management systems are coming into more widespread use at the program-management level, and more interest is apparent at top policy-making levels in such things as revenue-estimation and priority-programming methods.[30] An integral part of the thrust toward better tools to help management gain more direction and control over programs is the concept of performance monitoring—that is, developing systematic information on the progress and outcomes of program activities. This type of information feedback can be used to assess program effectiveness and, in a formative sense, to suggest ways of improving effectiveness. One report on monitoring the effectiveness of state transportation services suggests several uses of the outcomes data:[31]

1. Review of progress and trends in the provision of transportation services
2. Provide guidance for resource-allocation decisions
3. Budget formulation and justification
4. Indepth program evaluation and program analysis
5. Encourage employee motivation
6. Assess the performance of contractors
7. Provide quality-control checks on efficiency measurements
8. Improve communication between citizens and government officials

As evidence from a different perspective of the importance of performance monitoring to transportation programs, the Federal Highway Administration (FHWA) has recently introduced a system for monitoring the adequacy of the nation's highway system over time.[32] The Highway Performance Monitoring Systems (HPMS) is conducted by state and local transportation and planning agencies for FHWA, and is intended to provide guidance for future federal funding and programming policy, most of which flows through state transportation agencies. In developing performance indicators for a state department of transportation (DOT), therefore, HPMS should be considered as a potential data source given the parallel interests in maintaining and upgrading highway systems.

Elements of a PMS

A system can be thought of as a set of interacting elements working toward the accomplishment of explicit objectives.[33] This "system" aspect of performance monitoring will be discussed more fully later, but it must be stated at the outset that the purpose of performance monitoring is to provide relevant information to decision makers to enable them to take appropriate action to improve program performance. At an intermediate stage, the effectiveness of a performance-monitoring system (PMS) would be indicated by the extent to which the results are reflected in managers' decisions and actions. Ultimately, its impact would be measured by the observable improvement in program performance that can be directly traced to this utilization of PMS results.

A PMS consists of three major components: the data component, the analysis component and the action component.[34] As represented in figure 1-1, these components are logically sequenced, with their particular elements established by management decisions that are part of the monitoring *process* but not part of the performance monitoring *system* itself.[35] Policymakers and managers have responsibility for setting objectives and at least the outline of program elements and strategies aimed at achieving them. Together with evaluators or staff analysts, these policymakers and managers develop a consensus about the kinds of performance indicators to be included in a monitoring system and the intended uses of the PMS.

As shown in figure 1-1, the configuration of the data component will be dictated by the managers' choice of indicators and intended uses. The indicators govern what kinds of data will be routinely collected by the PMS, and the intended uses will determine the frequency and scope (or coverage) of the data input. Even the methodological procedures for operationalizing certain measures will sometimes be strongly influenced by intended uses. Once the data have geen gathered, they need to be processed—usually edited and computerized—before they can move into the analysis component. The purpose of the analysis is to summarize and interpret the data in terms of current performance levels and various types of comparisons. These results then feed into the action component, which should lead to decisions regarding the objectives themselves, program elements and strategies, and subsequent monitoring and evaluation activities. The primary intended outcome of such action is of course improved programs performing at higher levels of effectiveness and efficiency. However, a secondary effect, represented by the feedback loop in figure 1-1, would be changes in the original parameters governing the PMS itself. As the PMS produces results and more is learned about the program and the factors influencing its performance, managers may modify the indicators and specific intended uses of monitoring, with the overall PMS being modified accordingly.

The Data Component

The data component is obviously important because having data that are reliable, valid, and appropriate measures of performance is essential if a PMS is to impact on improved program performance. In addition, data collection and processing require substantial time and effort and typically consume the lion's share of the total cost of implementing a PMS. Thus to be

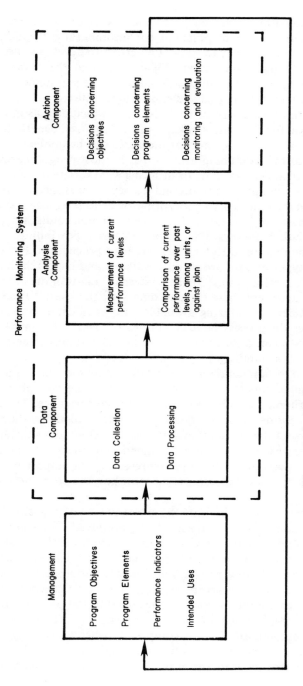

Figure 1-1. Performance-Monitoring-System Logic

cost-effective, the PMS must be geared to the selective acquisition of "good" data with maximum potential for meaningful utilization. Conversely, there is no better way to subvert an effort to develop a monitoring capability than to incur substantial dollar cost—and the organizational strains that sometimes arise from additional reporting requirements—in the collection of data that do not have demonstrable utility.

Given a sound framework of indicators to be included, as opposed to "generating data for the data's sake," the effort may benefit from the multiple uses to which many kinds of measures can be applied. The most striking aspect of the data component is that in most program areas, relevant performance indicators come from such a wide variety of data sources. These range, for example, from internal agency records, accounting data, administrative data reported to sponsoring or central agencies and such, through client-based or "caseload" data, observational counts and physical inspections, to citizen surveys. Each entails different possibilities and constraints and thus requires different measurement procedures. Fortunately, many of these types of data are readily available and incur relatively little additional cost for reformating. While "external" kinds of data are usually desirable to complement these existing data sets, the overall PMS can be made more efficient by utilizing available data as much as possible. Frequently agencies do process large quantities of data with only marginal returns. If a PMS can utilize these particular data sources, there may be mutual benefit all around.

The most important consideration in developing the data component is what kinds of indicators to include, and this in turn depends on what kind of evaluative criteria are to be used to monitor performance. The relevant variables to be considered can be identified through a model of the program logic that explicates the assumptions of cause/effect relationships by which a program is expected to produce its intended impacts.[36] Such a model would include "outcomes" measures representing the impact of the program, as well as "process" measures that show how the program is intended to operate.

Effectiveness measures indicate the extent to which program objectives are being met and how much impact is being produced. These are the most important set of performance indicators to be incorporated in a monitoring system. A comprehensive monitoring system would also encompass key process measures reflecting program activities and outputs. More important, the system might also incorporate measures of efficiency showing the ratios of inputs to outputs, resources consumed to the products resulting. *Internal-operating-efficiency* indicators represent the relationship between costs and the amount of activity completed, whereas *cost-effectiveness* measures relate costs to the direct effects or impacts produced by the program.[37] A PMS that incorporates process and related efficiency measures along with the effectiveness indicators will be more complicated to develop, but it will also be much more useful as a diagnostic tool for suggesting actions for improving program performance.

In a large-scale PMS, the data component consists of numerous data sets that are updated and processed at regular intervals. Each set of measures that forms part of the overall system can be thought of as an element of the PMS, and each of these data sets will have its own collection procedures, processing routines, and schedules. It is by no means necessary that they all be tied to the the same schedule. For some a semi-annual or even annual update may be appropriate, whereas others may warrant weekly or monthly data input, depending on the nature of the measures themselves and the uses to which they would be put. In any case, data processing is usually required to prepare for analysis. This usually includes editing or "cleaning" the data and organizing it into computer files but may also entail manipulating the data into higher levels of aggregation.

The Analysis Component

The analysis component is conceptually the most critical in that raw data are often relatively meaningless in terms of identifying problems or suggesting corrective actions. The data are typically too detailed and disaggregate to present a picture of performance, and looking at data for any one time period or organizational unit seldom provides a frame of reference for interpreting individual numbers as representing good or poor performance. Furthermore, individual indicators often must be related to one another in order to construct performance indicators such as efficiency measures.

The purpose of the analysis component is to distill the data into intelligible form, essentially to translate data into information. In part, this may be a matter of "data reduction," for example, aggregating cases to fewer, larger groups to simplify a review of performance on a practical level that is meaningful to top management. Similarly, the data reduction may consist of combining several indicators into composite measures or indices, again to deemphasize the detail and minutiae and make the data comprehensible.

For the most part, however, the data are made interpretable in a practically significant way by analysis that focuses on performance comparisons. While the data component consist of the activities that make up a PMS, the analysis generates the comparisons that are really the products of the monitoring system. Various benchmarks for comparison are suggested in figure 1-1. Given the function of a PMS to track performance over time, the most natural kind of comparison, and the most frequent, is the comparison of current or most recent performance levels with similar figures for past periods. This facilitates an interpretation of performance in terms of "how well is the program doing relative to this time last year?" and provides a perspective of performance trends over the long run.

A second basis for comparison is an analysis of actual performance levels as opposed to planned or budgeted amounts. Regardless of past performance, targets may have been set for the current or most recent period that were thought to be reasonably attainable. This "actual-versus-plan" kind of comparison then provides a very direct indication of how well managers and/or programs are performing. A related basis for comparison examines actual performance against some specified standard. Evaluating the quality of outputs, for instance, might be based on a comparison against some stated standard operating procedure, while efficiency could be evaluated by comparing actual output against the amount of output that would be expected given a standard of "X number of units of output per staff week," and so forth.

Finally, managers often find it useful to have performance evaluated in terms of comparisons among geographic or organizational units. Such cross-sectional comparisons may involve only the most recent time period or may actually consist of comparing trends or changes in performance among these decentralized units. On the one hand, these kinds of comparisons may serve to explain macro-performance trends, for example, marginal improvement overall turning out to be the net effect of substantial improvement in some areas or units diluted by lack of improvement or retrogression in others. Furthermore, when operating responsibilities are decentralized to regional or organizational units, performance trends at this level are directly relevant to top management.

Whatever the frame of reference—over time among units, or against plan—care must be exercised in interpreting the results. As discussed earlier in this chapter, performance monitoring is different from intensive evaluation in a very fundamental way. Since indicators are being monitored but not intensively analyzed as a rule, the underlying cause/effect patterns are not always apparent. While the results do often directly represent the outcomes of program strategies, many other factors come into play. These so-called environmental factors that are not part of the program itself but rather characterize the contest within which it operates may also be shifting over time or account for basic performance differentials among geographic or organizational units. Therefore, external factors should be taken into account where practical, and judgment must be used in actually assessing performance on the basis of selected indicators.

The Action Component

The "action component" refers to management's use of the performance-monitoring system. If the data collection incorporates the most appropriate indicators of performance and the analysis focuses on the most relevant comparisons, then the results—positive or negative—should be relevant to top executives and program managers. The overriding purpose of a PMS is to supply relevant information to enhance decision making in order to improve program performance. While the results produced by the analysis component constitute the direct products of a PMS, decisions made by management that are based partially or in full on these results represent the outcomes of the PMS. The impact of the monitoring system then is measured by the degree to which the performance-oriented information it generates is reflected in subsequent decisions about the program, and ultimately in the extent to which such decisions result in improved effectiveness and efficiency.

The types of decisions prompted by the results of monitoring concern program objectives, program elements of strategies, and the monitoring and evaluation process. They do not necessarily involve policy shifts or decisions to change programs. When results are uniformly positive, this tends to reinforce policies already in effect and generally would be interpreted as supporting a "decision" to continue on the same course. This is not a nondecision, but rather reflects a management-by-exception approach in which standing decisions are left in force unless challenged by negative results. Positive results, however, may prompt more proactive decisions along the lines of giving greater priority or increased financial support to programs or intervention strategies that appear to be working well.

By contrast, negative results reflecting poor performance usually suggest the need for change, or at least looking into whether or not alternative approaches are in order. At the risk of oversimplification, the kinds of decisions suggested by negative feedback tend to fall into the following four categories:

Modify program objectives and/or standards

Modify program activities and/or pursue alternative strategies

Undertake intensive evaluation

Change the measures included in the PMS

The possibility of changing program objectives as a valid response to negative results should not be overlooked. Performance monitoring implies the use of "performance targeting" as a strategy for productivity improvement, whether in support of a formal management system such as PPB or MBO or not.[38] What needs to be understood is that monitoring contributes to such systems by keying in two ways on the use of explicit objectives. Not only does the monitoring track performance to determine whether objectives are being achieved, it also provides a frame of reference that can be helpful in establishing objectives in the first place or modifying them later on. The data base that accumulates with an ongoing monitoring system can provide a basis for assessing the magnitude of needs and the severity of problems, and comparisons of progress over time and across units may help gain insight into how much improvement can be reasonably expected. In some instances, continuing failure to attain objectives may lead to the conclusion that the objectives themselves are the problem—unrealistically ambitious, collectively inconsistent, or not worthwhile in relation to costs. This applies to work standards concerning efficiency. Thus negative results may lead to decisions to modify the specifics in certain objectives or to shift priorities among them.

The most frequent kind of decision triggered by negative feedback concerns a change in program activities or intervention strategies. When it is clear that objectives are not being met, the reasons why can sometimes be tracked to program failure or theory failure.[39] Briefly, if the program has not been implemented correctly, or if ongoing activities are not being conducted as planned, the problem is program failure. This would suggest a need to remedy these problems so that the program operates according to plan and then check to see if effectiveness improves. This is probably the most typical kind of corrective action arising in a PMS. On the other hand, if program routines are operating according to plan but objectives are still not being met, then theory failure is indicated—that is, that the underlying logic of the program strategy for accomplishing those ojectives is faulty in some way. This would signal a need to overhaul the program activities in a managerial sense as much as to rethink the intervention strategy on which these activities are based. Thus one important kind of decision concerns shifting to alternative means for moving towards the same objectives. As will become clear later in this book, isolating the sources of poor overall performance requires that process measures be monitored along with effectiveness indicators.

Other decisions concern the monitoring and evaluation process itself. While the action component refers to devising and implementing remedies for improving program performance, these changes may not be suggested directly by the results of the PMS. More often, these results will identify problems but not provide clear solutions. In such circumstances, the main outcome of the monitoring may be to prompt the undertaking of an intensive evaluation designed to probe the reasons for poor performance and develop corrective action. In this mode, performance monitoring is part of a larger "sequential-purchase-of-information" strategy in which the evaluation resources of an agency are targeted to the most pressing and potentially most promising issues.[40] Finally, negative performance-monitoring results that are totally at odds with other signals indicating strong performance may raise the issue of whether the problem lies with measurement instead of actual performance. If the validity or reliability of the indicators is questionable, then the results may be a decision to change the measures used in the PMS and monitor further to check the congruence.

In practice, these different decision situations are not always as clearly differentiated as the preceding categorization might suggest. Indicators of poor performance might not make it clear whether the diffuculty lies primarily with the objectives, the program configuration, or the measures used. In this context, it is important to remember that a PMS generates evidence that accumulates over time. Given difficulty in sorting out explanations for poor performance, one pragmatic approach is to "wait and see" as the data acquire more stability. Furthermore, the ongoing nature of performance monitoring allows or encourages "experimenting" loosely with programs and measures in an attempt to better understand how to improve performance.

Performance-Monitoring Systems

The word *system* really has two different connotations within the context of managing public programs, concerning structure and function. First, we can think of an agency or a program design as a system, a goal-seeking entity composed of various interacting parts. Second, we think of a system as a method or a methodological way of proceeding as opposed to a process of going through repetitive routines without direction or purpose. Performance-monitoring systems reflect both of these meanings. A well-designed PMS is an organized and routinized set of activities constituting a coherent enterprise in which data collection, analysis, and action are the primary components. It is also a systematic, methodical tool aimed at basing program and policy decisions in part on observed performance as opposed to ad hoc considerations.

Performance-monitoring systems should not be confused with management-information systems (MIS), a generic tool consisting of "an integrated, man/machine system for providing information to support the operations, management, and decision-making functions in an organization. The [MIS] utilizes computer hardware and software, manual procedures, management and decision models, and a data base."[41] The development of an MIS may emphasize housekeeping functions, data-bank management, model building, or process control. However, the intended use from a management perspective is to provide relevant information to appropriate levels of management to aid decision making with regard to analysis, policymaking, program management, operating control, and planning.[42]

An MIS is a data-processing and information management tool that may or may not directly involve performance monitoring.[43] There is a two-directional relationship between these systems in that a performance-monitoring effort is likely to both draw from existing MISs for data input and utilize MIS in order to be activated. Large agencies often maintain numerous management-information systems geared to different decision-making processes, and data from these may be extracted and reformated if necessary to feed into the performance-monitoring system. This is simply an efficient use of data-collection resources. Moreover, the performance-monitoring system itself may well be embodied in an MIS; the data-collection and -analysis components are very likely to be operationalized by a computerized MIS aimed at feeding information (not raw data) into the action component at requisite time intervals.

Purpose and Approach

The immediate concern of this book is the development and utilization of performance-monitoring systems (PMS) for state transportation programs. It is based on a project conducted by the author for the Pennyslvania Department of Transportation, which was designed to apply state-of-the-art management technology to help gain direction and control over ongoing programs. This work draws on the experience of other states as well as currently evolving approaches to performance measurement and evaluation, and thus should be of generalized interest to a fairly broad audience.

The primary purpose of the book is to present a systematic approach to developing performance-monitoring systems and to illustrate its application in one major transportation agency. Implicitly the book is intended to help make the case for the potential of performance monitoring in government by illustrating the varied uses that can be made of performance-monitoring systems. The particular PMS discussed in this book is designed to contribute to a number of functions, including needs assessment, programming, budgeting, program evaluation, and management control.

PennDOT

More than either the federal or local levels of government, the states have the major responsibility for transportation programs, and the Pennsylvania Department of Transportation (PennDOT) is itself a noteworthy case study. The Department is responsible for some 45,000 miles of highway—one of the largest and most difficult networks in the country to maintain—and has also been a leader in innovative transit programming.[44] It is indeed a major transportation agency, with roughly 15,000 employees and an annual operating budget on the order of $1.5 billion. By reputation, Pennsylvania has one of the worst highway systems in the nation—it is sometimes referred to as the "pothole capital of the world"—and according to *Engineering News Record,* in 1979 this situation appeared to have passed the point of no return: "Pennsylvania's highway system is marked by such disrepair, disrepute, and disarray that restoration seems all but impossible."[45]

After years of policies that emphasized new construction at the expense of maintaining existing roads, the highways and many of the state's bridges had deteriorated to a deplorable state; the Federal Highway Administration estimated that 29 percent of Pennsylvania's bridges were outdated and were candidates for collapse without major rehabilitation efforts. There was a legitimate question as to whether the entire system was indeed "unmanageable," as 13,000 of the 45,000 miles were basically local-use roads that should not really be the responsibility of the state government.[46] In addition, PennDOT's work force had become overgrown, largely as a result of the patronage system, and employees were generally characterized by low productivity and low morale. Futhermore, PennDOT was plagued with corruption, waste, and abuse, and the overall situation was summed up during the most recent gubernatorial campaign as a Department characterized chiefly by "patronage, payoffs, and potholes."[47]

The situation is dynamic, however, in that the current administration of Governor Dick Thornburgh came into office determined to turn the Department around. The new theme became "service and credibility," and the new top-management team in PennDOT is known in the profession for its performance orientation and the use of sophisticated management technology. PennDOT is now committed to increasing productivity and thereby improving its effectiveness through a set of policy shifts aimed at "doing more with less." Through a number of actions aimed at reducing the overall complement of employees, increasing production quantity and quality, cutting expenses and building better management systems, the new administration is intent on improving service delivery in an era of reduced resources.[48] Thus PennDOT is a perfect model for illustrating the development of a PMS, given the obvious need for improved performance and a general management philosophy that is consistent with this approach.

Analytical Approach

The overall objective of the project that provides most of the material in this book was to develop a comprehensive set of performance indicators for all of the Department's major programs so that management can stay well informed as to what is being accomplished with monies being spent.[49] A monitoring system for the highway program was undertaken first because it is by far the biggest and most complicated program and has clear priority in terms of top management's objectives.

The performance indicators were developed with a dual purpose keyed to different levels of intended use. First, much of the data will be used to provide various levels of management with information to help them operate programs more effectively. Second, stemming from the "report-card" concept proposed by an earlier fiscal review,[50] the system is being designed to communicate selected key indicators to external audiences such as the legislature, the Office of Budget and Administration, and the public to document the Department's track record. The two are closely related in that the internal management uses require the processing of substantial amounts of data—much of it readily available—in order to build a sufficient information base for analyzing performance and recommending program adjustments. The indicators to be reported to external audiences will be skimmed off the top of this data base as general, highly aggregated measures; this would not be possible if the detailed data were not in place.

Implementing and maintaining a performance-monitoring system begins with developing data sources, and moves through data collection and analysis to the presentation of findings to intended users.[51] The basic approach to developing a monitoring system should proceed through the following five steps:

1. Identify the program's objectives and outline the program design; how is it supposed to operate and what is it supposed to accomplish?
2. Given objectives and program rationale, determine what kinds of measures would be most suitable as performance indicators.
3. Identify potential data sources within and outside the Department and assess their quality and appropriateness.
4. Where feasible, begin data processing and/or reformating to obtain initial output, and assess the appropriateness and workability of those particular indicators.
5. Refine these data elements and develop the overall performance-monitoring system in terms of data processing, analysis, reporting formats and frequencies, channels of communication, and intended use.

The primary strategy employed was to rely on existing departmental data bases as much as possible. State DOT's generate vast quantities of data and typically maintain many large record-keeping systems. Often there are few linkages among them; separate data banks with incompatible formats are used by different organizational units, and there is little exchange or integration of information. Part of the effort lies in evaluating the potential worth of existing data sources and ways of improving the utilization of information they contain. Where necessary, however, new data-collection procedures have been devised, as discussed below.

The development and evaluation of specific measures was based on the following considerations: (1) reliability—how dependable and consistent are the procedures for collecting data; (2) validity—how accurately and directly does the proposed measure represent that aspect of performance being examined; and (3) sensitivity—how responsive is the measurement scale to what may be small but real changes in actual performance as opposed to the influence of environmental shifts?

Outline of the Book

The chapters of this book describe in some detail the development of performance-monitoring systems for PennDOT, centering particularly on the highway programs, and present results from some of the components that have been implemented. Following the steps identified previously, chapter 2 discusses a systems approach to explicating the underlying logic of programs and develops the overarching model of the highway programs that serves as a conceptual framework for most of the rest of the book. The model incorporates both the process side and the effectiveness side of the program logic. Chapter 3 then elaborates the process side of the model, using measures of resources and outputs and illustrates the kinds of efficiency comparisons that can help management bring program operation under control.

Chapter 4 moves beyond program activities and work completed to the effects on highway condition itself. A trained-observer survey of road conditions is developed that has numerous managerial uses in addition to tracking the Department's progress in maintaining or upgrading highway conditions over time. Chapter 5 presents findings from the first few cycles of this condition survey, and shows how the results can provide a basis for decisions to improve program performance. Chapter 6 then turns to elaborating the effectiveness side of the model developed in chapter 2 and discusses the use of a variety of data sources to track the impact of programs.

Following this piecing out of a highway program performance-monitoring system, chapter 7 presents a parallel model for tracking the performance of the state's mass-transit programs. This area is fundamentally different from the highway programs in that the state supports rather than operates local-transit systems. Chapter 8 discusses the development and results of the piloting of a large-scale statewide citizen survey aimed at making available to decision makers "external" feedback from citizens to complement the more immediate program operation and condition data discussed earlier. Finally, chapter 9 discusses barriers and strategies concerning the implementation of performance-monitoring systems and draws some conclusions about the state of the art, the costs, and the usefulness of instituting and maintaining this kind of management tool.

Notes

1. A.W. Steiss and G.A. Daneke, *Performance Administration* (Lexington, Mass.: Lexington Books, D.C. Heath, 1980), p. 2.

2. J.D. Waller, D.M. Kemp, J.W. Scanlon, F. Tolson, and J.S. Wholey, *Monitoring for Government Agencies* (Washington, D.C.: Urban Institute, 1976).

3. Donald L. Grant, *Monitoring Ongoing Programs* (San Francisco: Jossey-Bass, 1978).

4. Joseph A. Maciariello, *Program Management Control Systems* (Wiley, 1978); Robert N. Anthony and Regina Herzlinger, *Management Control In Nonprofit Organizations* (Irwin, 1980).

5. L.L. Morris and C.T. Fitz-Gibbon, *How to Measure Program Implementation* (Beverly Hills, Calif.: Sage, 1978); W. Williams and R.F. Elmore, eds., *Social Program Implementation* (New York: Academic, 1976); P.H. Rossi, H.E. Freeman, and S.R. Wright, *Evaluation: A Systematic Approach* (Beverly Hills, Calif.: Sage, 1979).

6. J.D. Waller, et al., *Monitoring for Government Agencies* (Washington, D.C.: Urban Institute, 1976); Joseph S. Wholey, *Evaluation: Promise and Performance,* (Washington, D.C.: Urban Institute, 1979), chap. IV.

7. H.P Hatry, S.N. Clarren, T. van Houten, J.P. Woodward, and P.A. Don Vito, *Efficiency Measurement for Local Government Services* (Washington, D.C.: Urban Institute, 1979); H.P. Hatry, L.H. Blair, D.M. Fisk, J.M. Greiner, J.R. Hall, Jr., and P.S. Schaenman, *How Effective Are Your Community Services?* (Washington, D.C.: Urban Institute, 1977).

8. A.H. Schainblatt, *Monitoring the Outcomes of State Mental Health Treatment Programs* (Washington, D.C. Urban Institute, 1977); A.H. Schainblatt, *Monitoring the Outcomes of State Chronic Disease Control Programs* (Washington, D.C.: Urban Institute, 1977); L.H. Blair, H.P. Hatry, K. Bunn, L. Stevens, and K. Parker, *Monitoring the Impacts of Prison and Parole Services* (Washington, D.C.: Urban Institute, 1977); A. Millar, H. Hatry, and M. Koss, *Monitoring the Outcomes of Social Services* (Washington, D.C.: Urban Institute, 1977).

9. The Urban Institute works most closely related to the system overviewed here are *The Status of Productivity Measurement in State Government,* prepared for the National Center for Productivity and Quality of Working Life, Department of Health, Education and Welfare and U.S. Department of Transportation (Washington, D.C.: Urban Institute, Sep-

tember 1975); J.M Greiner, J.R. Hall, Jr., H.P. Hatry, and P.S. Schaenman, *Monitoring the Effectiveness of State Transportation Services,* prepared for the U.S. Department of Transportation, DOT-TPI-10-77-23 (Washington, D.C.: Urban Institute, July 1977).

10. *Improving Program Performance,* District of Columbia Government Report for Fiscal Year 1977 (District of Columbia Government, Executive Office of the Mayor, January 1978).

11. See *1979 Program Strategies: Policy, Budget Objectives,* Office of Management and Budget, Dayton, Ohio; 1978 Dallas City Profile: Results and Findings, Office of Management Services, Dallas, Tex.

12. Rackham S. Fukuhara, "Productivity Improvement in Cities," *The Municipal Year Book* (Washington, D.C.: International City Management Association, 1977), chap. E-3, pp. 193–200.

13. C. Windle and S.S. Sharfstein, "Three Approaches to Monitoring Mental Health Services," *New Directions for Program Evaluation* 3 (1978): 45–62.

14. J.M. Greiner, J.R. Hall, Jr., H.P. Hatry, and P.S. Schaenman, *Monitoring the Effectiveness of State Transportation Services.*

15. See, for example, the Section 15 reporting requirements established by the Urban Mass Transportation Act of 1964, as amended.

16. *Total Performance Management: Some Pointers for Action,* prepared by the National Center for Productivity and Quality of Working Life in cooperation with the Office of Policy Development and Research, U.S. Department of Housing and Urban Development and the U.S. General Accounting Office (Washington, D.C.: Government Printing Office, 1978).

17. Wholey, *Evaluation: Promise and Performance,* p. xiv.

18. Theodore H. Poister, "Performance Monitoring in the Evaluation Process" (Paper delivered at the Third Annual Conference of the Association for Public Policy Analysis and Management, Washington, D.C., October 1981).

19. See Theodore H. Poister, *Public Program Analysis: Applied Research Methods* (Baltimore: University Park Press, 1978), chap. 7, for explanation of these alternative research designs.

20. Wholey, *Evaluation: Promise and Performance.*

21. Hatry, Blair, Fisk, Greiner, Hall, and Schaenman, *How Effective Are Your Community Services?,* pp. 195–199.

22. For general reference to the development of program budgeting systems, see Robert D. Lee, Jr., and Ronald W. Johnson, *Public Budgeting Systems* (Baltimore: University Park Press, 1977), chaps. 4 and 5; Fremont J. Lyden and Ernest G. Miller, *Public Budgeting: Program Planning and Evaluation* (Chicago: Rand McNally College Publishing, 1978).

23. Rodney H. Brady, "MBO Goes to Work in the Public Sector," *Harvard Business Review,* March–April 1973, pp. 65–74; George L. Morrisey, *Management by Objectives and Results in the Public Sector* (Reading,

Mass.: Addison-Wesley, 1976); George S. Odiorne, "MBO in State Government," *Public Administration Review* 36 (January–February 1976): 28–33.

24. Bruce H. DeWoolfson, Jr., "Public Sector MBO and PPB: Cross Fertilization in Management Systems," *Public Administration Review* 35 (July–August 1975):387–395.

25. For general discussion of the Program Evaluation Review Technique (PERT), see Jack Byrd, Jr., *Operations Research Models for Public Administration* (Lexington, Mass.: Lexington Books, D.C. Heath, 1975), chap. 3; Christopher K. McKenna, *Quantitative Methods for Public Decision Making* (New York: McGraw-Hill, 1980), chap. 12.

26. John M. Greiner, Harry P. Hatry, Margo P. Koss, Annie P. Millar, and Jane P. Woodward, *Productivity and Motivation: A Review of State and Local Government Initiatives* (Washington, D.C.: Urban Institute, 1981); Research and Policy Committee of the Committee for Economic Development, *Improving Productivity in State and Local Government* (New York: Committee for Economic Development, 1976); Fukuhara, "Productivity Improvement in Cities"; Richard F. Keevey, "State Productivity Improvements: Building on Existing Strengths," *Public Administration Review* 40 (September–October 1980):451–458.

27. Heinz Heckeroth, "The Changing California Highway Program," *Transportation Research Record,* No. 654 (Washington, D.C.: Transportation Research Board, 1979), pp. 23–27; also see Marshall F. Reed, Jr., "Transportation Programming in Today's Rapidly Changing Fiscal Environment," *Transportation Research Record,* No. 680 (1979); pp. 20–22; also see R.D. Juster and W.M. Pecknold, "Improving the Process of Programming Transportation Investments," *Transportation Research Record,* No. 599 (1976), pp. 19–24; also see Ronald R. Knox, Theodore K. Martin, and William J. Yuskus, "Programming Highway Improvements in the New Funding Environment," *Transportation Research Record,* No. 599 (1976), pp. 7–12.

28. T.H. Poister, T.D. Larson, and S. Rao, "Fiscal Planning and Highway Programming: The Pennsylvania Response to a Changing Environment," *Transportation Research Record,* No. 654 (Washington, D.C.: Transportation Research Board, 1977), pp. 16–22; S. Rao et al., "New Directions for PennDOT: A Fiscal Review," Pennsylvania Transportation Institute, University Park, Pa., PTI 7616, October 1976.

29. See set of articles in "Maintaining Decision Making and Energy Use, Roadside and Pavement Management, and Preferential Bridge Icing," *Transportation Research Record,* No. 674 (Washington, D.C.: Transportation Research Board, 1978). Also see W.R. Hudson, R. Haas, and R. Daryl Pedigo, *Pavement Management System Development,* National Cooperative Highway Research Program Report 215 (1979), and Mohamed Y.

Shahin, *Components of a Pavement Maintenance Management System* (U.S. Army Construction Engineering Research Laboratory, Champaign, Ill., 1980).

30. J.H. Batchelder, et al, "Applications of the Highway Investment Analysis Package," *Transportation Research Record,* No. 698 (Washington, D.C.: Transportation Research Board, 1979), pp. 1–5; also see the article by C.V. Zegeer and R.L. Rizenbergs, "Priority Programming for Highway Reconstruction," *Transportation Research Record,* No. 698 (1979), pp. 15–23; "Evaluating Options in Statewide Transportation Planning/Programming: Techniques and Applications," National Cooperative Highway Research Program Report No. 199, Transportation Research Board, March 1979; S.J. Bellomo et al., "Evaluation and Application of a Priority Programming System in Maryland," *Transportation Research Record* No 680 (1978), pp. 8–15.

31. *Monitoring the Effectiveness of State Transportation Services,* DOT-TPI-10-77-23, pp. 3–6.

32. *Highway Performance Monitoring System: Field Implementation Manual,* U.S. Department of Transportation, Federal Highway Administration, Program Management Division, Washington, D.C., January 1979.

33. C.W. Churchman, *The Systems Approach* (New York: Dell, 1968).

34. Stan Altman, "Performance Monitoring Systems for Public Managers," *Public Administration Review* 39 (January–February 1979):31–35.

35. Wholey, *Evaluation: Promise and Performance,* pp. 117–119.

36. Poister, *Public Program Analysis: Applied Research Methods,* chap. 2.

37. These and other evaluative criteria are discussed more fully in Poister, *Public Program Analysis: Applied Research Methods,* chap. 1.

38. John M. Greiner, Harry P. Hatry, Margo P. Koss, Annie P. Millar, and Jane P. Woodward, *Productivity and Motivation: A Review of State and Local Government Initiatives,* chaps. 8–12.

39. Carol H. Weiss, *Evaluation Research: Methods of Assessing Program Effectiveness* (Englewood Cliffs, N.J.: Prentice-Hall, 1972), pp. 38–39; see also Poister, *Public Program Analysis: Applied Research Methods.*

40. Wholey, *Evaluation: Promise and Performance.*

41. Gordon B. Davis, *Management Information Systems: Conceptual Foundations, Structure, and Development* (New York: McGraw-Hill, 1974), p. 5.

42. Kenneth L. Kraemer and John Leslie King, *Computers and Local Government Volume 1, A Manager's Guide* (New York: Praeger, 1977), chap. 1.

43. For general references on MIS, see S. Atre, *Data Base: Structured Techniques for Design, Performance, and Management* (New York: Wiley-

Interscience, 1980); Gordon B. Davis and Gordon C. Everest, *Readings in Management Information Systems* (New York: McGraw-Hill, 1976); K.J. Radford, *Information Systems for Decision Systems* (Reston, Va.: Reston Publishing, 1978); Kenneth L. Kraemer, William H. Dutton, and Alana Northrop, *The Management of Information Systems* (New York: Columbia University Press, 1981).

44. V.R. Vuchic, E.L. Tennyson, and W.C. Underwood, "Application of Guidelines for Improving Transit Service and Operating Efficiency," *Transportation Research Record,* No. 519 (Washington, D.C: Transportation Research Board, 1974), pp. 66–72; Theodore H. Poister and Thomas D. Larson, "Administering State Mass Transportation Programs in Pennsylvania," *Transportation Research Record,* No. 603 (1976), pp. 1–7.

45. As quoted by Secretary Thomas D. Larson in an address before the National Conference on Local Transportation of the American Road and Transportation Builders Association, Pittsburgh, Pa. (October 1979).

46. Theodore H. Poister and Thomas D. Larson, "The Return of State Highways to Local Government," Pennsylvania Transportation Institute, University Park, Pennsylvania, PTI 7426, December 1974; Srikanth Rao and Thomas D. Larson, "Rationalizing the State Highway System: A Study of Transferring Some Roads to Local Governments," Pennsylvania Transportation Institute, University Park, Pa., PTI 7718, September 1977.

47. Repeated by Secretary Thomas D. Larson in an address before the 68th General Assembly of Boroughs, Hershey, Pa. (June 1979).

48. J.I. Scheiner, "Productivity Improvement in the Pennsylvania Department of Transportation," *Public Productivity Review* 5, no. 1 (March 1981):14–20; Scott Kutz, "Programmed Project Management in Pennsylvania: Statewide Data Access," (Paper delivered to the 60th Annual Meeting of the Transportation Research Board, Washington, D.C., January 1981).

49. Theodore H. Poister, "Development of Performance Indicators for the Pennsylvania Department of Transportation," in *Public Productivity Review* (forthcoming); also see Pennsylvania Transportation Institute, PTI 8012, University Park, Pa., September 1980.

50. *New Directions for PennDOT: A Fiscal Task Force Review,* Pennsylvania Department of Transportation, Harrisburg, Pa., April 1976, p. 16.

51. Wholey, *Evaluation: Promise and Performance,* p. 137.

2

Model Development

Since the purpose of performance monitoring is to track program operations and accomplishments over time, it is important to begin with a clear understanding of the program itself: what it is, how it works, and what it is supposed to be producing. Thus the first step in developing a PMS is to construct a sound model of the overall program design to which the subsequent development and analysis of performance indicators will be keyed. As indicated in chapter 1, this means identifying the program's objectives and outlining the overall rationale of what the program consists of and how it is expected to operate to pursue these objectives.

This model-development stage is critical because it identifies those important facets of program performance that should be included in a monitoring system. The model is a simplified representation—usually in diagrams with supporting narrative—of the program design, showing its major elements along with their intended products and some indication of the logical linkages by which they are supposed to accomplish their objectives. Many public programs are necessarily complex in terms of both operations and underlying logic, and it is easy to get bogged down in the detail of routine operations at the expense of the real purpose. Developing an overall program model takes a more global view toward outlining the program logic spanning from operations to final impacts, although this is often followed up with more specific models of particular components.

Summarizing an overall program design in a model entails the identification of the critical variables, the roles they play and the presumed cause/effect relationship among them, all of which describe *what* the program is intended to accomplish and *how* it is expected to do so. While this process may appear to be a simple exercise of reducing an obvious reality to a few charts, in practice it is often not so easy. In fact, one of the major barriers to conducting worthwhile program evaluations has been found to be the absence of a common understanding of what the underlying program logic is.[1] There is a tendency in large organizations managing complex programs to lose sight of long-range purpose in favor of short-term objectives and to overemphasize immediate managerial objectives at the expense of real impacts. Thus thinking through—or in some cases, reconstructing—a comprehensive program logic in order to develop the model may be healthy in its own right in terms of restoring a proper perspective on what performance really is or should be.

At any rate, building the model is a crucial step in the development of a performance-monitoring system because it provides the basic framework for determining what aspects of program operations and performance should be examined, what kinds of indicators need to be monitored and how they should be analyzed. If there is not a good fit between the model and reality—if the model is not accurate in terms of what the program is or if it is not plausible with respect to intended means/ends relationships— then a lot of effort may later be wasted in the collection, analysis, and reporting of information that will not be able to contribute significantly to improved program performance.

The Systems Approach

The most direct way of describing a program design—what goes into it, how it operates, and what is supposed to come out of it—is to outline it as a goal-seeking system.[2] Any public program should be designed to accomplish certain specified objectives, producing real physical, economic, social, or attitudinal changes out in the environment. Thus specifying a program's design is a matter of identifying its inputs, components, or activities, outputs, intermediate results, and intended effects as they all relate to the underlying program logic of how the objectives are expected to be accomplished. In the case of the Pennsylvania Department of Transportation, the overriding objective is quite clear; the legislation that created the Department in 1970 states that it is responsible for providing "fast, safe and efficient transportation."[3]

Developing the model of the major program variables and the relationships among them is greatly facilitated by sorting through the myriad factors that might be relevant to differentiate among a few major categories of variables that play different roles in the overall program logic. Figure 2-1 is an abstract systems model showing the major features of a program's design and underlying logic. When the variables that are obviously relevant to program operation and performance are organized according to this model, either the program logic emerges or gaps in the logic are identified. When the latter occurs, the partially completed model at least serves to focus questions about the validity of assumptions underlying logic. The major features of this program/systems model are briefly described here with reference to a highway program.[4]

Inputs or Resources

The inputs into the program are resources in the form of personnel, materials, equipment and facilities and other expenses that are consumed by the

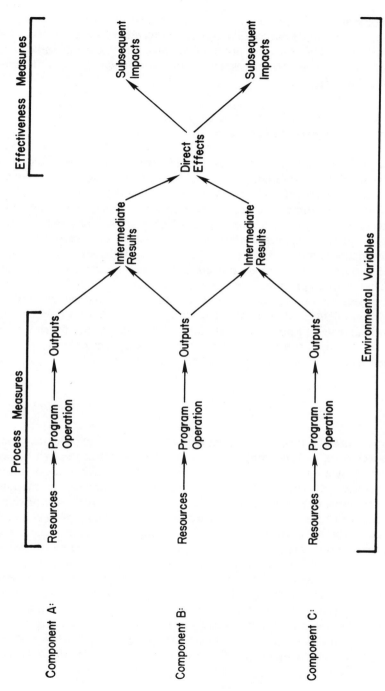

Figure 2-1. Program-Logic Systems Model

program operations. These resources can all be measured in their own natural units, but for some purposes it is more convenient to convert them all into dollar terms. The resources going into a program are prime indicators of level of effort and are also necessary in conjunction with other indicators for monitoring efficiency.

Components, Elements, and Activities

Complex programs are often structured in hierarchies of systems and subsystems that might be thought of as consisting of programs, components, elements, and activities. Components are basically subsystems of the larger program or system and are geared to more specific objectives that contribute to accomplishing the program's overall objectives. For example, the highway-construction program consists of new construction, reconstruction and betterments components. Each component and element can be elaborated if necessary, in terms of objectives, resources, activities, and outputs. They may also produce separate intermediate results or direct effects or their objectives may converge at these points. The indicators used to identify components and elements or to describe the activities they consist of are called *program-operation variables*. Performance monitoring may emphasize individual components, elements, and activities or may be more concerned with their interaction and combined impacts.

Outputs

The outputs are the most direct products of program components. They often reflect workload measures of amounts of programmed activity completed, and they are usually the best indicators of how much work or activity has been conducted under various program components. In human-service programs, output is usually measured by unit of treatment or some other indicator of the amount of service provided. Outputs represent a critical point in the program logic because, although they do not have any inherent value, they are necessary to trigger some causal sequence in the environment by which the desired effects are expected to materialize.

Frequently outputs can be represented either with more of a cost orientation or a product orientation. For example, the output of a resurfacing activity might well be the number of lane miles resurfaced indicating how much work was completed. Alternatively, the output might be measured by how many gallons of material were placed on the surface, which would depend on both the lane miles resurfaced and the thickness of the overlays.

Each version may be useful for certain purposes, but in general, the more product-oriented expression of outputs is preferred.

Intended Effects or Impacts

Programs are designed to meet specified objectives that usually refer to target areas or target populations in the field outside the program and agency themselves. These direct effects are tangible, observable improvements in the environment of a physical, economic, social, or psychological nature. The benefits that accrue with the accomplishment of these objectives are the justification for the program in the first place, and thus measuring the effects of immediate objectives as well as possible further impacts is at the heart of performance monitoring. The overall objective from which the impacts of the highway program are derived has been established above as the provision of fast, safe, and efficient transportation. An example of a subsequent impact would be an improved economic climate to which improved transportation will contribute.

Intermediate Results

Frequently the logic that connects a program's outputs with its intended impacts moves through intermediate results as represented by *linking variables*. These linking variables represent real changes in the target population or target area that are expected to occur as a result of program activities, but in their own right, they do not represent the attainment of objectives. Rather, they are necessary intermediate effects that are necessary in order to lead to the accomplishment of the real outcomes-oriented objectives. The outputs of the maintenance program, for instance, are aimed at improving the condition of the highway sections where work is performed; this improved condition is an intermediate result. Hopefully, this improved condition then will contribute to faster, safer, and more efficient transportation.

Environmental Variables

Programs operate in environments characterized by physical, financial, legal, social, economic, and psychological attributes, and these environmental characteristics—external to the program itself—often heavily influence program performance. To be successful, program designs must be well suited to their environments, aimed at overcoming some of the more malleable constraints, and able to accommodate to the hardcore "uncontrollables." Performance-monitoring systems sometimes track changes in these environmental conditions as moderating variables that may help to interpret trends in other performance indicators. For example, monitoring the efficiency of the highway maintenance program might be tempered by trends observed in the escalating costs of raw materials beyond the Department's control.

Collectively, the different types of indicators describe a program's intended design. The logic moves from resources to program components, conversion processes that produce outputs. The outputs in turn trigger a causal sequence intended to accomplish basic objectives. These means/ends streams of the separate components work individually, but at some point they converge in pursuance of common impacts. Resources are consumed by activities that produce direct outputs such as lane miles reconstructed, safety projects completed, and tons of patching material placed in the roadway. If these activities really contribute something, it should be evident in a well-maintained or upgraded highway network. Developing indicators of the condition of roads and the adequacy of the highway system in terms of lane widths, passing opportunities, surface conditions, and so on, provides a means for determining whether these assumed relationships hold up. Finally, if such improvements are worthwhile, they should impact in the field in terms of working toward the department's objectives of fast, safe, and efficient transportation.

Overview of the Program Logic

The basic logic underlying the highway program is that the Department's construction and maintenance activities will be effective in providing fast, safe, comfortable, and reasonably inexpensive transportation to the motoring public. While this general logic is common to most transportation programs, it often is not explicated in terms of direct causal linkages between activities and effects. Many highway agencies do not test the validity of the causal assumptions that constitute this logic. Rather, they are presumed to hold up at face value. The thinking seems to run that the consequences of these activities are obvious: Good programs produce better highways, which in turn translate into improved service to users.

In practice, developing an outline of a program logic is frequently a matter of identifying a sequence of causal assumptions in a de facto sense in the absence of written statements in planning documents or some unwritten version of a program rationale that is subscribed to widely within the agency. Given a set of program activities along with a consensus on generalized objectives, what is the plausible logic that would reflect a causal connection running from the former to the latter? With respect to the Pennsylvania DOT's highway programs, this process of reverse thinking led to a simplified but explicit statement of an acceptable program rationale, an overview of the program logic. This logic model was never fully detailed due to the exceeding complexity of the program structure itself, the superficial redundancy among many program elements, and then finding that many elements could be expected to contribute to numerous and overlapping effects. Moreover, the generalized overview was totally sufficient as a framework for identifying the program logic and developing performance indicators.

Program Components and Resources

Specifying the underlying logic begins with an understanding of the program itself, the resources used and the activities conducted. Figure 2-2 outlines the overall highway program including the three major subprograms: maintenance, highway construction, and safety construction. Following the Planning Programming and Budgeting System (PPBS) in use in the state government, these three programs are futher defined in a subsystem structure in terms of components and elements.

The resources used by these programs are commonly classified according to personnel, operating expenses, materials, and equipment. In the accounting system, of course, these items are specified much more precisely, with personnel costs, for example, broken down into salaries, wages, and various overtime rates. Operational expenses would include such items as travel and subsistence, freight charges, professional services, utilities, rents, and repairs. The materials and equipment refer to various aggregates and particular machines actually used in building and maintaining highways. This detail, however, is not usually necessary for performance-monitoring purposes.

It is important to note though that these resources might be measured in two different ways. While they are often represented in dollar terms for efficiency analysis, it may be more useful in some instances to use their natural measurement units. Thus personnel can be measured in dollar costs or in terms of production hours, support hours, and administrative hours. Furthermore, these resources might belong to the department or purchased from private contractors. The manhours in question may pertain to departmental work forces or to private construction companies, and materials consumed may be from department stockpiles or purchased from vendors. Similarly, equipment used on road projects may be owned by the Department or rented from private vendors.

The three major programs—maintenance, construction, and safety construction—are closely interrelated and share many common elements.

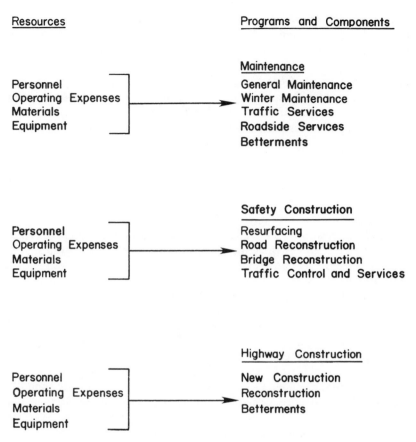

Resources   Programs and Components

Maintenance

Personnel   General Maintenance
Operating Expenses   Winter Maintenance
Materials   Traffic Services
Equipment   Roadside Services
                                   Betterments

Safety Construction

Personnel   Resurfacing
Operating Expenses   Road Reconstruction
Materials   Bridge Reconstruction
Equipment   Traffic Control and Services

Highway Construction

Personnel   New Construction
Operating Expenses   Reconstruction
Materials   Betterments
Equipment

Figure 2-2. Highway Programs, Components, and Resources

Resurfacing projects, for instance, are carried out under all three programs. Nevertheless, they clearly are three separate programs in pursuit of distinct but related objectives. The maintenance program is geared to the continuing regular maintenance and upgrading of the nearly 45,000 miles of existing highways. The objective is to keep the roads open and serviceable to the motoring public, to counteract the normal wear and tear due to usage and environmental factors in order to preserve highways in their "as built" condition. The purpose of the maintenance program is not to alter the basic character of the road or to extend its design life.

The general-maintenance-program component includes most of the routine maintenance work performed on the roadway surface, shoulders, and drainage features as well as routine maintenance and repairs on bridges.

The winter-maintenance component includes the erection of snow fences, putting material on roads to prevent freezing, and snowplowing. Routine upkeep of appurtenances—subordinate features of thoroughfares such as pavement-marking signs, guardrails, and lighting—makes up the traffic-services program, whereas *roadside services* refers to the maintenance of fences and facilities such as roadside rests. The betterments component consists of relatively small projects intended to upgrade the quality of a section of highway such as paving the shoulders of an older road or installing additional drainage structures. All these components are further defined by the elements they consist of. For example, the general-maintenance component has surface-maintenance, shoulder-maintenance, and drainage-maintenance elements that in turn are further broken down by work activities, methods used, and so forth.

The safety-construction program also focuses on the existing highway network but is aimed at making changes at selected sites in order to remove hazards and reduce the potential for accidents. Much of this effort is devoted to resurfacing highway sections where existing surfaces are slick and prone to skidding. The road-reconstruction component improves the basic design of a section in order to make it safer; this might mean straightening a road alignment, widening a road, smoothing grades to increase slight distances, or improving shoulders. It could also include projects designed to improve the geometrics of intersections to reduce the likelihood of accidents. The bridge reconstruction component of the safety-construction program is aimed at correcting the deficiencies that make many of the existing bridges on the state system unsafe, closed, or restricted to limited use. The traffic-control and services component includes numerous kinds of projects to install or improve guardrails, median barriers, pedestrian walks, route markers, traffic signs and signals, and lighting in order to make the roads safer.

The objective of the highway-construction program is to improve the overall level of service provided by the entire system through expansion, building new links or expanding existing roads in order to improve travel times, reduce congestion and increase connectivity from place to place. This includes construction of new highways (primarily the completion of missing links in the interstate system), the relocation of existing state highways, reconstruction (for example, replacing an old two-lane road with a new four-lane road) and betterments such as adding a third lane to an existing pavement or resurfacing an entire section of highway. These construction projects include bridges as well as roadways and are designated as urban versus rural and attached to a particular functional classification, interstates through collectors and local roads.

Although the safety and highway-construction programs involve many of the same elements, the critical difference is that safety projects are intended to improve the safety aspects of existing facilities, whereas the construction program is aimed at expanding the carrying capacity of selected portions of the system. In a similar vein, both the maintenance and construction programs include betterments, but the difference is mainly a matter of scale. Maintenance betterments projects are small (usually involving 500 feet or less of roadway) and do not make any appreciable impact on system capacity.

Intended Linkages

Figure 2–3 shows an overview of the logic by which the three major programs, with resources represented as dollar costs, are linked to effective performance. The most direct products of these programs are outputs. The Bureau of Maintenance uses the term *production units* to refer to the unit for measuring the amount of output for its various activities. These would be such measures as lane miles that have been surface treated, tons of patching material used to fill potholes, the number of signs installed and feet of guardrail replaced, indicators that represent how much work is actually completed in a given time period. The output for the highway-construction program can be measured by linear miles or lane miles of new construction. Because the safety-construction program includes such a heterogenous mix of activities, they would require varied indicators or outputs; one uniform count would be the number of projects.

Assuming some relationship between resources and products, dollar costs would constitute another common denominator for comparing the magnitudes of different projects, but this would beg the question of efficiency. It should be noted, however, that many of the maintenance-program production units are measured by amounts of material utilized. Although material is one type of resource, this is one indicator of how large maintenance projects are and how much work is accomplished—unless substantial amounts of material are being wasted.

The combined effect of the outputs produced by the maintenance and construction programs should be the improvement of the quality of the state's highway system. This improved quality is not really an end in its own right but rather the necessary means toward the goal of fast, safe, and efficient highway transportation for its users. Thus system adequacy is actually an intermediate result, a linking variable that constitutes the logical connection between the program outputs and the indicators of effectiveness.

Quality of the road system has traditionally been evaluated with sufficiency ratings that are based on an assessment of various highway features that fall into three categories: condition, safety, and service. In this sufficiency-rating framework, *condition* refers, for the most part, to the "as-built" condition of the road surface, foundation, drainage, and shoulders, the primary object of the maintenance program. The safety category in-

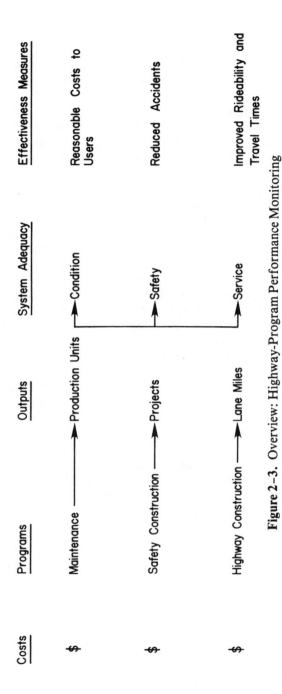

Figure 2-3. Overview: Highway-Program Performance Monitoring

cludes lane, shoulder, and median widths along with uniformity in the highway design, stopping-sight distances, and hazards, all of which are concerns of the safety program. Service pertains to access control, alignments, passing opportunities, rideability, amenities, and signs and pavement markings, all relating to the basic original design, which is in the province of the construction program.

There are no unique one-to-one relationships between the three programs and their respective outputs with these three categories of system adequacy, although there are predominant linkages as represented by the parallel lines in figure 2-3. Thus condition of the roads would be dependent primarily on the maintenance program: safety features would be primarily dependent on safety-construction projects; and service aspects of the road system would depend mainly on the highway-construction program. However, there are direct relationships that cross over these lines, and in particular, it should be noted that the maintenance program actually impacts on all three categories of sufficiency. Activities such as patching potholes, removing obstructions from the pavement and shoulders, and regrading shoulders to eliminate dropoff—not to mention snow and ice control in the winter-maintenance program—are all aimed in large part at reducing safety hazards, while much of the surface maintenance serves to improve rideability and travel times. Thus at a macro level, it is difficult to isolate cause/effect relationships between program outputs and highway-system adequacy. Changes in the ratings of safety aspects, for example, cannot automatically be attributed solely to the safety-construction program.

Given the overall objective of fast, safe, and efficient highway transportation, the most straightforward measures of effectiveness would relate to the costs incurred by users, accident rates, and travel times or rideability. Reduced travel times would be a quantitative indicator of effectiveness whereas improved rideability—how smooth a ride does the motorist get—is a qualitative indicator of service to users. As before, there are no unique one-to-one relationships between the three system adequacy categories and the three types of effectiveness measures. Safety features, for example, will impact on user costs and travel times as well as on accident rates. Yet user costs might be expected to depend primarily on road conditions, whereas accident rates would depend on safety features and travel times would depend mainly on service levels.

In this context it is important to note the essential compatibility among the highway program's three objectives. For the most part, smooth-riding well-maintained roads provide good service to users in terms of comfort and travel times. By the same token they entail less exposure to obstructions that can cause accidents and lower user costs in terms of vehicle operating expenses and repairs. While priorities among the three major programs obviously must be set, sorting out their individual effects is less critical here than in a program area characterized by conflicting objectives.

In summary, then, figure 2-3 shows the general underlying logic by which the effectiveness of the Department's highway program might be improved. If more funds were made available for the maintenance and construction programs, or if ways were found to utilize existing resources more efficiently, then program outputs should increase. If this occurs, then system adequacy and sufficiency ratings should improve over time, or at least should stabilize instead of deteriorate. Ultimately, if system adequacy does improve substantially, then PennDOT should maintain or improve its present level of effectiveness in terms of holding the line or reducing costs to users, containing or reducing accident rates, and shortening travel times.

Finally, it should be noted that the dimensions of the highway program that are shown in figure 2-3 relate both to efficiency and effectiveness. In general, the left-hand side of the figure, relating costs to outputs, is concerned with "process" and the internal operating efficiency of these programs. On the other hand, the right-hand side of the diagram focuses on effectiveness, achieving the objectives of improving the adequacy of the highway system, and impacting more favorably on users. Furthermore, responsiveness would relate to the degree to which the public is concerned about making the kinds of improvements and whether motorists are sensitive to the impacts that do occur.

Improving the efficiency of the highway programs is clearly important for PennDOT at the moment, but that really will have no particular value if it cannot be translated into improved effectiveness. While the program logic just explained seems obvious at first, it should not be construed as evidence that conducting program activities will automatically produce the intended effects. For instance, maintenance outputs could be produced very efficiently at low cost, but if the Department is resurfacing roads that are already in relatively good condition while other highway sections in poor shape go untreated, there will be little improvement in overall system adequacy. Furthermore, the Department could be producing the outputs both efficiently and on roads where condition really was poor, but if these projects are programmed for lightly traveled, lower-order roads while similar problems exist on heavily traveled higher-order highways, then the impacts on users in terms of costs, accidents, and travel times would still be very slight. Finally, there are numerous environmental variables such as harsh climatic factors and heavy-traffic volumes, that can negate effects of program outputs.

Data Sources and Evaluability

The information that would be required to fully operationalize this model for monitoring the performance of the highway programs would encompass a large assortment of data sources and varies widely in terms of availability. With respect to the maintenance program, for instance, the Department already had a detailed reporting system in place concerning the output and efficiency of many activities. Process data for the safety and construction programs were basically available but not well organized for the purpose of performance monitoring. By contrast, the kinds of data needed for the more effectiveness oriented performance monitoring were scattered or non-existent.

Selecting Indicators

As indicated in chapter 1, the primary strategy in developing performance indicators was to rely on existing departmental data bases as much as possible. Much of the effort lies in evaluating the potential worth of existing data sources and their appropriateness for operationalizing the basic performance-monitoring model. Where existing data are not available, of poor quality, or not tailored well enough to the purpose, new data-collection procedures may have to be devised. In some cases, it may be decided that the utility of collecting additional information is not worth the cost; the overall model does not necessarily have to be fitted out completely in order for the performance feedback to be useful.

The development and evaluation of specific measures were based on the consideration of their reliability, validity, and sensitivity as defined in chapter 1. Potential indicators must be assessed not only in terms of their consistency and dependability but also in terms of what they actually represent, what other measures they are related to, and what factors can cause changes in the values these performance indicators take on. Balancing off these considerations of the quality and usefulness of information is the cost of data collection. The difficulty of obtaining indicators that are strong in light of these measurement criteria and the tradeoffs among them that may arise are illustrated in subsequent chapters.

Evaluability Assessment

Most of the rest of this book is devoted to the process of actually developing performance-monitoring tools keyed to the kind of program-logic model presented in this chapter—refining the linkages and characteristics to be analyzed, developing and evaluating data sources and indicators, analyzing the results and developing ways to facilitate the conversion from performance feedback into improved program management. Early on in the process, a basic question emerges: What aspects of program performance should be monitored closely as opposed to other aspects for which monitoring might not be so productive?

Clearly, it is likely to be more important to monitor the performance of some parts of a program than others, and some aspects of a program are more susceptible than others to monitoring and evaluation. The effort to develop monitoring tools should focus on aspects of program performance that have a high potential for being useful, and managers should implement only those monitoring systems that have a clear potential for providing useful information. Thus, although complete coverage might be desirable, the work to develop performance indicators and reporting systems should concentrate on those areas in which the expected payoff to management is the greatest.

The concept of evaluability⁵ can be of assistance here. Basically, programs are considered to be evaluable if they have clear-cut objectives, if the underlying assumptions linking programs to objectives are plausible, if valid measures and evaluation tools are available, and if the intended uses of evaluative information by management are well defined. Applying this line of thinking to the identification of those aspects of program performance to be emphasized in a monitoring system would require, in addition to clear objectives and underlying logical connections, that substantially improved performance in a given area be seen as a realistic possibility, that sound evaluation of such performance is viable, and that management has given priority to this improved performance.

Given this approach, the development of monitoring systems for Penn-DOT concentrated heavily on some areas of performance and only touched on others lightly. In fact, this evaluative consideration is what led to focusing on the highway programs in the first place. Within the highway program, attention focused first on the efficiency type of analysis because a major priority of the new administration was to eliminate waste and generate more product with existing resource levels. Second, much of the effort concentrated on system adequacy because the first priority in the Department was to reverse the trend of deterioration in the state's highway system and begin to improve the physical highway network. This concern, however, focuses on the more dynamic aspects of system adequacy—particularly road condition—which should be sensitive to program initiatives, and de-emphasizes some of the more static elements such as lane width and other design features.

As will be seen, somewhat less attention focused on the true effectiveness elements of the general program-performance model. In large part, this was because the program rationale that holds that increased highway-system adequacy will lead to decreased costs to users, reduced accidents, and improved travel times is somewhat tenuous. The problem is twofold. In addition to the Department's programs, these impact conditions are subject to numerous external factors such as fuel costs, the mix of vehicles using the system and traffic volumes to name a few. While these "environmental givens" do not appear in figure 2-3, their influence may be overwhelming. Within this larger causal context, the program activities may have little chance of dramatically impacting on these outcomes.

Second, the elasticity of impacts to outputs may be relatively low on a statewide basis. While current expenditure levels may be sufficient to prevent significant worsening of these outcomes, for example, quantum increases in expenditures may be required to produce only marginal improvements in these outcomes. Relatively high output levels may well be necessary to maintain the status quo, but it may not be feasible for program outputs to generate real impact on a statewide basis. Concentrated outputs at site-specific projects should produce real impact in terms of user costs, travel time, and accidents, but translated to the statewide network level, the overall impact may be minimal. It is still important, however, to monitor some general indicators of effectiveness to determine whether these outcome conditions are holding their own or worsening over time, as indicators of needs. Viewed as impact measures, most of the effectiveness indicators must be interpreted in light of trends and levels of key environmental factors.

This leads to a second problem, namely, that evaluating impacts in this more wide-open context with limited sensitivity of impacts to program outputs is much more difficult. Indicators and analytical approaches are needed which can assess the effects of specific program factors while "controlling" for the major influencing variables. Such high-powered discriminating tools are beyond the analytical rigor usually associated with performance monitoring. Most important, however, monitoring the final effectiveness elements was not of primary interest to the policymakers because they did not question the basic logic that improvements in highway condition that are targeted to heavily used highways in a "worst-first" approach will ultimately produce real benefits to users. Thus, while monitoring effectiveness in terms of user costs, accident rates, and travel times was definitely a part of this effort, it is not the most important element in terms of the effort going into the development of new data sources and the analysis of performance trends.

Notes

1. P. Horst, J.N.Nay, J.W. Scanlon, and J.S. Wholey, "Program Management and the Federal Evaluator," *Public Administration Review* 34, no. 4 (July–August 1974):300–308.

2. C.W. Churchman, *The Systems Approach* (New York: Dell Publishing, 1968).

3. Act No. 120, Laws of the General Assembly of the Commonwealth of Pennsylvania, S. B. 408, Vol. 1, 1970.

4. See T.H. Poister, *Public Program Analysis: Applied Research Methods* (Baltimore: University Park Press, 1978), chap. 2 for a more complete discussion of this systems approach. For illustrations of the approach as applied to various local governmental programs, see T.H. Poister, J.C. McDavid, and A.H Magoun, *Applied Program Evaluation in Local Government* (Lexington, Mass.: Lexington Books, D.C. Heath, 1979).

5. J.S. Wholey, *Evaluation: Promise and Performance* (Washington, D.C.: Urban Institute, 1979), chap. 2; L. Rutman, Planning Useful Evaluations: Evaluability Assessment (Beverly Hills: Sage, 1980).

3 Process Monitoring

Tracking the implementation and continuing operation of programs and components is called *process monitoring*. This concern spans the left-hand side of figure 2-3 relating to resources, costs, activities, and outputs. Although these indicators do not directly represent outcomes, process monitoring is important because it provides an indication of the quantity and perhaps the quality of work completed under various components and elements.

In an organization responsible for massive public programs beset by bureaucratic drift and sluggish productivity, gaining control over the programs must be a top priority of any new management team that is serious about improving performance. Top management cannot set new directions and be assured that they are being pursued effectively unless there is clear information ont he status of existing programs and trends in program operations. This requires good data on the mix of ongoing activities, de facto priorities among them, how resources are being utilized, how much of different kinds of products are being generated, and how well they are being produced. Linkages with true-effectiveness measures cannot be established until basic information regarding internal-program operations is available.

Process monitoring involves the tracking of resource availability and utilization, varying levels of effort in different program areas, and changes in the way specific activities are conducted, as well as the outputs that are produced. As indicated in chapter 2, how well managers meet output targets should be assessed in two ways; (1) quantity—does the amount of work completed equal, exceed, or fall short of the amount programmed, and (2) quality—how well is this work done, and is it performed in accordance with standards? There is often a tendency to emphasize the quantity of outputs at the expense of the quality dimensions simply because the former kind of data are typically available, whereas quality measures are often more difficult to define and collect. However, it is important to include quality indicators where possible because they sometimes shed a very different light on performance. In fact, there are frequently inverse relationships between the two such that when the quantity indicators point to apparent high productivity, the real explanation may be that a lot of quick-and-dirty production was completed with the effect of boosting volume at the expense of quality.

45

Another aspect of process monitoring concerns the time dimension. Simply determining whether activities are proceeding on schedule is frequently a major managerial concern. Rather than serving as an independent indicator of performance, time-based measures usually have a complementary or reciprocating relationship with quantity or quality indicators. For example, output quantities are totaled for given time periods such as the number of lane miles resurfaced in a month, a quarter, a four-month maintenance season, or a year. Conversely, interest might center on the number of months or years required to catch up with some specified backlog of resurfacing projects. With respect to quality of outputs, how well winter-maintenance functions are performed might be measured by the amount of time it takes to clear a road after a major snowfall, while the duration in hours or days that a travel lane is out of service while maintenance work is going on would be an indicator of inconvenience to motorists due to the maintenance program.

The main evaluative criterion in process monitoring is internal operating efficiency, and this can generally be measured on both a time basis and a cost basis, which again are two sides of the same coin. The primary measures of efficiency are ratios of resources or costs to outputs such as the average cost per foot of guardrail replacement or the cost per lane mile of resurfacing over some specified time period. Focusing on a resource unit such as a crew, however, might lead to measuring efficiency in terms of the feet of guardrail replaced or the lane miles of road resurfaced per week. For some activities, productivity is best measured by the amount of time elapsed from beginning to completion of an activity.

Clearly, there are various ways to monitor efficiency, and the approach to developing indicators for the design and construction program is necessarily different than for the maintenance program because of the different nature of the work. Each project moving through the design and construction phases of the safety- and highway-construction programs is unique, while maintenance activities are much more routine and permit more direct comparisons. As will be seen below, the selection of efficiency indicators must be tailored to management's specific concerns about overall program performance.

Global Program Monitoring

Process monitoring is more common than true effectiveness monitoring in public organizations because ongoing operations are the most immediate concern of managers at many levels. Second, while effectiveness indicators often derive from external sources, for the most part, process monitoring relies on routine program-operation data that are maintained and utilized internally for accounting and line-management purposes. When desired process measures are not readily available or are not maintained in a format or at a level of aggregation that is useful to management, it is usually not too difficult to develop a reporting system that will generate the requisite information. Since process monitoring is basically a matter of keeping counts on internal program activities, the source data are usually a matter of record at the operating levels. Thus, although reliability may present problems and reporting formats may need to be reconfigured, data availability is usually not a problem in process monitoring. For these same reasons, process monitoring is often conducted in greater detail than is effectiveness monitoring.

Top-Level-Management Targets

While detailed process monitoring tends to occur at operating levels where concern centers on the performance of operating units, a more useful stance from a policymaking perspective is a macro-level monitoring for the organization as a whole. As part of the move of top management to strengthen control over all transportation programs, for example, PennDOT has established a *Management Objectives Report* that tracks key process indicators for all programs on a monthly basis. For the first time, basic data on personnel complements, expenditures, and program activities are presented together in one place in a format that is updated monthly to show progress over a fiscal year. The indicators that are included represent very generalized levels of effort or specific aspects of program performance that have been identified as priority areas. For each indicator the *Report* compares actual amounts with planned or budgeted amounts for the month. It also shows cumulative figures in conjunction with comparable data for the previous year, allowing management to track the progress of organizational divisions and programs in terms of input and output—how many resources are going into these programs and how much the programs are producing. This type of data provides a quick picture of how much activity is going on and how much is being accomplished.

The kinds of highway-program indicators included in the *Management Objectives Report,* often referred to as the "Bluebook," are directly tied to the systems model discussed in chapter 2. Since the safety-construction and highway-construction programs are so similar in process—and since at this time the construction program consists mainly of reconstruction and betterments projects on the existing network as opposed to building totally new highways—they are tracked together in the report. Resources for these programs are indicated by the total number of personnel working in highway and safety improvements and total expenditures for the month broken down by salaries and fringe benefits, operating expenses, engineering consultants, right-of-way (ROW) acquisition, and construction contracts.

The amount of activity going on in these programs is represented first by the number of active projects in the design stage, the right-of-way stage, and the construction stage. One indication of wasted effort in this process is given by the number of projects in the design or ROW stages that have become inactive. Since the number of bridges that are closed because they are unsafe, restricted from use by heavy vehicles, or otherwise deficient is such a great problem in the Pennsylvania system, the number of bridge projects underway is called out for specific attention. The report also includes the number of new projects that have been put out to bid and the dollar value of new-construction projects for which contracts have been awarded. These indicators represent outputs of the design process, and serve to preview levels of construction activity coming on-line in the near future. Total output of the overall program is indicated by the number of projects that were completed in the given month either in the design stage, right-of-way acquisition, or actual construction. Since a priority in the reconstruction area, from both a safety and service standpoint, is to resurface roads that are of poor quality, a specific output indicator included in the report is the miles of highway that have been overlayed, broken down by classification from interstates to local roads.

Actual service provision differs fundamentally between the safety and construction programs as opposed to the highway-maintenance program, in that while all construction work is done by private contractors, most of the maintenance work is performed by Departmental labor forces working in the county maintenance units. However, in an effort to increase maintenance levels and at the same time make operations more efficient, there has been a move to expand maintenance capabilities through contracting with private operators to supplement the efforts of Departmental work forces. Thus resources going into the maintenance program are tracked in the *Management Objectives Report* by an indicator of the dollar value of maintenance work contracted out as well as the total complement of maintenance personnel and the dollar value of maintenance materials, equipment, and supplies. The amount of activity is represented by the number of maintenance contract awards to private firms and the number of contracts with municipal units of government for snow removal, pothole patching, and comprehensive maintenance. The monthly outputs of the maintenance program are shown—separately for Departmental forces and by contract—by selective indicators representing the miles of road that have been surface treated, and the total production units completed statewide in terms of miles of shoulder cutting, the number of drainage pipes repaired or replaced, and the tons of manual patching material used to fill potholes.

Utilization of Macro Process-Monitoring Data

The *Management Objectives Report* is keyed directly to the MBO system in use in the upper tiers of the Department. The purpose of the MBO system is to set performance targets for executives and major program managers in the form of agreements between supervisors and subordinates, and then to base appraisals of individuals' performance in light of these targets. These assessments of program performance then are used in personnel decisions, but more important, they form the basis for continuing or revising targets and defining new priorities. Many of the items included in the report relate directly to the targets established in the MBO process and are used to evaluate managers' success in meeting them.

This link between MBO and process monitoring is natural because for the most part, the performance targets refer to internal operations and outputs rather than effectiveness and external impacts. Managers clearly should be responsible for the ongoing operation of their programs as well as the quantity and quality of the outputs they produce, but it is sometimes difficult to hold them accountable for achieving specific kinds of desired impacts which are influenced not only by the program, but by numerous other influences beyond the managers' control. For example, a manager may be responsible for completing a certain number of safety-improvement projects that should reasonably be expected to reduce accidents and eliminate some projected number of fatalities or injuries and property damage over the long run. Accident reduction may not be apparent in the short run, however, and in any case, the manager cannot be held fully accountable for lowering an accident rate that is largely a function of vehicle condition, driver behavior, weather conditions, and so on. While activities and outputs are only justifiable on the basis of contributing directly to improved impact conditions, the process measures provide the firmest basis for evaluating managers' performance.

Although the information provided in the *Management Objectives Report* is basically descriptive, it serves a program-performance-evaluation function in a number of ways. While the amount of funds expended on a given activity or the amount of work completed under that activity simply describes workload levels, this kind of information takes on an evaluative aspect when compared against planned expenditure or output levels. If less money is being expended on new activities or programs slated for increased emphasis, it may signal problems in implementation, whereas overspending may well indicate managers' difficulties in holding costs down. Similarly, output levels substantially below planned amounts usually flag problems either of unrealistic programming or failure in the field to manage work crews and operations so as to achieve desired production levels.

In addition to presenting these data, the first page of the report notes major variances between planned versus actual expenditures, activity levels, or outputs. This calls problems or potential problem areas to the attention of top executives as well as the managers responsible for these activities, to whom copies of the report are distributed. For instance, a substantial shortfall in manual pothole-patching activity below planned production would be noted as an unfavorable variance, and this would likely trigger a follow-up investigation of why production was low or whether the shortfall was concentrated in a few large counties. Favorable variances are also reported as an indication of performance exceeding expectations.

These planned and actual values of important process indicators have further evaluative meaning in terms of comparisons over time and across organizational units. By showing each indicator on a month-to-month basis, improving or worsening trends can be identified, sometimes permitting more serious problems to be anticipated and possibly counteracted. Furthermore, each indicator is presented as a cumulative measure and compared with cumulative levels for the same month in the preceding year. This shows current performance compared with prior performance on a deseasonalized basis. Major variances between current and prior-year performance are also noted in order to call attention to any substantial gains or losses in expenditures or production.

A third evaluative aspect of the process monitoring appearing in the *Management Objectives Report* involves comparisons among organizational units. While the report contains only aggregate data for monitoring status and trends on a statewide basis, companion reports are prepared and distributed at the same time on an engineering district and county basis. The *District Management Summary* shows many of the same kinds of indicators broken down by the eleven districts, and the *County Objectives Report,* called the "Redbook," does the same thing for the sixty-seven counties in the state. In a management system characterized by decentralized decision making and line management within a framework of centralized policymaking and control, these disaggregated reports that facilitate comparisons across regions and county, organizational units are crucial. They enable district engineers and county maintenance managers to see how their units are performing in comparison with other parts of the state, and they show management at the department level how performance levels and trends vary across the state.

Monitoring Design and Construction Activities

Although the safety-construction and highway-construction programs are parallel programs with distinct purposes—reducing accident potential versus increasing travel capacity—as noted earlier, they move through a similar process from design to final acceptance of projects, which, for the most part, consist of alterations and improvements to existing highway sections. For both kinds of projects (some projects may have elements of both improved safety and increased capacity), the actual construction is contracted out to private firms, but departmental personnel are responsible for the construction-management process from design through completion of the project and putting the facility into service. This design and construction process involves a lengthy set of activities from planning and programming approvals, through final project design, ROW acquisition, reviews, bid solicitations and awards, construction, inspection, and final audit.

Figure 3–1 traces a project through a simplified flow diagram of the design and construction activities of the Department. The final decision on design comes at the end of a long process involving the preparation of environmental-impact statements, public hearings, and initial project funding. The final design of a project is undertaken by the Engineering District Office or a consultant, depending on workload and the technical expertise available to the district. At the same time the right-of-way is secured and utilities are relocated, if necessary, in anticipation of construction. The design is reviewed at various stages by all interested state and federal agencies. These usually include the state Department of Transportation, the state Department of Environmental Resources, and the U.S. Environmental Protection Agency. The Federal Highway Administration has granted to the state "certification-and-acceptance" authority for most highway projects.

Upon completion of the design, the project is reviewed by the Bureau of Highway Design; on the basis of its recommendations, the Deputy Secretary for Highway Administration authorizes the solicitation of bids by the Bureau of Highway Design's Contract Division. The bids are opened and reviewed by the Contract Division, and a recommendation is made for award or no award. The Federal Highway Administration approves the Department's recommendation to award, and a contract is negotiated. During construction, inspections are conducted by personnel from the Engineering District Office. The Bureau of Contract Quality Control oversees district inspection while contract work is progressing, and it reviews all contract changes. When the work is completed, a final audit is conducted by the district and reviewed by the Bureau of Contract Quality Control. The entire process can take from several months to several years.

Project Monitoring

Even with the construction programs scaled down somewhat in relation to the priority placed on maintenance, PennDOT has a few thousand projects

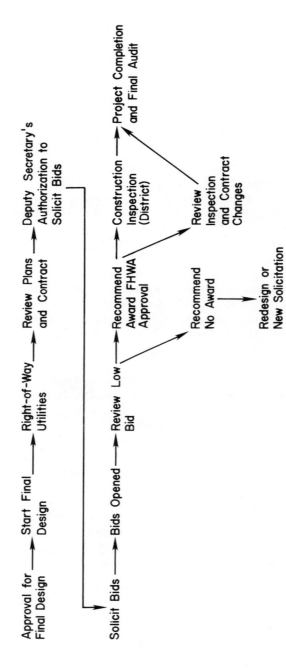

Figure 3–1. Project Flow: Highway Design and Construction

in the pipeline at any time, ranging from small betterments efforts on short sections of highway, to multimillion-dollar major reconstruction projects and large-scale new-construction projects aimed at filling in missing links on the interstate system. With so many and diverse projects at various stages throughout the design and construction process, simply tracking their status for top-level decision makers and others is a very difficult job. Until recently all record-keeping on these projects was done manually, and aggregated data on sets of projects—if it were available—were not usually considered to be reliable. Furthermore, it was virtually infeasible to classify and sort projects to facilitate the standard kinds of analyses and comparisons that decision makers would want to see.

Recognizing the basic inadequacy of the existing bookkeeping process to provide reasonably quick and reliable responses to questions about the status of projects of a certain type, in a given geographic area, or at a particular state in the overall design and construction process, PennDOT's new administration has developed a Project-Management System as part of its effort to exert control and direction over the safety and construction programs. This Project Management System is a "computerized information system which integrates project-related data from the engineering and planning communities with accounting data from the financial community. These data are stored in a common data base and are accessed by users located both in the Department's Central Office and the eleven Engineering Districts. The PMS has enabled people in the various branches of the Department to obtain consistent information on all projects because everyone is accessing the same data base."[1]

The Project Management System is intended to identify projects included in the Department's overall program, to monitor the status of their federal funding, and to track the physical and fiscal progress of each project by maintaining information concerning previous activity, current status, and future estimates. For the first time, each project entering the pipeline is assigned a unique identifying number that remains the same throughout all phases of planning, design, and construction, including activities undertaken at the district as well as the departmental level. The kinds of information on each project contained in the system include basic descriptive data (type of project, funding category, functional class of highway, project length, traffic volumes, and so on), project location, the accounting charge numbers related to the project, overall costs for engineering, ROW and construction, milestone-achievement dates for all steps in the design and construction process, and the senatorial and legislative districts. This system, for the first time, permits managers to quickly obtain more refined information on active projects in design, ROW or construction, for example, the number of projects at some particular stage in the overall process, the number located in a given district, those utilizing a certain category of federal funding, the number aimed at making safety improvements or the number programmed for a particular class of highways such as principal arterials.

Although the Project Monitoring System has numerous applications involving the obligation of federal funds, the development of a schedule for letting contracts, and the development of cash-flow estimates, its greatest utility in terms of performance monitoring concerns the tracking of construction and particularly preconstruction activities—all the hurdles a project must get over in order to be advertised for bids. Each step in the design and construction process overviewed in figure 3-1 is specified as a milestone, beginning with the approval of the project for design by the Program Management Committee and terminating with the issuance of an acceptance certificate. For each project in the system, milestone dates are posted as either estimated, actual, or not applicable. As the project moves through the process, the actual milestone dates are entered, and estimated dates for further milestones may be revised; all updating is done "at the source" by the organization unit responsible for each particular activity. Because the PMS can aggregate projects into so many different groupings, it is highly suitable for monitoring the status and progress of the overall program in addition to keeping track of individual projects. For example, top management might be interested in knowing the total number and dollar value of projects for which contracts can be expected to be awarded within the next six months.

Design and Construction Efficiency

Measuring the quality of outputs for the design and other preconstruction activities is difficult. Although the quality of the output of construction activities—the actual bridge, intersection, or highway section that is completed or altered—should really be assessed in terms of serviceability over time, when construction is completed to the Department's satisfaction, the certificate of acceptance is supposed to affirm that the product does conform with bid specifications. Literally, there is a concrete, tangible product, the quality of which can be assessed. On the other hand, the outputs of the design process are "paper products" such as plans, designs, environmental reviews, and contracts, whose quality is not so apparent.

One indication of how well preconstruction work is performed, however, focuses on the relationship between the cost estimates originally developed for an individual project and the actual bids received from contractors interested in doing the work. For all projects that are bid out to contractors, the *Management Objectives Report* shows the number of cases in which the lowest viable bid received deviated from the estimated cost by 15 percent or more in either direction. These indicators are monitored on the theory that if the low bids come in consistently at 15 percent or more above or below programmed costs, the highway-design staff are being too generous in setting expected costs or unrealistically stingy in estimating the cost for which the project could be built.

With respect to efficiency, there are a few measures that might be used to monitor design and construction activities. The first is the average number of days required per project from approval of final design to project completion. This could be broken down by the average number of days required for each design and construction-milestone per project, for instance, the average number of days spent by other agencies in reviewing the plans and contract documents prior to advertisement. In this case, as the number of days decreased, the design process would be viewed as becoming more efficient. Also, bottlenecks in the design or construction process could easily be identified. For the entire process, efficiency should result in a decrease in the total time required from approval of final design to project completion. Although this information is not developed at present, the Project Management System could easily be used to generate an average total time from approval of the design until project completion and an average number of days or weeks spent working on each milestone. These data would further lend themselves to the type of analysis usually associated with PERT (Program Evaluation and Review Technique), which is intended to find ways to collapse the overall time required to complete specified activities.

Another method of measuring efficiency in design and construction activities is to monitor the average number of mandays expended by the Department on each project. These data are kept by the Department on a cost basis, that is, the cost of design and construction services for each project. Manhours spent per project would have to be collected manually under present payroll-processing procedures, but cost data are available and would probably closely parallel the manhour statistics. However, there are some problems with measures of the type proposed here. Smaller projects may take as long to design and as much effort to administer as larger, more costly projects. It is possible that by observing differences in time or manhours spent per project, the measures will reflect differences in project characteristics rather than efficiency. Interpretation of this kind of indicator could be greatly assisted by analysis of the ratio of design costs to actual project costs. Such analysis would show whether this relationship is constant, as assumed in architects' billing practices, or whether scale economies result in larger projects having lower ratios of design costs to the value of contracts that are awarded.

The California Department of Transportation has been successful in developing a means for controlling for the effects of different sizes of projects on labor demands. For projects involving less than $200,000, several cost categories or ranges were established. Information on the total manhours required for each project was collected and aggregated for the appropriate category. Data on labor requirements for projects over $200,000 were aggregated by type of project rather than by costs. This procedure was used to derive an average cost per project for budgeting Departmental design and construction activities. Estimates have been accurate to within 5–10 percent. The threshold of $200,000 may be raised as a result of inflation, but the distinction between major and minor projects would still be maintained. This procedure should eliminate major biases arising from project characteristics and permit the use of average time and average manhour measures to monitor the efficiency of design and construction activities in the Department.

Another problem, more difficult conceptually, is that a reduced number of manhours per project or total time per project may result in higher costs due to changes to contracts, or projects that are inadequately designed and inspected, ultimately resulting in a reduced project life. Emphasizing apparent design efficiency could produce designs and projects that are suboptimal in the long run. It would therefore be desirable to link improved efficiency in the immediate design process, as described previously with some measure comparing project life with the expected or design life of the project. No information of this type exists at present, and undoubtedly it would be difficult to collect. Nevertheless, some measure of the long-term efficiency of cost effectiveness of the design and construction processes should be available for monitoring purposes.

In strictly financial terms, design efficiency on an organizational-unit basis can be measured by the percentage of total design-staff-salary cost that is charged to ongoing projects as opposed to general overhead. The *Management Objectives Report* monitors this overhead-charging factor for all units in the planning and highway divisions as an indication of how much relative effort is actually going into the production of designs.

Monitoring the Efficiency of the Maintenance Program

Early in the performance indicators project, it was decided to concentrate efforts on the highway-maintenance program for a number of reasons. First, maintenance is a big program in terms of both manpower and expenditures—maintenance has been made a top priority and accounts for approximately 60 percent of the Department's budget. Second, in recent years the Department has had difficulty financing the maintenance program at a level consistent with needs; as a result there has been a growing backlog of estimated maintenance deficiencies. Third, the maintenance program has high public visibility, in large part due to the relatively poor condition of many portions of the state-highway network. Fourth, there are apparent inefficiencies in the program, evidenced in part by a high degree of variation in unit costs among counties. In the past the overall efficiency of maintenance operations in the field has been suspect due, in large part, to the traditionally heavy influence of political patronage in hiring practices. The quality of work performed in some counties, and particularly for certain activities, has been notoriously poor. This leads to the fifth reason for the importance of looking at the maintenance program: the need to gain greater control over the separate county-level maintenance operations.

A final factor that made the maintenance program an attractive one to concentrate on in developing performance indicators is that the Bureau of Maintenance already had a good start on a monitoring system with its Highway Maintenance Management System (HMMS). With HMMS the bureau has an ongoing computerized information system for monitoring the internal operation of routine maintenance activities: general maintenance, winter-traffic services, traffic services, roadside maintenance, and maintenance administration. For the whole set of specific work activities or cost functions that make up these programs, HMMS reports monthly data on manpower, materials, and equipment costs as well as production on a county-by-county basis. For maintenance planning and control functions, a detailed-reporting format has been developed that is useful to districts, counties, and the central Bureau of Maintenance in managing this program.

Efficiency Indicators

For these programs, developing indicators of efficient performance is primarily a matter of selecting key activities from among the 143 originally contained in HMMS and developing a reporting form that would present maintenance-performance data in a more highly aggregated format useful to top management in monitoring the program on a monthly or four-month-maintenance-season basis. However, closer examination of HMMS output reveals that there are considerable problems concerning data reliability stemming mainly from reporting error and the merging of data from different sources. For example, while production information comes from the counties where the work is conducted, the financial data are obtained from the accounting system. To some extent these are not totally compatible because work completed is reported for the given month, whereas personnel costs are reported for pay periods and the two do not always coincide. With respect to reporting and processing errors, editing routines and tighter control on data input are now being established to improve the adequacy of HMMS data for aggregate comparisons.

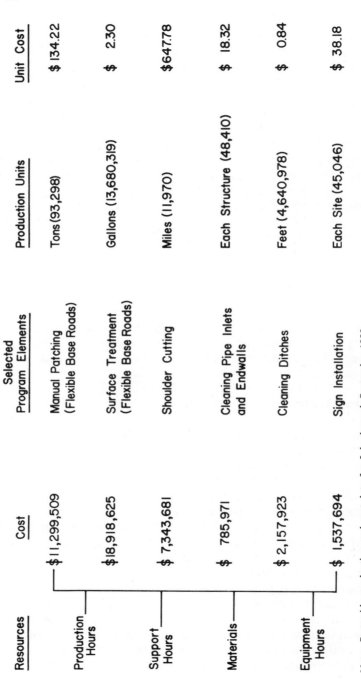

Resources	Cost	Selected Program Elements	Production Units	Unit Cost
Production Hours	$11,299,509	Manual Patching (Flexible Base Roads)	Tons (93,298)	$ 134.22
	$18,918,625	Surface Treatment (Flexible Base Roads)	Gallons (13,680,319)	$ 2.30
Support Hours	$ 7,343,681	Shoulder Cutting	Miles (11,970)	$647.78
Materials	$ 785,971	Cleaning Pipe Inlets and Endwalls	Each Structure (48,410)	$ 18.32
	$ 2,157,923	Cleaning Ditches	Feet (4,640,978)	$ 0.84
Equipment Hours	$ 1,537,694	Sign Installation	Each Site (45,046)	$ 38.18

Note: Statewide production and cost data for July through September 1980.

Figure 3–2. Illustrative Maintenance-Program-Efficiency Indicators

Figure 3-2 illustrates the framework for the maintenance-program-efficiency analysis for a sample of program elements, otherwise referred to as "activities" or "cost functions." The costs of production and support manhours, materials, and equipment can be measured in both their natural units or in dollars; both can be useful in developing efficiency indicators. Production hours refers to the number of manhours spent in actually performing the maintenance work, while support hours include the time spent for travel, safety, and training.

Ideally, outputs, or production units, should be measured in terms of both quantity and quality. HMMS reports output quantities in terms of tons of manual patching, gallons of surface treatment, miles of shoulder cutting, and feet of drainage ditches cleaned, and so on, a different measurement unit for each cost function. It should be noted that there are two types of output indicators illustrated in figure 3-2, those based on the amount of material that is put into place by maintenance workers, and those that indicate the amount of roadway or the number of facilities that have been treated. The former type is somewhat of a cost-oriented output indicator while the latter is more production oriented. The latter type is preferred, where feasible, because it comes closer to indicating the amount of improvement or betterment that has been accomplished.

Materials-based output indicators such as gallons of surface-treatment material applied to the road, are valid indicators of workload, but because of variation in lane width and thickness of the application, they do not always translate directly into how much improvement has been accomplished. Approximate conversion factors are available, but where possible, it would be preferable to report both the quantity of material used and the amount of improvement accomplished. For example, in addition to knowing how many tons of pothole-patching material were used to fill potholes, it would be useful to know how many potholes were patched or how many sections of highway were made free from potholes. This type of information is more difficult to obtain, however, and it does not provide an even interpretation of how much work was done. The tons-of-patching-material indicator is used because it is a common denominator whether small or large potholes have been patched and whether individual versus continuous clusters of potholes have been eliminated.

More important, quality measures for the outputs are not presently available. This is unfortunate because it is known that the quality of the maintenance work performed by the counties is uneven at best and varies from district to district. One of the priorities of the new administration in appointing county maintenance managers on a merit basis was to improve the quality of the maintenance work performed. PennDOT began to develop a quality-control program in which central-office inspectors would visit job sites in all counties on a random-sample basis to assess the quality of various activities completed by maintenance crews, but that effort was curtailed due to the difficulty and expense involved. Standard operating procedures have been defined for each maintenance activity or cost function, and the obvious basis for assessing the quality of work completed would be some sort of scale reflecting the degree of compliance with these procedures.

The most direct measure of efficiency, disregarding quality, is the unit cost or the dollar cost per production unit, as shown in figure 3-2. A complementary indicator that measures the labor productivity of the maintenance crews irrespective of the dollar costs of personnel, materials, and equipment would be the number of units produced per hour, or the ratio of production units to production hours. These measures can be used to provide benchmarks at one point in time, or more interestingly, to make comparisons among counties or districts and to gauge trends in efficiency over time. The unit-cost indicator relates directly to the primary concern in maintenance programming: How much production can be expected with a given amount of funding? However, the production-units-per-production-hour measure provides a better basis for comparing the managerial effect on maintenance efficiency because it is not confounded by external factors such as cost differentials among regions or uncontrollable price escalations over time.

Analyzing trends in unit costs or comparing them across counties in the absence of any quality indicator presumes that this unmeasured quality factor is similar across all observations. If the Department is successful in greatly improving the quality of maintenance work performed and if site visits and other appraisal methods show that within some range of tolerance, work is being completed in compliance with standard operation procedures, then an alternative is to assume that all work is done in accordance with standards and to interpret the unit cost comparisons in their own right. This essentially is what is being done at present. While the Department is moving in the direction of higher-quality maintenance work, however, it is by no means clear that this goal has been fully realized. This begs the question then of what the quality indicators would look like and reaffirms that some type of quality indicators need to be developed. Instead of site-visit inspections, for example, one possible indicator at least for certain kinds of activities would be the frequency with which repeat applications of the same maintenance treatments are applied to the same highway sections. The theory is that if the work is done according to standards, repeat applications will not be necessary as soon as when poor-quality work is done. If such quality indicators become available, they can be combined with the production data in a quantity/quality index of outputs, or they can be used separately to help interpret the analysis of comparative unit costs.

Cross-Sectional Comparisons

The Department has implemented a system to monitor production units and costs for individual counties on a monthly basis, in large part to compare efficiencies among counties and districts. In the spirit of emphasizing the "important few" at the expense of the "trivial many," fourteen activities have been selected and combined from among the 143 original cost functions in order to present a manageable picture of the most important activities from a departmentwide perspective. These items comprise the main indicators in the *County Objectives Report* (the "Redbook") discussed earlier. In addition to unit costs computed for the fourteen maintenance activities, counties are also compared in terms of completed production units for these cost functions against planned production, and in terms of actual manhours related to standard manhours, that is the number of manhours that would have been required to complete a certain number of production units if standard production rates prevailed.

While these are the most appropriate indicators of efficiency, it is important to recognize that many factors other than managerial competence influence the productivity levels attained by counties. This includes environmental (external) influences such as climatic conditions and topography, average travel volumes and the cost of materials, all of which vary substantially around the state. Costs can also be expected to vary with the size of the road network in a county, the overall scale of operations, and the extent to which specialized crews perform the work, a more feasible alternative in the large counties than in the smaller counties.

In comparing total costs or unit costs among counties, it is necessary to take volume of production into account since counties can be expected to achieve economies of scale and operate more efficiently at higher levels of output. Figure 3–3 shows the regression of total cost of surface treatment on a $\log_{10}$ transformation of production units that have been converted from gallons and tons to linear miles. This curve, showing costs increasing with production but at a diminishing rate, fits the data better than a linear model. The figure also shows a "tolerance band" within ± 20 percent of predicted cost; counties falling above the band would appear to be the least efficient on that cost function and would warrant some investigation. (Similar analysis could be applied to unit-cost models as opposed to total cost models.)

The predictability of the cost of specified maintenance activities incurred by counties can be improved with multivariate models that incorporate the kind of environmental variables mentioned previously. This is generally the approach taken by an earlier study that included other operations and environmental variables in developing cost models for five selected cost

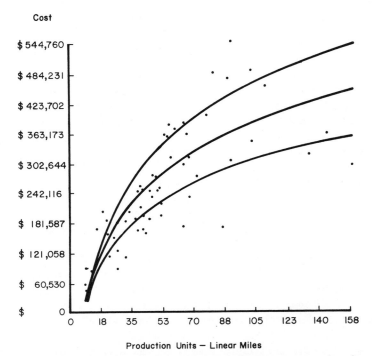

Cost

Production Units — Linear Miles

Note: Upper and lower curves show ± 20 percent from average cost based on production. Production units in tons (for plant mix) and gallons (liquid bituminous) have been converted to linear miles.

Figure 3–3. Surface-Treatment Costs by Production Level

functions.[2] When the study's results were pursued by field investigations, however, it became apparent that to some degree there was an inverse relationship between efficiency and actual quality of work, that is, some counties looked efficient because they were doing quick but low-quality work. Thus it is clear that some type of quality assurance is needed.

Over the past two years, top-management personnel have instituted a practice of executive visits intended in part to prod maintenance managers into assuring that work is completed according to standards. If it does not become apparent that the situation is improving, it may be necessary to develop actual measures of work quality, as discussed earlier, and to incorporate the results into the kind of productivity analysis overviewed in figure 3–2.

Cross-sectional analysis of maintenance productivity on a county basis incorporating qualtity measures could follow the model outlined in figure 3–4. A budgeted total-dollar cost will purchase some mix and quantity of

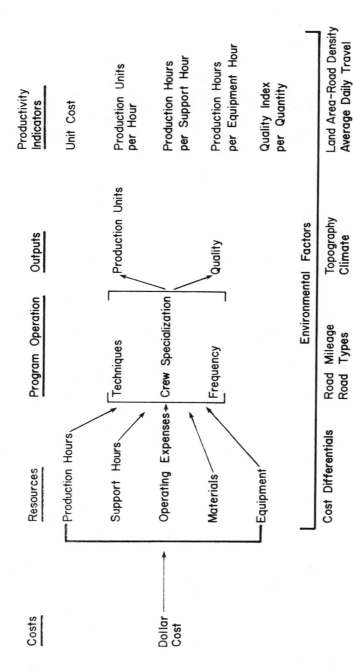

Figure 3–4. County Highway-Maintenance-Productivity Model

resources broken down by production and support hours, operating expenses, materials, and equipment. These resources can be used to complete production units, ideally measured with both quantitative and qualitative indicators. The productivity of these operations could be measured not only by unit costs but also by production units per hour. Such indicators as production hours to support hours, production hours to equipment hours, and quality/quantity ratio are further efficiency measures that can help to interpret or explain county-productivity comparisons. Managers can influence productivity through manipulation of such overt factors as techniques, crew specialization, and frequency of given operations, as well as through more subtle managerial style. In addition, productivity can be influenced by uncontrollable environmental factors such as cost differentials in purchasing materials, the mix of different types of highways in the county, topography, and such climatic factors as precipitation and the number of freeze-thaw cycles, as well as general indicators representing the scale of maintenance operations in a county.

While HMMS tracks production units and costs on a monthly basis, use of the univariate curvilinear regressions or multivariate models keyed to figure 3–4 is probably more appropriate when conducted on the basis of the three separate four-month construction/maintenance seasons because short-term fluctuation will have less influence on relative performance among counties. Additional efficiency indicators that can be examined on either a monthly or seasonal basis include the following: (1) completed compared to planned production, (2) actual manhours compared to "standard" manhours, (3) the ratio of manhours to the cost of materials, (4) total project costs as a percentage of total maintenance budget, and (5) ratio of administrative and support cost to one hundred manhours of production. These measures can be used to compare the efficiency of counties and/or districts and to track overall efficiency in the Department's maintenance program over time.

Trend Analysis

While examination of process data for a given time period can be very useful from the standpoint of comparing current performance against plans or standards, this kind of analysis takes on added significance when the data span a few years, therefore permitting a monitoring over time. This time dimension is really the essence of performance monitoring, that is, tracking key indicators over time to determine whether performance is remaining stable, deteriorating, or improving, particularly when operating methods or management strategies have been changed. Such trend analysis can be conducted in the aggregate or broken down geographically by organizational unit.

Essentially, accumulated data on the costs, production levels, and internal operating efficiency of the maintenance program provide a natural basis for time-series analysis generally using either a continuous or an interrupted time-series design. The latter is appropriate when definite changes have been implemented—new policies or strategies—and the purpose of the analysis is to compare preintervention trends with postintervention trends.[3] Examining HMMS data on a monthly basis for a period stretching over a few years would lend itself to classic time-series analysis using fairly high-powered statistical techniques.[4] Alternatively, the data can be aggregated to an annual or maintenance-season basis and evaluated more descriptively.

In any kind of time-series analysis, two possible sources of extraneous influence should be kept in mind, seasonal variation and environmental factors. If monthly, quarterly, or maintenance-season data are being observed, care must be taken not to draw conclusions about real changes in performance that actually result from seasonal differences. Fair comparisons equate similar seasons such as surface-treatment production in fall 1980 against that of fall 1979. Second, environmental factors beyond management's control may shift over time and exert a strong influence on performance trends. In the highway-maintenance area, the cost of raw materials has risen dramatically in recent years so that unit costs will increase if actual productivity levels are static. Thus unit-cost comparisons must be complemented by analysis of other indicators to provide a complete picture of process-monitoring trends.

This is illustrated in table 3-1, which shows production and cost data over four fiscal years for one maintenance activity, cutting shoulders. In accordance with the new administration's position that shoulders and drainage generally had been neglected in the past and that related activities should be emphasized in planned-maintenance programs, production in-

Table 3-1
Shoulder-Cutting Cost and Production Data

	Fiscal 1978	Fiscal 1979	Fiscal 1980	Fiscal 1981
Production units (miles)	11,561	15, 557	17,974	21,001
Total costs	4,539,440	6,014,707	10,915,873	14,217,654
Unit cost	392.65	386.62	607.31	677.00
Personnel costs	3,108,999	4,147,107	6,140,856	7,551,372
Production hours	182,070	222,002	271,496	308,371
Support hours	191,010	250,518	351,919	414,515
Units per hour	0.03	0.03	0.03	0.03
Units per production hour	0.06	0.07	0.07	0.07

creased dramatically. The number of miles of shoulders cut in fiscal 1981 exceeded the figure for fiscal 1978 by 82 percent. However, the total cost of that activity statewide more than tripled over the same three years, and the unit cost therefore increased by 72 percent. On this measure alone, internal operating efficiency would appear to have worsened, but this is basically a function of escalating costs. Personnel cost per hour, for example, rose from $8.33 in 1978 to $10.45 in 1981, and the cost of materials and equipment increased considerably more. Labor productivity, measured by the production units completed per hour or units per production hour, was very static over the three-year period. Thus although unit costs went up significantly, internal operating efficiency remained constant in terms of actual resource utilization.

Table 3-2 shows similar data for one of the surface activities emphasized most heavily by the Department—surface treatment (liquid bituminous) on flexible-base roads. Both production and total costs increased from fiscal 1978 to fiscal 1981, but costs increased at a faster rate, so that unit cost increased by more than 20 percent. Although total cost increased substantially, support hours and particularly production hours decreased significantly over this period, and therefore personnel costs decreased.

This activity was targeted by the Department for improved performance in that productivity had been far below standards in the past. For example, the standard that had been set for surface treatment was one gallon of output for each 0.0075 production hours of activity time; this converts into an expected standard of 133.3 gallons per production hour. In fiscal 1978, the actual figure was only 38.6, rising to 98.8 in 1979, and approaching the standard with 127.2 gallons per production hour in 1981. Therefore, crew productivity increased dramatically and offset the increased costs of materials and equipment.

Table 3-2
Surface-Treatment Cost and Production Data

	Fiscal 1978	Fiscal 1979	Fiscal 1980	Fiscal 1981
Production units (gallons)	8,817,851	8,791,148	9,565,222	10,090,362
Total cost	9,785,254	8,539,983	10,693,867	13,803,543
Unit cost	1.11	0.97	1.12	1.37
Personnel costs	3,630,993	2,166,649	2,328,118	2,571,214
Production hours	228,236	89,009	82,901	79,301
Support hours	168,663	110.559	127,727	132,794
Units per hour	22.22	44.05	45.41	47.57
Units per production hour	38.63	98.77	115.38	127.24

Note: Data apply to liquid bituminous on flexible-base roads only.

A more typical pattern of trends over time is that for guardrail repair, shown in table 3-3. Production in 1981 was 15 percent above 1978, but total costs increased more, and unit cost went from $2.33 to $2.59, an increase of 11 percent. This apparent loss in efficiency masks the fact that crew productivity, measured by production units per production hour, increased by 58 percent.

A final example, shown in table 3-4, illustrates a response pattern that raises performance questions that would be of concern to top management. The total cost of manual patching—filling potholes—increased marginally from 1978 to 1980, while production units completed dropped by 55 percent. Thus unit costs more than doubled. Furthermore, production hours dropped by 27 percent, and total activity hours decreased only slightly, 19

Table 3-3
Guardrail-Repair Cost and Production Data

	Fiscal 1978	Fiscal 1979	Fiscal 1980	Fiscal 1981
Production units (feet)	500,427	456,156	602,411	575,931
Total cost	1,164,279	1,108,434	1,630,332	1,488,801
Unit cost	2.33	2.43	2.71	2.59
Personnel costs	687,770	668,825	930,322	765,588
Production hours	60,094	52,742	60,604	43,811
Support hours	21,321	21,209	32,554	29,935
Units per hour	6.15	6.17	6.47	7.81
Units per production hour	8.33	8.65	9.94	13.15

Table 3-4
Manual-Patching Cost and Production Data

	Fiscal 1978	Fiscal 1979	Fiscal 1980	Fiscal 1981
Production units (tons)	507,867	460,291	285,407	227,371
Total cost	30,875,855	32,770,770	36,881,525	33,422,861
Unit cost	60.77	71.20	129.22	147.00
Personnel costs	20,202,956	20,397,862	21,602,568	19,982,329
Production hours	1,544,048	1,424,667	1,293,838	1,132,281
Support hours	842,886	844,101	888,222	802,602
Units per hour	.21	.20	.13	.12
Units per production hour	.33	.32	.22	.20

Note: Applies to flexible-base roads only.

percent, indicating that crew productivity had decreased by more than one-third.

These last findings illustrate the importance of the "everthing-else-equal" assumption concerning efficiency analysis relying solely on quantitative indicators. The results in table 3–4 indicate that the efficiency of the maintenance crews decreased dramatically, assuming that the quality of the work completed remained the same over the time period in question. In fact, it probably did not. The quality of the Department's pothole-patching work was legendarily poor, characterized by "dump-and-run" operations and "election-day-specials." The new administration initiated a training program and stressed a "do-it-right" policy aimed at placement patches that would last. One interpretation of table 3–4 is that it illustrates the trade-off between quantity and quality. Incorporation of quality indicators in the efficiency analysis along the lines discussed earlier would permit verification of this premise. Beyond that, if indeed the crews are now doing more effective pothole patching even though their production levels are down, the results should show up in terms of an improved condition of roadway surfaces, discussed in chapters 4 and 5.

Notes

1. Scott Kutz, "Programmed Project Management in Pennsylvania: Statewide Access" (Paper delivered to the 60th Annual Meeting of the Transportation Research Board in Washington, D.C., in January 1981).

2. *An Evaluation of the Production Cost of Highway Maintenance in Pennsylvania* (Pennsylvania Office of the Budget, Harrisburg, Pennsylvania, 1978).

3. T.H. Poister, *Public Program Analysis: Applied Research Methods* (Baltimore: University Park Press, 1978), chap. 9.

4. Thomas D. Cook and Donald T. Campbell, *Quasi-Experimentation: Design & Analysis Issues for Field Settings* (Chicago: Rand McNally College Publishing, 1979).

4

Linking Variables: System Adequacy

The intended linkages between the outputs of the construction and maintenance programs and real impacts in terms of user costs, accidents, and service are represented by measures of system adequacy, as discussed in chapter 2. For instance, as a result of placing a certain number of tons of patching material on the roadway, the number of potholes should be reduced over a period of time and in turn contribute to a reduction in vehicle operating and maintenance costs. Similarly, adding center turn lanes at busy intersections or paving the shoulders along highways should help to minimize exposure to accidents.

Monitoring the status of the physical highway network should obviously be at the core of any information system intended to provide feedback on the performance of the construction and maintenance programs. State and local transportation agencies are charged with responsibility for the continuing development, upgrading, and maintenance of highway systems; keeping track of the adequacy of the system in terms of condition, safety, and serviceability is the most direct means of assessing how well they are meeting this responsibility. Evaluating program operations in terms of whether key activities meet production targets and whether outputs are produced efficiently is clearly important from a line-management perspective, as discussed in chapter 3, but on a larger scale these activities are worthwhile only if they make a demonstrable difference in the actual status of the highway system. Thus monitoring-system adequacy on an ongoing basis is central to the whole idea of performance monitoring for highway programs.

Highway Characteristics and Indicators

Potential indicators of system adequacy run the full gamut of measureable changes in the physical design and condition of the highways. A comprehensive list of features would include, first of all, a number of design characteristics of the roadway itself such as number of lanes, lane width, pavement type, shoulder type, grades, curvature, the geometrics of intersections, access control, and whether there is a division between travel directions. Beyond this would be various types of drainage structures and numerous types of appurtenances—that is, supporting facilities such as traffic-control devices, signs, pavement markings, median barriers, guardrails, and roadside rests. Although these features are off the roadway proper, they are important from both a structural integrity and a safety standpoint. For all of these characteristics, we might be interested in both their design (does the particular highway segment have guardrails and, if so, what type are they?) and their present condition (are they structurally sound and fully functional?).

Principal concern, however, focuses on the actual pavements, including surface and foundation, because they actually carry the traffic. A wide variety of measurement tools are currently used by highway engineers to obtain readings on four different aspects of pavement adequacy: (1) structural capacity, (2) skid resistance, (3) condition, and (4) rideability.[1]

Structural capacity concerns the ability of the pavement to adequately support a particular weight or carry a given load and depends on how well the road was built, the thickness of various layers in the subbase, base, and surface, and the properties of materials used. It can be measured by looking at core samples taken from the road or can be inferred indirectly by the pavement's response to nondestructive tests using equipment such as a Benkelman Beam, Dynaflect, or a Road Rater. Skid resistance refers to the friction or abrasive elements of the pavement surface that are intended to prevent skidding. This can also be measured by mechanical equipment such as a skid trailer, from which "skid numbers" are derived.

Condition and Rideability

Pavement condition is usually measured in terms of distress, observable deterioration, or accumulated damage in the pavement. This would include such observable conditions as potholes, cracking, "blowups," and deteriorated joints. A wide array of condition or distress surveys, most of them involving physical inspection by trained observers, are presently in use in different states. More recently photologging has been introduced as a way to speed up the fieldwork necessary for a condition survey.[2] Because maintenance work is often performed in response to distress, some condition surveys count evidence such as patches and sealed areas as indications of distress.

Rideability refers to the riding quality and riding comfort of a given section of highway. It is usually measured in terms of roughness rated by response-type measuring systems such as a Mays Meter, PCA Meter or roughometer, or by actual profile as measured by a Profilometer.[3] The raw data obtained from these mechanical measuring devices are often converted into a present serviceability index (PSI) ranging from 0 to 5, representing very low to very high levels of service, respectively. The concept of "serviceability" reflects the quality of the road and the level of service it affords *as perceived by the user.* Panel ratings have been found to correlate quite highly with roughness measures, and serviceability is sometimes thought of as representing the motorist's perspective on rideability and distressed conditions.[4] Continuing this line of thought, pavement "performance" reflects serviceability over time, the history of a given highway section's serviceability from construction through its design life. Thus effective highway-construction and maintenance programs should ultimately pay off in terms of improved pavement performance.

Although these concepts are often confused, it should be clearly understood that rideability and condition data measure two very distinct attributes of road quality. Condition indicators represent the actual physical characteristics of a section of highway, its state of repair or deterioration at a given time, whereas rideability or PSI represents the ride quality it provides. Condition pertains to the quality of the road itself, while PSI relates to the behavior of a vehicle driving on that road. The two are of course connected, inasmuch as poorer surface condition—more potholes, cracking, joint deterioration, surface obstruction, and so on—can be expected to reduce the quality of the ride. However, a road section could be in good condition in terms of having no surface distress but still have a low PSI due to the lack of good profile or simply a rough layer of surfacing material. Thus condition and ride are clearly complementary measures of road quality.

It should also be pointed out that pavement performance in its broadest sense—including structural capacity and skid resistance in addition to rideability and distress—must be evaluated in light of the type of road in a given highway section and its functional class, the purpose it was designed to serve. In other words, the minimum acceptable levels of structural capacity, skid resistance, and rideability are necessarily much higher for four-lane, divided highways that carry heavy traffic volumes with a high percentage of trucks than for lower-order farm-to-market roads carrying relatively light traffic. Similarly, greater distress levels are acceptable on lower roads than on higher-order roads. Specification of both design standards and performance standards varies widely across different classes of highway. Therefore, pavement-performance data must be analyzed in terms of functional classification, travel volumes, and pavement type in order to evaluate overall system adequacy.

Federal HPMS

During the initial stages of developing performance indicators for Penn-DOT, the Federal Highway Administration (FHWA) issued guidelines for implementing a Highway Performance Monitoring System (HPMS).[5] The purpose of HPMS was to establish a data base for the continual monitoring of the nationwide highway system as an aid to investment planning and programming and as a data source for numerous studies required by federal legislation. In implementing HPMS, each state DOT is required to maintain a fairly comprehensive data base on a preselected sample of highway sections and to update the information annually using a mix of routinely available secondary data and primary data obtained from field observations. Thus each state now has a permanent sample data base that could be used for monitoring pavement performance over time, and that can be combined by FHWA for monitoring overall trends in pavement performance on a nationwide basis.

The Pennsylvania DOT is required to supply FHWA with updated data on a sample of roughly 5,000 sections of highway including interstates and other freeways, principal and minor arterials, and urban collectors. The information reported is quite comprehensive in some respects, including descriptive characteristics such as functional class, federal-aid designation, and local jurisdiction, along with design features such as length, access control, number of lanes, lane width, median width and type, shoulder width and type, surface type, number of intersections, and traffic control. Other factors include type of operation (one way or two way), carrying capacity, travel volumes and traffic composition, speed limits and average speed. The reporting form also calls for structural number, skid number, and an indication of "pavement condition," although this last item has not been standardized among the states and allows PSI to be used instead of a condition index.

In developing indicators of system adequacy for PennDOT, careful consideration was given to the possibility of using HPMS as the basic data source since essentially HPMS incorporates much of the relevant kinds of information and because the Department was already required to collect and report these data items from FHWA. However, it was decided that although the coordination of the two efforts was certainly desirable in principle, HPMS would not suffice as a means for tracking the Department's progress in improving Pennsylvania's highways. The reasons are twofold. First, while performance monitoring can be based on sample data, a constant or permanent sample is not desirable because as the highway sections included in the sample become known, and as the purpose and process of performance monitoring become better understood, this could create a serious problem of reactive measurement. If, for instance, counties or districts wanted their performance to look good, the permanent sample sections might turn into "showcase" highways upgraded to the extreme at the expense of other, possibly more important roads. Conversely, district and county managers could react by letting the permanent sample sections deteriorate faster than other roads in an effort to assure higher allocations of maintenance funds. Second, HPMS does not include any comprehensive and well-defined indication of road condition, probably the most important aspect of highway quality in Pennsylvania.

At this point, it should be clear that there are myriad types of measures and specific indicators representing various aspects of highway-system adequacy, and that a monitoring system that attempted to incorporate all possible measures in a "cafeteria approach" would probably be cumbersome and inefficient. Decisions about which characteristics to monitor and what indicators to develop depend on the purposes of the monitoring system in the first place, as well as the priorities placed on different parts of the agency's overall highway program. In general, macro-level performance monitoring will not require all the detailed data that are necessary in project-design work. For example, structural-capacity information is obviously necessary in considering whether to overlay or rebuild a section of road, but this usually occurs only after other indicators have made it clear that some major corrective action needs to be taken. Along the same lines, skid numbers are needed to evaluate whether some type of surface treatment is necessary to increase skid resistance, but this may come into play only on sections that have been already identified as hazardous locations.

Furthermore, many of the attributes identified above as comprising system adequacy are basically design features such as number of lanes or shoulder width, which may be fairly static. In other words, from an aggregate monitoring perspective, these features may not be substantially altered in the short run as a result of program activity. On the other hand, such aspects of road quality as condition and rideability may be highly variable in the short run, being sensitive to numerous kinds of program activity. Selecting the most relevant types of indicators depends in large part on the current status of the system and the mix of objectives and program activities in the Department. To the extent that the safety and construction programs are aimed at upgrading the overall highway system, some of the design features may predominate, whereas emphasis on maintaining and restoring the existing system as designed would tend to be reflected in terms of improved condition and rideability.

Sufficiency Ratings

As indicated in chapter 2, the usual means of monitoring system adequacy is to use sufficiency ratings. These ratings involve the inventory and assessment of numerous highway features often grouped in the categories of condition, safety and service. Different versions of sufficiency ratings have been used by many states, and in recent years considerable work has been done on developing procedures that could be applied nationwide.[6]

In general, sufficiency-rating measures monitor the change in substandard highway characteristics over time in order to show the effects of the Department's activities on the road system. For most of the measures, substandard characteristics have been defined in terms of current design standards. These standards will inevitably change, and the proposed measures should remain current with the state of the art in highway design. Care should be exercised not to compare data from years in which the design standards have changed. When standards do change, a new data base should be accrued so that those measures affected by the change can be compared. The sources of information required to generate these measures may also change as more sophisticated and accurate reporting mechanisms are introduced into the Department's management-information system.

A list of highway features commonly incorporated in sufficiency-rating methods is presented in table 4–1 grouped into the three broad categories of condition, safety, and service. Also shown in table 4–1 are measures commonly employed for each variable, and the data bases that either were existing at the time when the performance indicators were being developed or had been identified as potential new data sources to support the performance-monitoring effort.

In a full-fledged application of sufficiency ratings, measurements for these features would be taken on a periodic basis and combined into a single index to permit comparisons across districts or over time. A weighting scheme would be devised to reflect the relative importance of the three categories—usually the heaviest weight is placed on condition—as well as the individual features within each category. The whole rating is usually keyed to an index ranging from 0 to 100, with 100 representing highway segments with perfect scores in all three categories. These summary ratings are developed for individual highway sections, but they can be obtained for counties, districts, or states and interpreted in terms of average ratings or the percentage of roads below specified values on the index.

PennDOT could operationalize such ratings on a limited basis using the HPMS data base, but their utility would be contingent on the reliability of the condition data and the adequacy of the sample. A full-blown sufficiency rating was *not* recommended at this point both because the necessary data would not be available or easily obtainable for the entire statewide highway system and because not all aspects of system adequacy were considered to be of equal interest in terms of monitoring change over time. However, similar indices are being established for some of the more variable aspects of system adequacy, to be discussed later. Nevertheless, the indicators shown in table 4–1 have been identified as relevant measures to monitor collectivity over time but not in a combined index.

Pavement Type. Present design standards do not identify circumstances in which rigid pavement (concrete) is required instead of flexible pavement (asphalt). However, the need to provide paved roads in the state system is universally accepted. Thus measuring the change in miles of unimproved roads would best reflect changes in the physical characteristics of roads with regard to pavement type. (Unimproved roads are basically dirt roads that have received no surface treatment other than grading.) Data on the number of paved roads can be found in the road log, which is maintained by the Bureau of Advance Planning. Information in the road log is updated annually from straight-line drawings provided by the districts. Understandably, the road log is only as good as the data provided by the districts. Although these data are not considered to be entirely accurate, they are in a computerized format and can be accessed with relative ease.

Surface Condition. At the outset of the performance-indicator project, the Department did not have a systematic means of assessing surface condition, either in terms of regional comparisons or tracking change over time. Two systems for collecting surface and other condition data were considered for possible implementation: a trained-observer survey and photologging. A trained-observer survey is a technique for collecting data on highway conditions. It employs trained professionals to physically observe conditions on a sample of road segments on a periodic basis. Typically, conditions are reported as "good," "fair," or "poor," and the prevalence of deterioration on a road section may be roughly approximated, but more precise counts can be used. Trained-observer surveys are sometimes criticized on the grounds that the data they produce are too judgmental or impressionistic, that individual observer biases can distort the results, and that often they are conducted on only a sample basis. The photologging technique uses a vehicle-mounted camera to take pictures of the roadway every 50 feet or so, and then interprets the photos to assess conditions. The Department could use either a trained-observer survey or photologging to evaluate the extent of distress in road surfaces and to monitor changing surface conditions over time. Possible distress includes potholes, cracking, rutting, and joint deterioration.

Foundation Condition. Data for this measure can also be derived from either a trained-observer survey or photologging. Changes in the number of reportable foundation conditions would indicate the success or failure of the design, construction, and maintenance activities of the Department in improving road conditions caused by foundation problems.

Drainage Condition. Drainage-condition information can also be derived from a trained-observer survey. Changes in average counts, broken down

Table 4-1
Typical Sufficiency-Rating Measures

Variable	Measure	Existing Sources	Potential Sources
Condition			
Pavement type	Miles of unimproved roads	Road log	TOS/photologging
Surface condition	Number of reportable surface conditions		TOS/photologging
Foundation condition	Number of reportable foundation conditions		TOS
Drainage condition	Number of reportable drainage conditions		TOS/photologging
Shoulder condition	Number of reportable shoulder conditions		
Safety			
Lane width	Lane miles of roads with lane width below design standards	Straight lines/HPMS	
Shoulder width	Lane miles of roads with shoulder width below design standards	Straight lines/HPMS	
Median width	Lane miles of roads with median width below design standards	Road log	
Consistency	Number of transition sections with inadequate capacity	Road log/Capacity program	
Stopping-sight distance	Lane miles of roads with stopping-sight distance below design standards	CGHGM/HPMS	
Potentially hazardous locations	Number of high-incident locations	LPR	

Service

Service		Source
Access Control	Lane miles of road without required limited access	Road log/HPMS
Alignment	Lane miles of road with horizontal curves below design standards	Straight lines/HPMS
Passing opportunities	Lane miles of road without passing opportunities	CGHGM
Rideability	Lane miles of road with PSI below a standard PSI value	Mays Meters
Obstructions	Unit count of obstructions per mile	TOS/photologging
Signs and pavement markings	Unit count of nonfunctional signs and markings per mile	TOS/photologging
Roads posted	Miles of posted roads	MOR
Bridges closed	Number of bridges closed	MOR
Bridges weight-restricted	Number of weight-restricted bridges	MOR

Sources: TOS: Trained-Observer System; CGHGM: Computerized Geometric Highway Graphic MAP.
HPMS: Highway Performance-Monitoring System; LPR: Location Priority Report.
MOR: Management Objectives Report.

by maintenance functional class (MFC), should indicate deterioration or improvement in drainage conditions on a random sample of road segments representative of the entire state-road network. The problems of definition changes and statistical sensitivity encountered in the measurement of surface conditions apply to these measures as well. A trained-observer survey also may produce a biased low count on drainage deficiencies since drainage problems are not readily apparent during periods of good weather. Once a trained-observer survey becomes routinized, the degree of bias would become more apparent and adjustments could be made. The photologging technique cannot provide information on most drainage conditions because the pictures that are taken do not show the area beyond the shoulders; even side-mounted cameras would not capture drainage pipes, inlets, and endwalls.

Shoulder Condition. Shoulder condition pertains to the shoulder surface, the slope of the shoulder away from the road, and the possible drop-off from the pavement down to the shoulder. These conditions could be assessed by either a trained-observer survey or by photologging.

Lane Width. A measure of the change in lane miles of road with lane widths below design standards would indicate whether the state was fulfilling the requirements of its design criteria. It is assumed that these criteria represent the physical characteristics that best satisfy the requirements for safety, speed, and efficiency on highways, but this may not necessarily be true. Recent reports have called for improvements in the cost effectiveness of highway-design standards.[7] California and Texas have revised their standards, adding flexibility for adapting the standards to the characteristics of a given road segment. Data on current lane widths are available from straight-line diagrams held by the Bureau of Advance Planning that updates them as information is received from the district offices.

The information on lane width would have to be collected manually and added to information from the road log in order to determine a design lane width. By determining which segments in the road log have insufficient lane widths, the total number of lane miles with lane widths below design standards can be computed. If lane width information were added to the road log, the computation of this measure would be significantly simpler. Of particular significance would be the number of high-travel-volume road sections with substandard lane widths. The same type of data would be available from the sample used for the federally mandated HPMS. However, whether the fixed sample is representative of the state system after the first year depends on whether the observed road segments receive the same treatment as all road segments in the state.

Shoulder Width. A change in the lane miles of roads with a shoulder width less than design standards should indicate the progress of the Department in eliminating the hazard posed by narrow shoulders. These data are available for the entire state system from straight-line diagrams. The design standard for shoulders is not as complicated as that for lane width, so use of the road log is not necessary. The data would have to be collected manually and updated regularly from revisions forwarded by the Engineering District Office. Like data on the lane-width measure, data on shoulder width could be collected from HPMS, taking into account the limitations described earlier.

Median Width. Median widths are given in the road log for all state highways. The design standards give some latitude to the designer by specifying acceptable ranges of median width for certain classes of roads with various traffic volumes. Once a specific standard is set, the number of lane miles of highway with inadequate medians could be derived.

Stopping-Sight Distance. Minimum and desirable values for stopping-sight distances have been established for all roads in the state according to road class, number of lanes, and rural/urban classification. At present there exists no inventory of stopping-sight distances for the entire highway network. It is possible that information about stopping-sight distances from the sample used in HPMS would be sufficiently representative of changes in the entire system. Another source might be the data collected under a pilot project administered by the Traffic Operations Division. Through the use of a Computerized Geometric Highway Graphic Map (CGHGM) process, this project is generating data for all two-lane, marked, rural, and semirural roads. (Stopping-sight distance is not so critical in urban areas.) Once this data base has been generated, it may be possible to update it on a project-by-project basis. In addition, data on three-or-more-lane roads should be included. Given its present format, the data from the CGHGM project may have to be collected manually.

Potentially Hazardous Locations. PennDOT's Bureau of Accident Analysis issues an annual Safety Investment Program Location Priority Report, which identifies, in each county, locations with abnormally high accident rates. The districts investigate the locations with the highest rates, and subsequently forward proposals for improvements to the Traffic Operations Division, which then uses the cost-benefit ratio of each project to select projects that can be undertaken within budget constraints. In lieu of the survey of the entire highway network for hazards, the annual inventory of potentially hazardous locations supplies an excellent tool for monitoring the results of Department activities relating to road hazards. By observing changes in the number of potentially hazardous locations, the ability of the Department to eliminate these hazards can be measured. A decreasing number of potentially hazardous locations would provide one link between accident rates and the outputs of the Department's activities. Another statistic that may prove useful in monitoring the backlog of safety projects is a measure of those locations that repeatedly appear on the list.

Consistency. *Consistency* refers to the elimination of sections of highway in which the number of traffic lanes changes. The term is also used when discussing changes from flexible to rigid pavement, but for the purposes of this study, changes in pavement type are not as significant as those involving the number of lanes. Simply monitoring the number of transitional sections in the system would not be an accurate method for obtaining information about the effect of consistency on users. The construction of additional highway lanes would increase the number of transitional sections but might also help to reduce travel time, accidents, and user costs. A more useful measure of consistency would be one that monitored the changes in the number of transitional sections having inadequate capacity. Transitional sections could be identified from the road log and the capacity for each calculated by a computer program maintained by the Traffic Operations Division. By comparing peak volumes on these transitional sections with their design capacities, the number of sections with inadequate capacity could be derived.

Access Control. Class 1 state roads and interstate highways are the only roads in Pennsylvania on which limited access is required. The change in lane miles of road without required limited access can be derived from the road log and from straight-line diagrams by identifying all interstate and Class 1 highways having volumes that require limited access. The straight-line diagrams of these roads can then be reviewed to determine the number of lane miles of road with at-grade intersections. If road construction is being performed in accordance with the Department's design standards, this measure should remain constant or decrease with time. This process may be unduly expensive, however, in which case data from the HPMS can be used. It should be noted that lowering the number of lane miles without required limited access will probably have a minimal impact on users.

Alignment. Alignment affects a road user's line of sight and thus the speed at which a vehicle can travel safely and comfortably. Projects undertaken by the Transportation Department should bring curves on all roads up to design standards. In time there should be a decline in the number of lane miles with horizontal curves below design standards. The design standards for degrees of curvature are keyed to road class. Roads with curves below standard should be easily identifiable from straight-line diagrams. Data on curves should be contained in the 1981 HPMS report, which should be an economical substitute for systemwide data taken from the straight-line diagrams. However, HPMS data may not represent actual changes in the statewide system, and the information is updated only on a two-year, or in some cases, on a four-year basis.

Passing Opportunities. The number of lane miles of road without passing opportunities is probably one of the most significant characteristics that influences average speed on two- and three-lane highways. The change in this measure is one that most users can understand. The Computerized Geographic Highway Graphic Map (CGHGM) system will indicate the number of lane miles without passing opportunities on two-lane marked roads. If these data are updated regularly, they will provide an accurate measure of passing opportunities on these roads. The number of lane miles without passing opportunities on three-lane roads is not available from any departmental reporting system. Also, some formula for determining lane miles without passing opportunities on unmarked two-lane roads should be developed.

Rideability. Rideability can be determined in several ways. In Pennsylvania, a Mays meter is used to record the roughness of the road surface for each one-tenth-mile section. From the roughness data generated by the Mays meter, a present serviceability index (PSI) is calculated—a single number that indicates the surface condition of each segment. Under its pavement-management system, the Department has set a terminal serviceability index (TSI) that serves as a standard for roughness ratings in the state. If the PSI falls below the TSI, resurfacing of the segment is required. The derivation of TSI has been questioned, and thus it may be more prudent to select some other design value for identifying segments with intolerable rideability. The Department is currently conducting research aimed at either validating current TSI's or establishing new rideability standards. When these Performance indicators were first being investigated, the Department used Mays meters to measure roughness but only on scattered road sections around the state that had been proposed as candidates for resurfacing; no systematic attempt was made to assess rideability on a representative statewide basis. However, the effort could be expanded to cover a random sample of highway sections or all the roads in certain functional classes.

Obstructions. Surface and shoulder obstructions are tires, tree limbs, dead animals, rocks, or other objects lying on the surface that would cause a vehicle operator to swerve in order to avoid the object. This condition could easily be included in a trained-observer survey, with the unit count for obstructions being reduced to an average unit count per mile for yearly comparisons.

Signs and Pavement Markings. Another measure that could be obtained from a TOS is a unit count of nonfunctional signs and pavement markings, which also could be reduced to an overall average per mile.

Roads Posted. Posted roads create a serious problem for heavy truck movements. The problem is particularly acute in the coal-mining counties of Pennsylvania. The change in the number of miles of posted roads serves as a useful measure for monitoring the magnitude of this problem.

Bridges Closed and Bridges Weight-Restricted. Pennsylvania faces a bridge-deterioration problem of historic proportions. As of February 1980, 47 bridges were closed and 1,122 bridges carried weight restrictions. Closed or weight-limited bridges frequently result in significant additional user travel costs for those who must find alternative routes. These routes usually involve many miles and hours of circuitous travel and inconvenience. In a few cases, bridges may be the sole means of access to homes, businesses, or recreational areas on river islands. To mitigate the problem, emphasis at both the state and federal levels is now being placed on special dedicated funding programs such as the Critical Bridge Program. Measures of closed and weight-restricted bridges, therefore, are timely linking variables for these programs.

The measures proposed here as linking variables by no means represent a complete list. Measures should be added or deleted in accordance with current research on highway characteristics that most significantly affect travel time, accidents, and user costs.

Although it was not recommended that PennDOT establish a full-fledged sufficiency-rating program, it is clear that many of these features should be regularly monitored to keep track of overall system adequacy. Data on many of these features are readily available within the Department, and the need for information about other key features warrants new data-collection activities. Many of the items shown in table 4–1 are basically design features (pavement type, lane width, shoulder width, access control, and alignment) that are relatively static over time. Data on most of these features are contained in the road log and straight-line diagrams; as improvements are made they are recorded so that cumulative changes in the adequacy of the network can be noted at six-month or yearly intervals. Data on the number of potentially hazardous locations have been computerized as part of the accident-analysis program and are easily accessed; data on stopping-sight distances and passing opportunities are contained in the Department's CGHGM program. Thus data on most of the features that reflect the adequacy of the network are available through the Department's routine reporting systems. The primary task that remains is to collect meaningful indicators from these sources and present them on a periodic basis in a common format.

Trained-Observer Survey

While data were readily available on design-related features, systematic data had not been developed for many of the more variable conditions or service features. The Department did not have a systematic, objective basis for evaluating the condition of roads in different classes or in different parts of the state. Therefore, a major effort of the performance-indicators project was to develop and test a road-condition survey.[8] In addition to a number of more specific uses, this survey, conducted on a periodic basis, is designed to provide information relating to surface, shoulder, foundation, and drainage conditions, as well as rideability and other service features, which is necessary in order to monitor changes in highway-system condition over time.

As indicated in table 4-1, with the exception of rideability, most of the desired indicators of system adequacy for which an existing data source was not available could be picked up by a trained-observer survey or by photologging. Photologging obviously involves a more sophisticated technology, and in comparison with trained observers, it can result in substantial cost savings in conducting the fieldwork.[9] However, the TOS data collected in the field can be computerized and processed quickly, while photologs have to be examined rather painstakingly by trained observers working in the office before computer processing.

A potential problem with any observer survey, as opposed to mechanical measurements, concerns reliability—will the trained observers all measure conditions exactly the same way so that the measurements are, in effect, interchangeable? Furthermore, if the definitions of distress do not remain constant as the survey is repeated year after year, then comparisons over time are more difficult. Yet these same problems apply to photologging since the data are still recorded manually by individuals who must observe the photologs and make interpretations about deficiencies. One major difference between the alternatives is that the TOS can incorporate drainage condition while the photologs cannot. This was an important consideration in this case because the prevailing thinking in the Department held that drainage had been neglected in past maintenance programs with the effect of undermining highway-surface and foundation conditions.

Ultimately the trained-observer approach was chosen because it could be tailored to fit the varied concerns of the maintenance program and because it could be geared up fairly quickly with no major capital outlay.

Patterned after a similar ongoing survey in Ohio,[10] the trained-observer survey entails the use of trained professionals who observe a number of highway-condition variables by walking a random sample of highway segments in each county on a periodic basis. The number of "reportable conditions"—deficiencies in surface, foundation, drainage, shoulder, and other safety features—can be used to obtain an overall rating of the "as-built" maintenance condition of the roads in each county and district.

The data generated by this system are intended to serve two purposes relating to needs assessment and performance monitoring. First, an analysis of reportable conditions and the overall maintenance ratings should improve the basis on which funds are allocated for maintenance activities. The results should show where the greatest needs for maintenance efforts are, and permit a better allocation of resources among counties and districts and a more efficient targeting of funds by type of highway and by maintenance-cost function.[11]

Second, the TOS will provide the Department with a means of tracking the effectiveness of the maintenance program. Since highways in each county will be sampled for observation on a periodic basis, this system will accumulate time-series data that can be examined to determine whether the number of reportable conditions is decreasing and whether the overall maintenance ratings are improving over time. Such measures of change over time can also be correlated with the extent and costs of selected maintenance activities in order to examine the impact of these activities.

Instrument Design

To determine what kinds of deficiencies should be included in the TOS and to define the reportable conditions to be noted, three criteria were taken into account:

1. The system should be comprehensive in terms of highway-maintenance concerns and should include measures representing conditions of major structural characteristics and major safety features.
2. The list of reportable conditions should include those that relate to the Department's high-cost maintenance activities (excluding winter maintenance) and should include only the deficiencies to which the Department responds. For example, the condition of surface flushing would not be included because the Department does not take action to directly counteract this problem.

3. The measuring instrument itself must be reliable, based on observable, tangible characteristics or conditions rather than on impressions. To assure inter-observer reliability, the system must be based on clearly defined reportable conditions that would be observed and counted in the same way by different individuals.

Offsetting these criteria is the need for an instrument that is not too cumbersome to use. The system needs to be workable in the field; an unduly complicated set of measures may make the observers' work tedious and time consuming. During pretesting, the instrument was simplified and streamlined to make the fieldwork smoother and quicker.

The set of reportable conditions included in the survey reflects the major structural and safety concerns of highway maintenance as grouped in the general categories of roadways (surface and foundation), shoulders, drainage, and appurtenances. Figure 4-1 shows the individual items or deficiencies that indicate given types of reportable conditions. For example, surface deterioration may be indicated by dust layering, slopes greater than 1/2 inch per foot, depressions, minor cracking or "map cracking," and gaps in transverse or longitudinal joints. Specific definitions of each type of deficiency have been established, and the observers have been trained to apply them before beginning actual fieldwork. A complete description of the reportable conditions is contained in appendix A.

An attempt has also been made to minimize problems of interobserver reliability by establishing criteria for the extent required of each type of deficiency for it to qualify as a reportable condition. The prevalence of each reportable condition is to be measured by the frequency with which the observers see that condition along the sample stretch of highway they are inspecting. The definition of each type of reportable condition specifies a minimum—how much of that condition must be observed in order to be counted. For instance, minor cracking must cover at least 1 square foot.

In addition, a unit count is specified for each deficiency. If a given deficiency extends for more than this unit count, it counts as more than one reportable condition. For example, the unit count for minor cracking is 25 lineal feet. Thus, if the observers encounter map cracking of 1 square foot or more that extends 12 lineal feet, this counts as one reportable condition. However, if the map cracking were found to cover 60 lineal feet, this would be counted as three reportable conditions. With this system the observers have much less responsibility for determining the severity of the problems they come across.

It should also be noted that some degree of continuity among the different reportable conditions is built into the system. For instance, small depressions or holes less than 2 inches deep count as surface deterioration; potholes 2 inches or more in depth count as surface obstructions as long

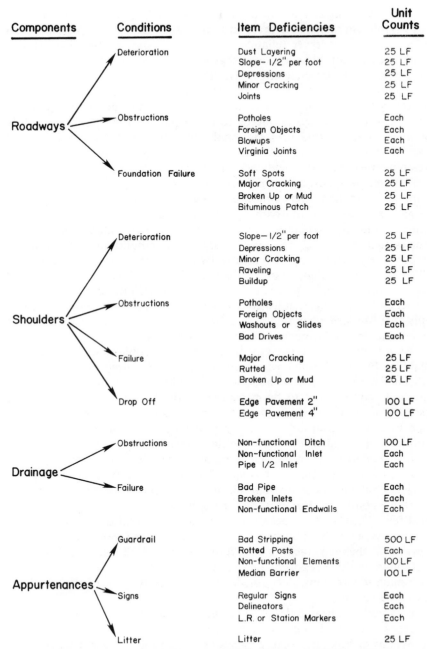

Components	Conditions	Item Deficiencies	Unit Counts
Roadways	Deterioration	Dust Layering	25 LF
		Slope— 1/2" per foot	25 LF
		Depressions	25 LF
		Minor Cracking	25 LF
		Joints	25 LF
	Obstructions	Potholes	Each
		Foreign Objects	Each
		Blowups	Each
		Virginia Joints	Each
	Foundation Failure	Soft Spots	25 LF
		Major Cracking	25 LF
		Broken Up or Mud	25 LF
		Bituminous Patch	25 LF
Shoulders	Deterioration	Slope— 1/2" per foot	25 LF
		Depressions	25 LF
		Minor Cracking	25 LF
		Raveling	25 LF
		Buildup	25 LF
	Obstructions	Potholes	Each
		Foreign Objects	Each
		Washouts or Slides	Each
		Bad Drives	Each
	Failure	Major Cracking	25 LF
		Rutted	25 LF
		Broken Up or Mud	25 LF
	Drop Off	Edge Pavement 2"	100 LF
		Edge Pavement 4"	100 LF
Drainage	Obstructions	Non-functional Ditch	100 LF
		Non-functional Inlet	Each
		Pipe 1/2 Inlet	Each
	Failure	Bad Pipe	Each
		Broken Inlets	Each
		Non-functional Endwalls	Each
Appurtenances	Guardrail	Bad Stripping	500 LF
		Rotted Posts	Each
		Non-functional Elements	100 LF
		Median Barrier	100 LF
	Signs	Regular Signs	Each
		Delineators	Each
		L.R. or Station Markers	Each
	Litter	Litter	25 LF

Figure 4–1. Trained-Observer Survey Reportable Conditions

as they are not larger than 2 square yards. Large potholes or depressions covering 2 square yards or more count as foundation failures.

In addition to visually inspecting the sample highway segments and recording the observed reportable conditions, for the first cycle, the crews doing the fieldwork rode each segment in a vehicle equipped with a Mays ride meter to obtain an indication of roughness. The Department had been using May meters on selected roadways and relying primarily on PSI measures to determine the need for resurfacing. Rideability is only one aspect of road condition, however, and the trained-observer counts on a variety of conditions should greatly improve the ability to discriminate between good and bad roads. More recently, the effort has been expanded to obtain PSI measures for all road sections on the higher-order systems.

Sample Selection

The trained-observer survey is to be conducted twice each year, in the spring and in the fall, with a floating sample; in other words, a new random sample of road segments will be selected for observation each time. While the sampling fraction must be low, given time and cost considerations and the fact that the system contains nearly 45,000 miles, data will build over time on most of the system. The use of floating samples is recommended in order to obtain more complete coverage in the span of a few observation periods, and to avoid possible problems arising from the targeting of maintenance activities to those few segments known to be included in a stationary sample.

Given the purpose of the trained-observer system as aiding in the allocation of maintenance funds, and monitoring the progress of the maintenance program across time, the development of a sample selection procedure was based on the following criteria:

1. The overall sample should be approximately representative of the statewide highway network in terms of the distribution across the sixty-seven counties and the eleven engineering districts.
2. Within individual counties the samples should provide for fairly precise estimates of the number of reportable conditions for the county as awhole.
3. While the samples will not be very reliable for a given type of road for any given county, the overall sample should provide reliability for a given maintenance functional code on a district basis.

Based on these criteria, it was decided that the most appropriate type of sample would be a random sample of the approximately 88,000 half-mile of observable segments, stratified by county and maintenance functional code (MFC). A separate sample is selected from each county, and within each county, care is taken to include sufficient examples of each road type. Since there are relatively fewer miles of the higher classes of highways, these must be sampled more heavily in order to have good sample reliability on a district basis. Therefore, while collectors and local roads were sampled at 2 percent for cycle 1 of the survey, the sampling fraction for interstate highways was 15 percent.

The Department's road logs were used to generate the sample. The road logs are organized by county, with sections of all state highways within a county arranged according to legislative route number. A given legislative route is broken down into small sections that are classified by a number of different indicators relating to location, structure, usage, and function. The sections vary in length; for example, in Lycoming County entries range from 0.02 to 7 miles. These extremes are not useful for the trained-observer system because the shortest sections would not provide sufficient length to detect all types of reportable conditions, and the longest would yield largely redundant information. Therefore, short contiguous sections or entries in the road log were combined, and a few of the longest sections were divided in an attempt to obtain segments of approximately 0.3 to 0.7 miles. In combining small sections, care was taken not to mix very dissimilar roads in the segments that would be used to draw the sample. Thus entries in the road log were combined only if they were part of the same legislative route, had the same urban/rural status, had the same classification according to the maintenance functional code, and fell within the same general range of average daily travel (ADT). The ranges of ADT established by Bureau of Maintenance personnel were: 1–1,499 vehicles, 1,500–2,999 vehicles, 3,000–4,999 vehicles, and 5,000 vehicles and above. Highway sections with ADTs of more than 5,000 vehicles could be combined only if the difference in ADT did not exceed 10,000 vehicles.

From the resulting file of 0.3- to 0.7-mile segments, roads were randomly selected for a sample that was stratified proportionately by county and disproportionately by MFC. The total mileage and number of sections sampled in cycle 1 for each MFC are shown in table 4–2. This overall sample of 3 percent contained a substantial number of highway segments to be observed; yet it was understood that if there were wide variation in the rate of reportable conditions, a larger sample might be needed to make statistically valid comparisons across districts and MFC categories.[12] Analysis of the results of the first three cycles has in fact indicated that larger samples are required in order to assure reliability at a county level. The sample size was expanded incrementally for cycles 2 and 3 and then doubled, using shorter sections, for cycles 4 and 5. As shown in table 4–2, the total sample size increased by a factor of two and a half from cycle 1 in the fall of 1979 to

Table 4-2
TOS Sample Selection Statistics

MFC	Total Mileage	Approximate Half-Mile Sections	Cycle 1 Sampling Fraction (Percent)	Cycle 1 Sections Observed	Cycle 5 Quarter-Mile Sections Observed
Interstate	1,060	2,120	15	339	1,092
Principal arterials	4,060	8,120	8	633	1,530
Minor arterials	8.460	16,920	2.5	399	1,373
Collectors	17,700	35,400	2.0	728	1,427
Local	12,780	25,560	2.0	482	1,170
Total	44,060	88,120	3.0	2,581	6,592

cycle 5 in the fall of 1981. In large part, this was made feasible by shortening the sections from a half-mile to a quarter-mile on the average since the early cycles showed that the half-mile sections were internally homogenous.

Conduct of the Fieldwork

Implementation of any new major data-collection effort intended to be conducted on a regular recurring basis requires considerable development, testing, and modification. The TOS developed for PennDOT has actually been in this formative or developmental mode through the first five cycles or so, encompassing a period of more than two years. The definitions of reportable conditions were field tested in a pilot program in Lycoming County, a rural county in north-central Pennsylvania that has one major city, Williamsport, and 869 miles of state highways. The pilot was conducted by the Operations Review Group, the unit given the basic responsibility for implementing the TOS. Lycoming was considered a representative county because, although it has no interstate highway, it has several four-lane roads. On two-lane roads, only one direction was walked and observations extended only to the center line. On three- and four-lane roads, both directions were walked and the data were combined for each section. Upon completion of the pilot program, staff from the Bureau of Highway Maintenance, and the Operations Review Group and the university consultants reviewed the results and made the following changes:

Several definitions were revised to reflect conditions as they were actually observed and to make reporting easier.

Unit counts were standardized for ease in observing and reporting.

Directions of walk were alternated to provide greater randomness and actual representation.

A two-man-team procedure for performing observations and recording data was established for the following reasons: (1) Use of a two-man team with two vehicles, one parked at each end of the section, saved considerable time previously lost by walking back to the vehicle at the starting point, and (2) many of the defined criteria are based on frequencies of occurrences within a 25- or 100-foot length. Through experimentation, the easiest method for tracking the distances was found to be with the use of a measuring wheel. One member of the team uses the wheel and notes distances and conditions, while the other member observes the conditions and records the counts on the chart.

The following standard packages were developed for each county for use by trained observers: (1) Straight-line diagrams for each section of roadway to be examined. These helped to locate roads in counties lacking station or legislative route markers. (2) County maps with all sections plotted in color to identify the approximate location of each section. This aids the team in planning a day's work with the minimal amount of travel time between sections. (3) Tabulation of sections by MFC, giving starting and stopping stations and length in feet and miles.

It was decided to inspect bridges with span lengths up to 20 feet because this was the cut-off length of the bridge-inspection team.

It was anticipated that a minimum of 5 two-man teams would be needed to complete the work before the winter. After initial training, new employees were assigned to work with the two engineers who had done the pretesting. When they became proficient, they were placed with other experienced employees. One of the engineers who performed the pilot in Lycoming County worked as the program coordinator during the entire cycle. He or his supervisor was available to answer questions concerning interpretations, definitions, and so on, either by telephone or on periodic visits to crews in the counties. Periodically, two or more teams were brought together to observe the same test sections in order to identify and correct any problems that resulted in differences in the way the teams were recording reportable conditions. This, along with periodic checks by the supervisors, produced a high level of inter-rater reliability.

To avoid weather problems, the survey started with counties in the northern and western part of the state and worked generally toward the southeast corner. Whenever possible, team members were rotated in a further attempt to prevent possible observer biases from solidifying. This helped to ensure uniform interpretation. At the completion of the first cycle and prior to release of the temporary personnel, a two-day seminar was held to discuss and revise, if necessary, each of the condition definitions, and to identify any potential problem areas that required attention before the next cycle.

The cost for the first cycle of field operations was approximately $200,000. In the second cycle, efficiency was increased by plotting all counties prior to starting fieldwork, and by dividing the state into five geographical areas. At the start of the cycle the teams were provided with all the packages for their assigned counties. This information permits the teams to be more efficient in the scheduling and conduct of their fieldwork. For example, instead of limiting a day's work to segments within one county, surveys can be made on the same day on segments near the common border of adjacent counties. Furthermore, data processing has been streamlined: In the process of selecting the sample, the computer prints all descriptive heading information, for example, length, traffic route, and stations, on the tally sheets for each survey. Therefore, the cost of subsequent cycles has gone up only incrementally even though the sample size has been increased. Because the results from the first three cycles have proven very useful, as discussed in the following chapters, PennDOT has made a longer-term commitment to TOS, and ways are now being analyzed to both strengthen its utility and expand its coverage.

Notes

1. For descriptions of the various aspects of pavement quality and their related measuring devices, see "Collection and Use of Pavement Condition Data," *NCHRP Synthesis 76,* Transportation Research Board, Washington, D.C., 1981; ARE Inc., *Pavement Management: Principles and Practices* (Prepared for U.S. Department of Transportation, Federal Highway Administration, Washington, D.C.).

2. Charles E. Dougan and Louis E. Sugland, "Photologging—A Maintenance Management Tool," *Transportation Research Record* 781 (1980):57–65.

3. T.D. Gillespie, M.W. Sayers, and L. Segel, "Calibration of Response-Type Road Roughness Measuring Systems," *NCHRP Report 228,* Transportation Research Board, Washington, D.C., 1980.

4. ARE Inc., *Pavement Management: Principles and Practices.*

5. *Highway Performance Monitoring Systems: Field Implementation Manual,* Federal Highway Administration, U.S. Department of Transportation (January 1979).

6. *National System Condition Index,* Final report prepared for U.S Department of Transportation, Federal Highway Administration, by Roy

Jorgensen Associates, Inc., Gaithersburg, Md., February 1978; *Performance Investment Analysis Process: Technical Report,* Federal Highway Administration, Washington, D.C., September 1978.

7. Christopher Fleet, Ed Kashuba, Glenn Jilek, and Richard Osborne. "Critical Issues in Statewide Transportation Planning," *Transportation Research Record* 710 (1979):1–7; S. Bellomo, et al. "Evaluating Options in Statewide Transportation Planning/Programming," *NCHRP Report 179,* Transportation Research Board, Washington, D.C., 1977; Jorgensen Associates, Inc., "Cost and Safety Effectiveness of Highway Design Elements," *NCHRP Report 197,* Transportation Research Board, Washington, D.C., 1978.

8. Theodore H. Poister and William R. Moyer, "The Pennsylvania DOT Trained Observer Survey: Design and Preliminary Results," *Transportation Research Record* 781 (1980):45–56.

9. Dougan and Sugland, "Photologging—A Maintenance Management Tool."

10. E.L. Miller, "A Method of Measuring the Quality of Highway Maintenance," *Transportation Research Record* 506 (1976):1–14; Byrd, Tallamy and MacDonald, *A Study of Highway Maintenance Quality Levels in Ohio,* Falls Church, Va., December 1970.

11. W.A. Phang, "Pavement—Condition Ratings and Rehabilitation Needs," *Transportation Research Record* 700 (1979):11–19; "Evaluation of Pavement Maintenance Strategies," *NCHRP Report* Transportation Research Board, Washington, D.C., 1981 (surveys used in maintenance programming); "Collection and Use of Pavement Condition Data," *NCHRP Synthesis 76* Transportation Research Board, Washington, D.C., 1981.

12. Texas Transportation Institute, *Measurements of Pavement Performance Using Statistical Sampling Techniques* (Austin, Tex., 1978), pp. 6–100.

5 Trained-Observer-Survey Results

The trained-observer survey (TOS) presented in chapter 4 has been adopted by PennDOT as a means of obtaining comprehensive and continually up-dated information on the more variable aspects of its 45,000-mile highway system. It is conducted twice annually at a total cost of several thousand dollars by the Operations Review Group, an auditing unit that reports to the Deputy Secretary of Administration. Because the trained-observer survey is so central to the performance-monitoring system developed in this book, representing the direct outcome of the maintenance program and the link-age between program outputs and effectiveness, the results of the first few cycles merit some attention. This chapter presents some initial results from cycle 1, followed by a discussion of changes in condition monitored over the first three cycles. It then moves to a discussion of the use of indices for com-paring counties, and concludes with remarks about additional modifica-tions and uses of this management tool.

Initial Results

Cycle 1 of the trained-observer survey was conducted in the fall of 1979 on a total of 2,581 highway segments averaging one-half mile in length. The cycle 1 data were of substantial interest to the Department, providing an initial picture of the overall pattern of variation of highway condition across the state, and serving as a benchmark for measuring progress in improving the roads. The preliminary findings presented here concern ratings of existing road conditions as well as estimates of total needs for maintenance work. The results pertain to statewide conditions and, in addi-tion, show comparisons across district and counties.

Overall Conditions

Figures 5-1 and 5-2 show aggregate statewide frequency distributions for four illustrative reportable conditions: surface depressions, minor cracking on the surface, pipe one-half full, and nonfunctioning guardrail elements.

93

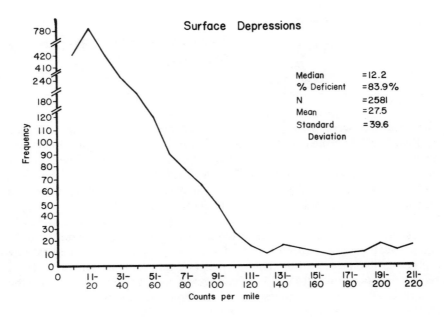

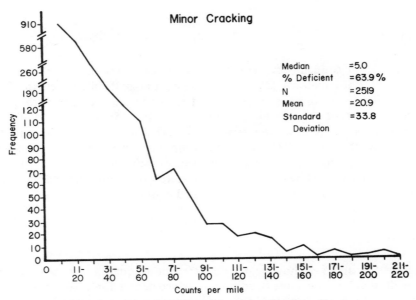

Figure 5-1. Illustrative TOS Cycle 1 Surface Counts

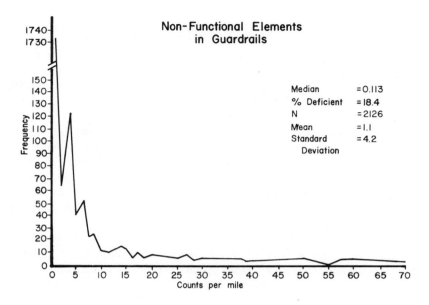

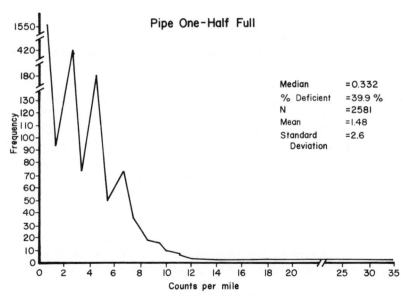

Figure 5–2. Other TOS Cycle 1 Condition Counts

The incidence of all conditions is reported on a count-per-mile basis. The most striking feature of these distributions is that they reflect widespread variation and are highly skewed to the right. For example, while roughly 16 percent of the 2,581 road sections inspected had no surface depressions, some had a moderate-to-heavy incidence of depressions and a few had the maximum possible, 211–220. On these highways, depressions were encountered in every 25-foot stretch that was observed.

That these reportable conditions are highly variable—and this characterizes almost all the items included in the survey—is further evidenced by the fact that the standard deviations exceed their respective mean averages by a considerable margin. The high degree of dispersion weakens sample reliability and makes it more difficult to compare means or obtain precise interval estimates. This was a strong indication that sample sizes should be expanded for future cycles of the survey.

The one-sidedness of these distributions, along with the skews toward extremely high values, makes the mean average less reliable as an indicator of central tendency. Median averages provide a more accurate indication of what values are taken on by the more typical roads for various conditions. It is also the case that on many of the indicators a significant number of roads have zero counts. Thus the percentage of road sections with some counts, or the percent deficient roads, is another measure worth examining. To concentrate on the extremely high values on the basis that in some respects the worst roads in a county or district are of greatest concern, the eightieth or ninetieth percentile might also be useful.

As can be seen in figure 5–1, surface depressions and minor cracking have similar distributions ranging from zero to the maximum, but a substantially higher percentage of all roads evidenced depressions (small potholes) than minor cracking. Comparison of the two medians also indicates that depressions were observed more often than minor cracking. Figure 5–2 shows that only 18.4 percent of the highway sections observed had nonfunctional guardrail elements and that the median was just slightly above .1 observed count per mile. The drainage condition of a pipe being half-full or more was encountered in nearly 40 percent of all sections, and the median was .33 counts per mile. The overall range of this condition is much less than for many others because along many stretches of highway, there are simply no pipes to observe.

The wide variability in the condition of Pennsylvania's road network is not surprising considering the inadequacy of funding for the maintenance program over the past decade and the great variety of roads included in the system. Unlike most states, which have responsibility only for trunk-line highway systems, PennDOT's system incorporates many lower-order collectors, farm-to-market, and small borough "local-use" roads that are not likely to stack up as well in terms of many reportable conditions. Given this context, the distributions seen in figures 5-1 and 5-2 are what might well be expected as a profile of the condition of the state's roads. Now that this profile is known, it raises questions about the preferred strategy for an improved maintenance program: Should the Department seek to steepen the skew by upgrading good and moderately good roads to zero deficiency, or should it concentrate on trying to eliminate deficiencies on roads in the worst possible condition? The development of such a strategy will depend largely on the pattern of variation in condition across different types of roads and geographic regions.

Maintenance-Functional-Classification Comparisons

Since programming and work planning are geared in large part to the maintenance functional class (MFC) of highway, it is worthwhile to make initial comparisons of reportable conditions by MFC. Table 5-1 shows the percentage of deficient roads as well as median averages for selected surface and shoulder conditions. On interstates and some other higher-order roads, the percent deficient will be overstated relative to lower MFC classes because four-lane highways were walked in both directions. There is little systematic variation in the percentage of roads deficient in depressions except that local roads have more deficient segments than the higher categories. However, looking at medians, it is apparent that the typical interstate has fewer depressions per mile than other roads and that this indicator increases with the lower order MFCs. Minor cracking and major cracking are more prevalent on lower-order roads than on interstates and principal arterials, as would be expected given maintenance priorities. However, the incidence of joint deterioration varies in the other direction, from forty-four counts per mile on the interstates and thirty-three per mile on principal arterials to being almost nonexistent on collectors and local roads. This is largely because joints are only observed on rigid-base and rigid-pavement roads, and these tend to be the higher-order roads. The 92 percent deficient on interstates and 73 percent on principal arterials would have to be considered an unacceptably high prevalence of joint deterioration.

Referring also to table 5-1, insufficient shoulder slopes are mainly a problem on collectors and local roads, largely because this condition occurs much less frequently on paved shoulders. Shoulder buildup varies in the opposite direction, perhaps reflecting the greater use of antiskid material on higher-order roads. It is interesting to note that although some shoulder buildup is encountered on a fairly high percentage of roads, the problem is not severe in that on the average there is substantially less than 1 count per mile. These reportable conditions are of great concern because they prevent adequate drainage of water away from the pavement, which can ultimately

Table 5-1
Median Counts per Mile and Percentage of Sections with Some Deficiency:
Surface and Shoulders

Maintenance Functional Class	Selected Surface Items			
	Surface Depressions	Minor Cracking	Joint Deterioration	Major Cracking
A Interstates	5.1 (83.5%)	0.5 (49.8%)	44.0 (92.0%)	1.2 (57.8%)
B Principal arterial	10.6 (81.8%)	2.5 (59.7%)	33.1 (73.2%)	2.8 (59.4%)
C Minor arterial	8.3 (78.4%)	7.7 (71.4%)	0.5 (49.6%)	10.9 (69.2%)
D Collectors	16.7 (83.6%)	9.2 (66.2%)	0.1 (16.9%)	8.5 (64.0%)
E Local	27.4 (91.7%)	13.0 (70.1%)	0.0 (5.6%)	12.1 (64.7%)

Maintenance Functional Class	Selected Shoulder Items			
	Shoulder Slope	Shoulder Buildup	Major Cracking	Shoulder Dropoff >4 Inches
Interstates	0.1 (8.3%)	0.5 (48.5%)	6.3 (60.5%)	0.0 (8.9%)
Principal arterials	0.3 (34.2%)	0.3 (38.8%)	0.4 (41.3%)	0.1 (16.1%)
Minor arterials	0.5 (48.9%)	0.3 (34.7%)	0.4 (45.1%)	0.1 (17.3%)
Collectors	14.9 (65.1%)	0.2 (26.6%)	0.3 (37.3%)	0.1 (20.2%)
Local	22.2 (69.7%)	0.2 (27.3%)	0.5 (59.3%)	0.1 (16.6%)

undermine the road itself. Shoulder dropoffs greater than 4 inches have the lowest incidence on interstates, as expected, and otherwise do not vary substantially by MFC. The low median counts are certainly favorable, but the moderate percentages of roads with some incidence of dropoff exceeding 4 inches are of concern because this reportable condition represents a severe safety hazard. The percent of roads with major cracking on the shoulders is substantially higher for interstates—at 60.5 percent—than for other roads that have fewer concrete and bituminous shoulders.

With the exception of interstates, the percentage of roads with nonfunctioning ditches is greater for the lower-order roads, as shown in table 5-2. On the other hand, the percent of roads with nonfunctioning inlets, as

Table 5–2
Median Counts per Mile and Percentage of Sections with Some Deficiency:
Drainage and Appurtenances

Maintenance Functional Class	Selected Drainage Items		
	Nonfunctional Ditches	Nonfunctional Inlet	Pipe Half-Full
Interstates	0.1 (22.4%)	0.1 (21.2%)	0.1 (20.9%)
Principal arterials	0.1 (15.3%)	0.2 (23.7%)	0.3 (40.9%)
Minor arterials	0.1 (19.5%)	0.1 (12.0%)	0.3 (37.8%)
Collectors	0.2 (25.1%)	0.1 (8.6%)	0.1 (45.3%)
Local	0.2 (25.9%)	0.0 (5.8%)	0.4 (45.4%)

Maintenance Functional Class	Selected Appurtenances			
	Bad Striping	Nonfunctional Guardrail Elements	Regular Signs	Litter
Interstates	0.0 (0.0%)	0.1 (21.4%)	0.1 (22.4%)	81.5 (100.0%)
Principal arterials	0.0 (4.4%)	0.2 (25.3%)	0.1 (19.6%)	64.7 (97.8%)
Minor arterials	0.0 (4.4%)	0.1 (21.8%)	0.1 (13.3%)	45.4 (95.5%)
Collectors	0.0 (7.1%)	0.1 (16.5%)	0.1 (13.3%)	32.0 (95.9%)
Local	0.2 (2.4%)	0.0 (7.7%)	0.1 (9.7%)	14.8 (89.2%)

well as the median average inlet deficiency, tends to decrease on lower-order roads. This is because the collectors and local roads have fewer inlets and endwalls at the ends of cross-pipes even though they tend to have more pipes per mile. Principal arterials are at the same level as interstates on this indicator, reflecting the fact that they have as many inlets but perhaps receive a little less maintenance effort. The prevalence of roads with cross-pipes that are one-half full or more is lowest for interstates, higher for arterials, and still higher for collectors and local roads that reflects the more numerous pipes on maintaining lower-order highways and the fact that less attention is given to pipes on these roads. Because the incidence of drainage problems is so heavily dependent on the actual numbers of ditches and structures, in subsequent cycles these totals have been tabulated and the deficiencies analyzed on a percentage basis.

Table 5-2 also shows median averages and the percent deficient on selected appurtenance conditions by MFC. Striping is good on the interstates and is only a minor problem on lower-order roads with the exception of local roads. While many local roads do not have striping, the level of maintenance is less on those that do compare with higher MFCs. The reportable conditions of nonfunctioning guardrail elements and missing or damaged regular signs are more frequent on the higher-order roads, largely because such roads have more of these appurtenances in place. The percentage of roads with some litter count is almost uniformly high (89 percent is pretty high except for local roads), but the median count decreases dramatically on the lower MFCs mainly as a function of their lower levels of usage. This reportable condition may need to be redefined in order to provide a more discriminating indicator.

Because some of the variation by MFC seems to be explicable in part by pavement type, it is interesting to look at some comparisons on this basis as illustrated by table 5-3. Median values and the percentage of roads having some potholes are highest for unpaved (dirt or gravel) roads and lowest for rigid-pavement roads, those with concrete slabs built over an earthen base. This might be expected given their respective design standards and maintenance priorities. Yet the most stark impression conveyed here is that the overall incidence of potholes is so high. Cracking—major and minor cracking combined—varies in the same direction although in a lower order of magnitude. While cracking is not applicable to unpaved roads, it was found in 64 percent of the flexible-base roads observed, 61 percent of the rigid-base roads, and in 24 percent of the rigid-pavement roads. The flexible-base roads, usually an asphalt or concrete pavement over a base of compacted crushed stone or other loose material, constitute over half of the state system.

District and County Comparisons

Table 5-4 shows the percentage of road sections with deficient shoulder slopes, as broken down by engineering district and MFC. In general, the pattern of shoulder-slope problems increasing with lower-order MFCs is replicated in the eleven districts, with some exceptions. In Districts 4 and 5, for example, there is less incidence of this problem on minor arterials than on major arterials. Overall, the percentage deficient ranges from 38 percent in District 5 to 61 percent in District 10. From a macro-level management perspective, this kind of information should be of primary importance in evaluating maintenance efforts over time. District engineers can then be

Table 5-3
Median Average and Percent Roads Deficient, by Pavement Type, Potholes and Cracking

	All Potholes		All Cracking		
	Md	Percent	Md	Percent	N
Rigid pavement	6.8	80.0	3.2	24.4	601
Rigid base	11.6	83.3	35.4	60.7	493
Flexible base	20.1	87.2	36.4	63.7	1,419
Unpaved	33.2	95.2	—	—	63

Table 5-4
Percentage of Roads with Deficient Shoulder Slope, by District MFC

District	Interstate (Percent)	Principal Arterial (Percent)	Minor Arterial (Percent)	Collectors (Percent)	Local Roads (Percent)	District Total (Percent)
1	17	48	54	72	67	53
2	0	10	52	57	83	40
3	0	10	35	59	62	43
4	11	57	30	60	68	45
5	6	33	24	57	63	38
6	0	50	70	52	45	49
8	8	23	38	62	66	45
9	0	31	32	68	70	52
10	8	27	64	77	90	61
11	7	45	74	88	82	59
12	14	37	77	73	76	59
MFC Total	8	34	49	65	70	49

called on to explain poor performance and to deal internally with problems in problem counties.

Figure 5-3 shows the geographic distribution of the percentage of roads on which nonfunctional guardrail elements were observed, by counties within districts. Many of the reportable conditions, particularly surface items such as major cracking, do not coincide with district boundaries to any substantial degree. The geographic distribution of some of the surface items do, however, correspond with topographical features, soil structure, or weather patterns. Other indicators are not directly explicable in terms of these environmental variables either, and essentially they represent scattered differences in county maintenance effectiveness.

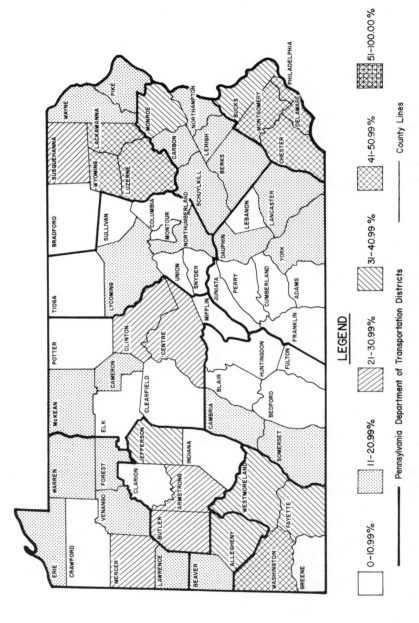

Figure 5-3. TOS Cycle 1 Nonfunctional Guardrail Counts by County

By contrast, the variation in the percentage of roads with nonfunctional guardrail elements coincides with district boundaries to a high degree. Districts 8 and 9 in the middle of the southern-tier counties, along with District 3 to the north, have almost uniformly low percentages of deficient roads. Districts with concentrations of counties in the highest ranges of percent roads with nonfunctional guardrail elements include District 6 around Philadelphia, District 4 in the northeast corner, and District 12 in the southwest. This kind of clustering would seem to reflect differences among districts in placing importance on the upkeep of guardrails and facilitates the delegation of responsibility for correcting problems to the district level.

Needs Assessment

A second major purpose of the trained-observer survey is to project maintenance needs on the basis of the estimated total amount of each deficiency in a district or county or particular MFC. This is done by applying the overall mean count per mile and the percentage of deficient roads to the total mileage of a particular MFC in a district or county. While the ratings discussed previously are based only on roads that are applicable for a certain condition—counts of nonfunctioning guardrail elements are recorded only for road segments that have guardrails, for example—for the purposes of estimating the total magnitude of a condition, rates, and percentages from the complete subsample (including "not appliables") are appropriate. Thus the issue for a given district is, how many counts of nonfunctioning guardrail elements on principal arterials are there, taking into account the fact that many road segments have no guardrail?

Table 5-5 illustrates these findings with respect to all potholes, shoulder washouts, bad pipes, broken inlets, and rotted posts in guardrails. Examination of the totals reveals that the overall sample has been expanded to the system's 44,209 miles by applying the original sampling fractions. Applying the mean counts per mile to each MFCs total mileage, the number of 25-foot sections with one or more potholes is projected to be 1,761,242; this would be the total estimated number of potholes or pothole clusters in the state system. Stated another way, if these 25-foot sections containing potholes were placed end to end, they would amount to 8,308 miles of highway, nearly 20 percent of the entire state system.

Similarly, the data show that as of fall 1979, there were an estimated 75,423 washouts or slides on shoulders, 7,628 bad pipes, 3,670 broken inlets to be repaired, and 43,707 rotted guardrail posts to be replaced. This gives the Department a better idea of the total magnitude of the problem in certain areas, and the breakdown by MFC shows whether these problems predominate on the more heavily or less heavily traveled roads. For example,

Table 5-5
Selected Deficiencies Estimated for Statewide Network, Cycle 1, Trained-Observer Survey

MFC	Total Mileage	Potholes[a]	End-to-End Mileage	Shoulder Washouts or Slides	Bad Pipes	Broken Inlets	Rotted Posts in Guardrails
A Interstates	1,139	12,012	57	1,153	10	40	133
B Principal arterial	4,301	98,758	466	5,409	231	278	2,209
C Minor arterial	8,159	214,388	1,011	16,052	572	1,297	11,591
D Collectors	18,531	688,443	3,247	32,417	3,294	1,756	19,692
E Local roads	12,079	747,643	3,527	20,392	3,522	299	10,082
Total	44,209	1,761,242	8,308	75,423	7,628	3,670	43,707

[a]Number of 25-foot sections with one or more potholes.

the interstate and principal arterial systems could be freed from bad pipes and broken inlets with relatively little effort, but to do the same for the collectors, those lower-order roads that carry traffic from local roads (including municipal streets and state-owned "local" roads) out to the trunk-line system, would be a massive undertaking.

Although not shown here, these same estimates can be developed on a district-by-district basis. This kind of output should be useful for programming because instead of showing the average condition on roads with certain design characteristics, it indicates the magnitude of deficiency across all highways in a given district. Depending on the size of the network of highways, in different districts, their relative magnitudes of needs may or may not conform to their ranking in terms of average condition. For instance, District 4 has a lower rate of potholes per mile than does District 12, but the total projected pothole count is nevertheless higher than in District 12. Districts 11 and 12 have the same rate of potholes per mile, but District 12 has twice the magnitude of deficiency. Similarly, Districts 5 and 8 have roughly equivalent ratings on potholes per mile, but District 8 has a much greater total need. When this kind of analysis is conducted for all reportable conditions, such comparisons should facilitate a more objective basis for programming maintenance activities. Staff should be cognizant of differences between districts on total projected counts of a given deficiency broken down by MFC, as well as differences across districts in the projected magnitudes of various kinds of reportable conditions.

Progress Monitoring

The trained-observer survey was designed principally as a tool for tracking the progress of the maintenance program over time. The results of the first cycle outlined previously reflected widespread variation in highway condition across a statewide system considered by top management to be generally unsatisfactory. When three cycles had been completed—in the fall of 1979, spring of 1980, and fall of 1980—the first comparisons over time were made to determine whether improvements in the system had been accomplished in accordance with management's priorities. Observed changes were interpreted in light of maintenance and betterments (major maintenance) outputs in order to assess the impact of maintenance efforts during the year on the incidence of reportable conditions.

Since seasonal variation would in many instances account for changes or the absence of change between fall and spring, the analysis focused on measuring progress or retrogression over the first full year that the TOS was in effect. Thus the following tables show mean counts of various reportable conditions for all three cycles, along with the percent change between cycles

1 and 3 (fall 1979 and fall 1980) and the significance level of a one-tailed difference of means test (two-sample *t*-test) between these two cycles.

Surface Conditions

Pothole patching became a primary focus of the maintenance program during the year spanning cycles 1 and 3. An additive index composed of three gradations of surface-pavement defects (depressions, potholes, and broken up with mud surfacing through) reveals a considerable decrease in "total-pothole" counts per mile for each road type. Although less effort was directed to lower-order roads and these roads still have a higher percentage of defective segments overall, table 5-6 shows statistically significant improvements in all categories averaging a 50- to 60-percent decrease in mean-deficiency counts. The smaller decreases between fall and spring, followed by more noticeable change over the spring and summer months, reflect seasonal variation in the condition itself and in the scheduling of major repairs.

Looking at the smallest and most prevalent potholes, surface depressions, a breakdown by pavement type appears to be consistent with findings according to functional class, as shown in table 5-7. Reflecting the greater amount of patching directed to higher classes of roads, greater improvement over time is evident for the rigid-pavement roads.

Minor cracking, left untreated, can be expected to result in major cracking and potholes over time. While a considerable reduction in major cracking, like potholes, can be observed on all roads, minor cracking worsened during the year on all but interstate highways. Even there the improvement was not statistically significant, as shown in table 5-8.

Because local roads carry relatively little truck traffic and less traffic overall, they would be expected to deteriorate more slowly than the higher-class roads. A somewhat smaller increase in minor cracking on these roads

Table 5-6
Total Potholes per Mile, by MFC

Maintenance Functional Class	Fall 1979 Cycle I	Spring 1980 Cycle 2	Fall 1980 Cycle 3	Percent Change	One-tailed Significance Level
Interstates	10.9	7.8	4.3	−60	.001
Principal arterials	23.1	17.0	10.5	−55	.001
Minor arterials	25.9	21.5	10.8	−58	.001
Collectors	36.8	30.5	19.7	−48	.001
Local Roads	60.6	46.8	29.6	−51	.001

Table 5-7
Roadway Depressions, by Pavement Type

Pavement Type	Fall 1979 Cycle I	Spring 1980 Cycle 2	Fall 1980 Cycle 3	Percent Change	One-tailed Significance Level
Rigid pavement	13.77	7.52	5.03	− 63	.001
Rigid base	26.78	23.53	11.27	− 58	.001
Flexible base	32.59	26.36	14.39	− 56	.001
Unpaved roads	53.42	69.07	41.94	− 21	—

Table 5-8
Surface Cracking, by MFC

Maintenance Functional Class	Major Cracking				
	Fall 1979 Cycle I	Spring 1980 Cycle 2	Fall 1980 Cycle 3	Percent Change	One-tailed Significance Level
Interstates	7.2	5.1	1.6	− 78	.001
Principal arterials	24.2	21.0	5.7	− 76	.001
Minor arterials	42.8	38.2	12.9	− 70	.001
Collectors	38.9	45.0	16.0	− 59	.001
Local roads	39.4	47.7	16.7	− 58	.001

Maintenance Functional Class	Minor Cracking				
	Fall 1979 Cycle I	Spring 1980 Cycle 2	Fall 1980 Cycle 3	Percent Change	One-tailed Significance Level
Interstates	8.1	4.8	5.7	− 30	
Principal arterials	17.6	12.9	18.6	+ 6	
Minor arterials	23.7	25.6	39.5	+ 66	.001
Collectors	24.6	25.0	37.3	+ 52	.001
Local roads	26.0	22.9	33.2	+ 28	.01

therefore may reflect less wear and tear rather than a greater amount of work done. Changes in traffic patterns to some extent may account for the high-percentage increases on minor arterials and collectors. Typically designed to the same standards as local roads with the expectation they would not be heavily traveled, many minor arterials and collectors now carry a traffic capacity that is marginal with their original design.

Increases in minor cracking in part may reflect deterioration of prior seal coating over major cracking now showing through as minor cracking. However, in departmental discussions concerning the development of a twelve-year improvement program, concern was expressed that the minimum amount of surface treatment needed to prevent minor cracking from becoming major cracking and potholes is not being provided. Although increases in minor cracking may be evidence that adequate preventive measures are not being taken, improvement on all pavement types in cycle 2, shown in table 5-9, suggests a prior program of skin patching may have left roads in good enough condition that resources were diverted to other problem areas during the summer months. Significant progress in major cracking and pothole repair came between spring and fall 1980. Because highways tend to be more heavily used during the summer, improvements may be the result of a concentrated effort being applied to those conditions considered most serious from the motorist's standpoint.

In general, the data seem to reflect a maintenance emphasis on the worst first, "worst" being defined by the comparative seriousness of the immediate condition and by the amount of wear and tear expected to leave some roads—that is, the more heavily traveled roads—in greater need of repair than others. Maintenance officials indicate that counties were, in fact, given lists of the 30 percent of the roads carrying 80 percent of the traffic and were advised to concentrate their efforts on that 30 percent of the system.

Although not a function of pavement condition, considerable improvement was made in the removal of objects creating safety hazards (for example, tree limbs, rocks, tires, dead animals) from the roadway surface. There is little systematic variation across road classes, pavement, or shoulder types in the amount of improvement observed, but in general, the percent change

Table 5-9
Minor Cracking, by Pavement Type

Pavement Type	Fall 1979 Cycle I	Spring 1980 Cycle 2	Fall 1980 Cycle 3	Percent Change	t	One-tailed Significance Level
Rigid pavement	7.7	1.8	3.5	− 55	3.84	.001
Rigid base	24.4	23.9	37.2	+ 52	− 4.86	.001
Flexible base	25.1	23.1	34.4	+ 37	− 5.76	.001
Unpaved roads	—	—	—	—	—	—

Table 5-10
Foreign Objects on Roadway Surface, by MFC

Maintenance Functional Class	Fall 1979 Cycle I	Spring 1980 Cycle 2	Fall 1980 Cycle 3	Percent Change	One-tailed Significance Level
Interstates	.15	.01	.03	− 80	.01
Principal arterials	.12	.06	.08	− 33	
Minor arterials	.16	.01	.02	− 88	.05
Collectors	.2	.04	.02	− 83	.05
Local roads	.47	.03	.03	− 94	.001

between fall 1979 and fall 1980 is dramatic, as shown in table 5-10. No explanation can be offered for the smaller reduction in surface object counts on *B* roads, but removal of such objects has been a departmental priority.

Shoulder Conditions

Changes in shoulder conditions were mixed—improvements being generally consistent with maintenance priorities but with deterioration, in some instances, difficult to interpret.

Shoulder depressions, shoulder potholes, and rutting were all reduced on the order of 50 to 60 percent, an outcome possibly attributed to the increased emphasis on shoulder work. Similarly, the reduction in shoulder-slope counts, shown in table 5-11, may reflect the new administration's emphasis on proper drainage as a means for minimizing pavement distress.

Table 5-11
Shoulder Slope, by MFC

Maintenance Functional Class	Fall 1979 Cycle I	Spring 1980 Cycle 2	Fall 1980 Cycle 3	Percent Change	One-tailed Significance Level
Interstates	1.9	2.8	1.6	− 16	
Principal arterials	12.8	11.6	4.4	− 66	.001
Minor arterials	25.4	22.7	9.8	− 61	.001
Collectors	42.0	26.7	25.5	− 39	.001
Local roads	50.0	49.3	24.9	− 50	.001

Shoulder shaping to allow water runoff from the pavement area resulted in a decrease in this reportable condition averaging 44 percent across shoulder types, while data by MFC show statistically significant improvement, from 39 to 66 percent fewer mean counts per mile, on the four road classes having the highest initial incidence of inadequate shoulder slope.

Shoulder cracking followed the same general pattern of change as cracking on the roadway surface. Across MFCs, major cracking was reduced by 50 to 70 percent whereas changes in the incidence of minor cracking was mixed. Although some improvement was made on *C* and *D* roads, minor cracking worsened considerably on interstates and principal arterials, resulting in an 85-percent aggregate increase in recorded deficiency. Lack of a regular program of maintenance for paved shoulders and a targeting of resources to the "worst first" would account for these observations, and would suggest similar trends be anticipated as long as current policies remain in effect.

Washouts and slides, considered a low maintenance priority as long as the travel way is not affected, were reduced on interstates but increased on all other road types. Although reportable conditions would be expected to vary with the amount of rainfall during any given period, increases may be partially explained by the neglect of sidedozing. The improvement on interstates again reflects the emphasis on higher-order roads, including attention to what, under most circumstances, are considered comparatively minor problems.

Shoulder dropoff, a dropoff between the pavement and the shoulder, is of concern from both a vehicle-maintenance and a safety standpoint. A program of grading and cutting is apparently responsible for the 39-percent reduction in dropoffs on unpaved shoulders, while improvement on paved shoulders may have come as a result of the Three R Program on interstates and principal arterials. Table 5-12 shows significant decreases in the counts

Table 5-12
Shoulder Dropoff Greater than 2 Inches, by MFC

Maintenance Functional Class	Fall 1979 Cycle I	Spring 1980 Cycle 2	Fall 1980 Cycle 3	Percent Change	One-tailed Significance Level
Interstates	2.9	1.5	1.9	−34	.01
Principal arterials	4.3	2.6	3.4	−21	.05
Minor arterials	6.4	3.2	3.0	−53	.001
Collectors	6.8	3.6	4.1	−40	.001
Local roads	4.2	2.7	2.8	−33	.001

Note: Shoulder dropoff is a composite of TOS indicators "Edge Pavement 2 to 4 Inches" and "Edge Pavement Greater than 4 Inches."

Table 5-13
Nonfunctional Ditch, by MFC

Maintenance Functional Class	Fall 1979 Cycle I	Spring 1980 Cycle 2	Fall 1980 Cycle 3	Percent Change	One-tailed Significance Level
Interstates	.70	1.90	1.10	+57	.05
Principal arterials	.82	2.80	1.60	+95	.001
Minor arterials	1.30	2.80	1.40	+8	
Collectors	1.40	3.10	1.80	+29	.05
Local roads	2.30	3.60	2.00	-13	

of shoulder dropoffs across all MFCs, with somehat higher percentage reductions on roads characteristically having unpaved shoulders. Lower counts on *A* and *B* roads in cycle 2, followed by increases in cycle 3, are presumably due to the normal swelling of paved shoulders during the winter months and their settling over the summer, which would leave a greater dropoff between the surface and the shoulder in the fall.

Drainage and Appurtenances

Despite increased productivity in ditch cleaning, pipe cleaning, and pipe replacement, progress in the drainage area was mixed. Nonfunctional ditches increased rather dramatically in cycle 2, perhaps due to the typical accumulation of standing water in the spring. Table 5-13 shows some lowering of mean counts on all roads by cycle 3, but the net change between fall 1979 and fall 1980 indicates a generally worsening condition. While no immediate explanation is offered, it is possible pipes are being cleaned with no provision for removing materials, or that as pipes are freed of dirt and sludge, water flow is impeded by materials deposited into the ditches and not removed. Based on the amount of ditch cleaning reported during the year, these findings are curious and need to be investigated further.

That pipes are in fact being cleaned is evident from the decrease in plugged-pipe counts on all roads. Because the total pipe count varies considerably across MFCs, table 5-14 shows cycles 1, 2, and 3 data presented as the percentage of all pipes on a given MFC observed to be at least one-half full. The somewhat larger percentage reductions in deficiency on lower-order roads may reflect more concerted effort being directed to those roads having the greatest total number of pipes.

A by-product of cleaning pipes is that the bottom of the pipes can be seen. A marked increase in bad-pipe counts on all roads may therefore be explained by the fact that pipes rusted or broken out at the bottom are now

Table 5-14
Percentage of Pipes One-Half Full, by MFC

Maintenance Functional Class	Fall 1979 Cycle I	Spring 1980 Cycle 2	Fall 1980 Cycle 3	Percent Change	One-tailed Significance Level
Interstates	.13	.09	.11	−15	—
Principal arterials	.21	.22	.20	−5	—
Minor arterials	.25	.26	.19	−24	.05
Collectors	.31	.29	.24	−23	.01
Local roads	.28	.29	.19	−32	.001

being observed and recorded. Although increases in bad pipes between cycles 1 and 3 were found on all MFCs, pipework on *C, D,* and *E* roads during the spring and summer of 1980 is reflected in the decrease in defective pipes observed on those roads between cycle 2 and cycle 3.

Appurtenances, in general, deteriorated between the fall of 1979 and the fall of 1980, with improvement coming only in litter pick-up and the replacement of broken or missing delineators. Table 5-15 shows a 55- to 60-percent reduction in litter across all functional classes, perhaps attributable to increased productivity of cleanup crews. In addition, the governor and the Department sponsored a cleanup campaign in which citizens were urged to get out and help pick up litter along the state's highways.

Being a relatively high expenditure item, it is difficult to explain the considerable deterioration in striping during 1979-1980. Fewer bad-striping counts were encountered on higher-order roads because these roads are automatically scheduled for painting once or twice a year. Seasonal change would account for deterioration between fall and spring, but the high-percentage increase on *B, C,* and *D* roads, and a significant worsening on interstates during a year in which production was at least equal to, if not greater than previous years, raises questions of whether the criteria for painting may have changed, whether crews were improperly supervised, or whether the Department may have received an unusually poor quality of paint, as some personnel have contended.

Guardrail deficiencies, median barriers, regular signs, and station markers also worsened during the year. Although a significant increase in defective guardrails was found on collectors and local roads, the only condition showing a statistically significant percent change on each MFC was the rise in missing station markers. A cutback in Department personnel has prevented systematic placement and replacement of location markers, creating a serious inhouse problem in that these serve to identify sites both for locating projects and recording accident data.

Table 5-15
Litter Counts, by MFC

Maintenance Functional Class	Fall 1979 Cycle I	Spring 1980 Cycle 2	Fall 1980 Cycle 3	Percent Change	One-tailed Significance Level
Interstates	88.5	56.1	38.5	−56	.001
Principal arterials	74.0	45.5	32.0	−57	.001
Minor arterials	61.0	37.8	26.4	−57	.001
Collectors	45.4	27.2	18.8	−59	.001
Local roads	25.0	14.6	11.0	−56	.001

Rotted posts and nonfunctional elements in guardrails are highly correlated with each other and are more prevalent on lower-order roads. There are few wooden posts on the newer sections of interstate highways, and those on minor arterials, collectors, and local roads are being replaced with steel posts. There is no immediate explanation for the statistically significant increases in deficiency on the lower-class roads, except that perhaps wooden posts are temporarily being left to deteriorate in anticipation of a systematic replacement effort.

County Rankings

The foregoing analysis of aggregate highway conditions and trends over time is useful to top management as a macro-monitoring tool. Central-office executives can see what kinds of problems are getting worse and what conditions are showing improvement on a statewide basis, and they can use these findings to assess the successes and failures of the Department's overall maintenance activities. In fact, the Secretary of Transportation drew such interpretations from the TOS cycle 1–cycle 3 comparisons presented previously and, based on these interpretations, reinforced some maintenance priorities and modified others in order to make the program more effective.

However, for other purposes the data need to be disaggregated to the county level. This is because the highway programs, and particularly the maintenance program, are implemented through a decentralized service-delivery system: county maintenance managers program their own activities and are directly responsible for maintaining the roads in their counties. Therefore, top management needs to be able to track the progress of individual counties if this information feedback is to be translated into action. Second, it naturally follows that central-office executives and district managers use the counties as building blocks in planning and managing the overall program. Objectives are set for individual counties, and funds are allocated first on a county basis. Thus it is crucial to know patterns and trends of highway condition and maintenance needs on a county basis.

While it is hoped that eventually the accumulated TOS data base will permit some detailed analysis for individual counties, the more immediate concern is to develop county rankings as an aid to the general prioritizing and allocation processes. Recent legislation requires that highway condition be built into a formula for allocating routine-maintenance monies among counties, but the specific means for doing so are still evolving. Moreover, top management needs to know the relative standing of counties for a variety of purposes ranging from personnel actions to the programming of major maintenance and reconstruction projects.

Overall Surface Condition

In developing schemes for ranking counties, two issues arise: (1) criteria, that is, on what basis (or items) should the counties be compared, and (2) sample reliability, that is, what sample sizes are required to differentiate with confidence among better and worse conditions. Concerning the substantive criteria, the counties can be compared on each of the forty-two TOS reportable conditions, and for certain purposes this is appropriate. However, this would yield forty-two different rankings, while for some purposes a single composite ranking is clearly preferable.

One approach to developing such composite rankings has been to combine TOS counts into four indices corresponding to roadway surface, shoulders, drainage, and appurtenances, and to further combine these into a single "maintenance-rating" index. The advantage of this two-tiered system is that it provides rankings on the four components of a roadway. The relationships and trade-offs among them often become relevant as well as a single summary measure that represents the ranking of counties by the overall condition of their highways.

Various means for deriving weights for the individual items (reportable conditions) to be used in computing these indices have been considered. These include (1) judgmental weights intended to reflect the importance of a given deficiency from the motorists' point of view, (2) judgmental weights reflecting their importance in terms of implications for preventive maintenance, (3) a statistical derivation, such as factor analysis, keyed to internal consistency, and (4) weights calculated on the basis of the cost of correcting various deficiencies. One set of indices that has actually been calibrated uses weights representing relative importance from a preventive-maintenance standpoint in the judgment of Bureau of Maintenance personnel. The surface-item weights were developed separately for each pavement type, and the shoulder-item weights separately for paved versus unpaved shoulders.

Table 5–16 shows the ranking of the sixty-seven counties from the highest to the lowest on the roadway-surface index, based on cycle 4 data collected in the spring of 1981. This measure was computed as

$$1,000 - \sum (\text{weight} \times \text{reportable condition count})$$

such that a value of 1,000 would reflect a county with perfect roadway surfaces—no counts of reportable conditions—while values approaching zero represent counties whose highways have severely deteriorated surfaces. The range is dramatic, from Franklin County with a mean surface rating of 971 to McKean County with a rating of only 23 out of 1,000. Table 5–16 shows the counties arrayed in four blocks because for macro-policy purposes, top management has found it convenient to work with quartiles thought of as the best counties, fairly good counties, fair-to-poor counties, and the worst counties.

Table 5–16
Roadway-Surface Condition by County, Spring 1981

Rank	County	Index Mean	Standard Deviation	N	95 percent Confidence Interval
Top Quartile, "Best Counties"					
1	Franklin	971	71	196	961 to 981
2	Union	944	98	90	923 to 965
3	Juniata	901	156	90	868 to 934
4	Adams	898	156	156	873 to 923
5	Perry	889	160	124	861 to 918
6	Cumberland	870	180	228	846 to 893
7	Montour	858	116	66	830 to 887
8	Fulton	854	212	120	815 to 892
9	Lycoming	849	185	198	823 to 875
10	Bedford	849	190	212	823 to 875
11	Mifflin	847	161	80	811 to 883
12	Dauphin	835	249	210	801 to 869
13	Snyder	833	207	88	789 to 876
14	Centre	812	234	236	782 to 842
15	Sullivan	803	199	60	752 to 854
16	Northumberland	798	243	156	760 to 837
17	Clinton	789	294	126	737 to 840
Second Quartile					
18	Lebanon	750	328	150	698 to 803
19	Columbia	741	324	154	689 to 792
20	Huntingdon	731	343	152	676 to 786
21	York	729	376	336	689 to 770
22	Blair	728	276	112	677 to 780
23	Tioga	714	325	178	666 to 762
24	Lancaster	707	320	334	672 to 741

Table 5-16 continued

Rank	County	Index Mean	Standard Deviation	N	95 percent Confidence Interval
Second Quartile continued					
25	Armstrong	693	314	182	647 to 738
26	Chester	684	365	340	645 to 723
27	Delaware	677	334	180	628 to 726
28	Potter	676	340	114	613 to 739
29	Carbon	659	346	76	580 to 738
30	Clearfield	658	420	284	609 to 707
31	Pike	644	315	142	592 to 696
32	Northampton	638	341	160	584 to 691
33	Monroe	630	343	204	582 to 677
34	Philadelphia	623	367	182	569 to 677
Third Quartile					
35	Montgomery	612	399	342	570 to 654
36	Bucks	612	345	352	576 to 648
37	Bradford	606	312	214	564 to 648
38	Allegheny	604	375	484	571 to 638
39	Wayne	602	359	170	548 to 657
40	Berks	582	393	340	540 to 624
41	Cameron	566	441	30	401 to 730
42	Lehigh	557	373	174	501 to 613
43	Elk	546	388	86	463 to 629
44	Schuylkill	533	390	254	485 to 581
45	Somerset	525	509	240	460 to 589
46	Luzerne	511	426	342	466 to 556
47	Fayette	496	377	212	445 to 547
48	Wyoming	490	427	82	396 to 584
49	Washington	484	586	366	424 to 544
50	Lackawanna	460	354	218	413 to 508
51	Lawrence	451	535	132	359 to 543
Bottom Quartiles, "Worst Counties"					
52	Beaver	425	410	190	366 to 483
53	Butler	420	527	260	355 to 484
54	Cambria	375	556	190	296 to 455
55	Clarion	351	608	178	261 to 441
56	Susquehanna	277	473	238	217 to 337
57	Jefferson	269	497	174	195 to 343
58	Erie	258	589	312	192 to 323
59	Venango	239	622	160	142 to 336
60	Greene	226	622	162	129 to 322
61	Forest	204	641	44	10 to 399
62	Indiana	153	954	218	26 to 281
63	Warren	119	643	116	0.4 to 237
64	Westmoreland	106	977	348	3 to 209
65	Mercer	92	477	284	37 to 148
66	Crawford	30	672	256	− 52 to 113
67	McKean	23	586	120	− 83 to 129

Note: The sample size for each county has been doubled in order to approximate the precision of interval estimates based on two cycles (one year's worth) of data.

Table 5–16 also shows the standard deviation for each county on the surface-condition index. It is very apparent that as the mean average surface condition increases, indicating counties with better overall surface conditions, the standard deviation tends to decrease. The coefficient of variation (standard deviation ÷ mean), therefore, decreases dramatically, indicating much greater uniformity in surface conditions in those counties with good roads. In the best counties the coefficient of variation is as low as .1, while in the worst counties it is as high as 20.1. As might be expected, "good" counties tend to have uniformly good roads whereas the "worst" counties have roads in very poor condition but also have some with surfaces that are very good.

Thus sample reliability, or the precision of interval estimates based on sample data, is the most difficult to achieve for those counties with the worst overall surface condition. Table 5–16 also shows 95-percent confidence intervals for estimating the true value of the index score for the county road system in its entirety. The sample sizes in cycle 4 were hypothetically doubled in this process in order to approximate the precision of estimates based on two cycles (one year's worth) of data. For the best counties, these intervals are easily within plus and minus 10 percent of the sample mean, but for the worst counties the precision is nowhere near that tight. Thus, while it is fairly clear which quartile each county falls into on a population basis, larger sample sizes are required to differentiate among counties in the same quartile, especially among the worst counties.

Other Indices

Similar indices developed for shoulders, drainage, appurtenances, and an overall maintenance rating show the same tendency for the best counties to exhibit greater uniformity. The rankings of the sixty-seven counties are similar, but not identical, across the four component indices. In some cases very notable differences occur, for instance, a county with generally good surfaces showing up with poor drainage or vice versa. This information is particularly useful to central-office maintenance staff because it allows them to flag priorities for surface work in some counties, drainage work in other counties and so on.

In the future, it may also be desirable to develop indices reflecting safety and service apart from "as-built" physical condition. The safety index, in particular, would be interesting and would incorporate the following reportable conditions: foreign objects on the roadway, pothole clusters, shoulder dropoff, rotted guardrail posts, nonfunctional guardrail elements, and damaged median barriers. Weights for these items could be based on research showing the probability of these hazards causing accidents and/or the expected dollar value of the damage incurred.

Conclusions

During its first two years in operation, the TOS has become established and accepted within the Department as a needed monitoring device. Increasingly, it is playing an important part in decision making. As the Secretary of Transportation stated in a memo to his deputies concerning the cycle 1–cycle 3 comparisons, "As time goes on and the data acquire more 'stability' the TOS will become an increasingly important management tool. All managers will be alerted to the fact that this tool is on hand and will be a force in departmental operations. Its use in describing the progress of this administration in an area which is vitally important to our economic goals will be pursued vigorously."

The evolving nature of the TOS as a management tool should be noted here. Results from the first cycle, and particularly across the first three cycles, gained the confidence of top management both by confirming widespread impressions about road conditions in general and on a district basis and by providing further insights as to precisely what kinds of reportable conditions were most prevalent in different geographic areas. Some of the results have been corroborated by corresponding patterns in the outputs of certain maintenance activities, while others have served to raise questions about maintenance policies and priorities.

Essentially, the findings from the early TOS cycles have confirmed PennDOT's need to retain such a monitoring tool on a continuing basis. The widespread variation in highway condition both among and within counties, the lack of predictability of condition based on functional class or pavement type, and the dramatic (but not universal) change in condition over time all indicate that highway condition in Pennsylvania is in a dynamic situation. Therefore, it is clear that the TOS needs to be continued and upgraded to assist in efforts to improve condition and track the success of these efforts.

Continuing Modifications

Beginning with the pretest and the initial cycles, the TOS has been continually modified in order to maximize the quality and usefulness of the data being generated. In addition to efforts to streamline the fieldwork and data processing, aimed in part at increasing reliability, several refinements have been made or are currently being suggested regarding both the content of the survey and the sampling strategy. Various items have been deleted, modified, or added to the survey to assure that the observers record the kind of information that has the greatest operational significance for the maintenance program. Based on findings from analysis of the relationship between surface condition and roughness, several modifications have recently been recommended to differentiate more clearly between various types of cracking and joint deterioration that result from different problems and require different corrective treatments.

Changes have also been made in the sample of roads selected for each TOS cycle. For cycle 4, the road sections were shortened and a much larger sample was taken in order to obtain a more representative cross-section. While sample reliability is very high for aggregate analysis or comparisons by MFC, it is not fully adequate for ranking counties or doing detailed analysis within counties, as indicated previously. Thus the next step, made possible in part by increased productivity in the field, is to move to an expanded sample in order to permit this county level analysis. Cycles 6 and 7 (spring and fall 1982) will each cover twice as many sections as did cycles 4 and 5; in effect one-third of all interstates, principal arterials, and minor arterials will be observed each year.

Additional Management Uses

The TOS was principally designed as a means for tracking progress over time, and that is still the major emphasis. Fall-to-fall and spring-to-spring comparison, as shown earlier in this chapter, are the most direct way to evaluate the net effect of program outputs on highway condition because they are not confounded by seasonal differences. They provide an indication of whether the roads are improving or worsening in the long run, particularly when they cover more than one year such as with a cycle 1–cycle 3–cycle 5 comparison. However, shorter-term comparisons can be useful from a different perspective. Looking at data from a spring cycle with reference to the preceding fall reflects in part the impact of the intervening winter weather on the highway system. Looking ahead at the following fall cycle in comparison with that same spring cycle shows the short-term effect of summer-maintenance activities.

In addition to providing an indication of how overall highway condition has been affected by maintenance activities and in the process contributing to the evaluation of county maintenance managers, the TOS data help in guiding the maintenance effort toward improving condition. The TOS is incorporated in a formula used to allocate funds among counties, and then counts of various reportable conditions are used by central-office staff in their review of the maintenance programs submitted by the counties that utilize these funds.

Potentially the TOS can play a more central role in managing the overall program. First, research is under way to develop cost models that would predict the costs of required maintenance activities in a county based on the counts of reportable conditions on its roads. While there are unique one-to-one relationships between certain reportable conditions and maintenance-cost functions—joint deterioration and joint sealing, for example—this is not the case for most deficiencies. For instance, knowing the number of potholes in a given road will not necessarily translate directly into a given number of tons of manual patching required because other conditions require patching and sometimes other treatments are needed. However, analysis of the multifaceted relationships involved may well provide conversion factors that could be used to set the optimal mix of activity in a county for a given season. Second, PennDOT is now embarking on the development of a comprehensive, integrated pavement management system that will rely on the TOS counts to sort out road sections requiring major maintenance or reconstruction versus continued routine maintenance. Thus the TOS is evolving into a major programming tool as well as an after-the-fact monitoring device.

6 Effectiveness Monitoring

Critical to the performance-monitoring concept is the ability to demonstrate the highway program's impact on users. Impact measures are usually the most difficult to interpret since they are often heavily influenced by other than program variables, and since the precise nature of the various linkages is generally not well known. Factors that relate to the transportation goals of fast, safe, and efficient service are essential in measuring the impact of any transportation services, and as discussed in chapter 2, in the highway area these factors translate into measures of user costs, accident statistics, and level of service. Table 6-1 identifies measures that might be used to quantify changes in these categories of impact along with possible sources of the data.

Accumulated research evidence shows clearly that under controlled experimental conditions, the sufficiency of highways in terms of condition, safety, and service features can and does make a difference in costs to users, accident rates and travel times.[1] Presumably, highway agencies are making their investments wisely and in ways that translate into system improvements and desired impacts on target conditions. The problem is in determining whether these linkages are actually holding up in practice with respect to a given DOT's programs. If, for example, the level of effort is weak or projects are not targeted on the worst conditions, these programs may not make a dent in the problems of inadequate roads and poor service to users.

In considering the measures shown in table 6-1, care must be taken to avoid "black boxing" the system and automatically concluding that observed changes in accidents, service levels, and user costs are direct results of improvements in the highway network. The problem is that these impact conditions are subject to a whole set of environmental variables, factors external to the highway program itself that may have strong cause/effect relationships with the outcome measures. Such factors as fuel cost and availability, vehicle-operating characteristics, driving behavior, traffic volumes, and composition may well have an overwhelming influence on accidents, service levels, and user costs. Within this context, desired impacts may be only marginally sensitive to programmed initiatives by the Department. Effectiveness monitoring requires tracking indicators such as those

Table 6-1
Effectiveness Measures

Indicator	Measure	Source
Accidents		
Number of accidents	Total number of accidents by type, extent of damage, and contributing factors. Accidents per 100,000 vehicle miles.	State Policy reports and DOT accident-analysis reports
Accidents at potentially hazardous locations	Change in number of accidents at potentially hazardous locations after project completion (standardized by ADT).	Safety-improvement program
Cost to users		
Vehicle-maintenance costs	Average cost per respondent of vehicle repairs caused by road conditions.	Citizen survey
Vehicle repairs	Percent vehicles requiring alignment or suspension repair.	Vehicle-inspection records
Level of Service		
Point-to-point travel time	Change in time spent commuting from residence to work.	Citizen survey
Average speed	Average speed in miles per hour or percent vehicles traveling below 40 mph.	Sample observations
Volume/capacity ratio	Rate of estimated thirtieth-hour peak traffic to design capacity.	48-hour traffic volume counts, HPMS
Traffic congestion	Percent responding that traffic congestion causes difficulties in getting to work or other places.	Citizen survey
Perceived road conditions	Percent indicating that road conditions have improved over the past year.	Citizen survey
Pothole encounters	Number of vehicles encountering potholes in one day.	Trained-observer survey

in table 6–1 and interpreting shifts over time in light of identifiable trends in this larger context.

Accidents

Measures relating accidents to the highway program are the most readily available within the Department. The Bureau of Accident Analysis maintains a computer-filed data base that is updated at least annually and that is used primarily to identify potentially hazardous locations as a basis for developing the safety-improvement program.

By observing the change from year to year in the total number of accidents per vehicle mile driven, some inference of the success of the safety aspect of the highway program can be made. This analysis can be made more detailed by observing the change in yearly accident totals broken down by type of accident (fatal, injury, or property damage) and by contributing factor (road conditions, driving while intoxicated, and so on). The contributing factors of greatest interest here, of course, concern road conditions.

Table 6–2 shows the total number of fatal, injury, and property-damage accidents for the statewide system for 1978 through 1981. To put these figures into perspective, given the 45,000 miles of highway in the system, accidents on the order of magnitude of 150,000 per year would signify that on the average, there are roughly three and a half accidents of some kind on each mile of roadway annually. The most notable finding is that there were 12 percent fewer accidents in 1981 than in 1978, with large reductions in both the property damage and injury categories. Accidents in all three cate-

Table 6–2
Statewide Total Accidents, by Type and Year

	Calendar Year			
Accident Type	1978	1979	1980	1981
Fatal	1,929	1,970	1,904	1,838
Injury	96,609	96,524	89,560	87,962
Property damage	59,823	58,370	51,025	48,964
Total accidents	158,361	156,622	142,489	138,764
Vehicle miles traveled (state system only)	74,838 m	70,286 m	71,332 m	71,508 m
Accidents/100 million VMT	212	223	199	194

gories decreased further in 1981 so that the overall trend across the four years has been toward substantially reducing total accidents in the state.

Since one environmental variable that influences accidents is travel volume—higher ADTs mean more exposure to potential accidents—highway-accident data are often standardized by vehicle miles traveled (VMT). This is particularly relevant here because one plausible explanation of the decrease in accidents is simply a drop in overall travel volumes because of higher fuel costs. Therefore, table 6-2 also shows VMT for each of the four years, as well as the number of accidents per 100 million vehicle miles traveled.

The results show a modest decrease in VMT over the four years in contrast to the slight drop in total accidents from 1978 to 1979 and the more pronounced drop from 1979 to 1981. This means that the accident rate of 212 accidents per 100 million vehicle miles in 1978 increased to 223 in 1979, but then dropped to 199 in 1980 and 194 in 1981. The 12 percent decrease in accidents per 100 million VMT from 1979 to 1981 is certainly notable and does coincide with the new administration's initiative aimed at "saving lives and reducing congestion." Given the highly significant reductions in reportable conditions on the state's highways between 1979 and 1980, as described in chapter 5, a conclusion of cause and effect between the Department's programmed activity and accident reduction is at this point at least plausible. While there has been no definitive study of the relationship between accidents and condition, prior research suggests that as PSI increases from 3.0 to 4.5, for example, accidents per 100 million VMT will decrease from 170 to 130.[2]

Accidents and Roadway Conditions

All accidents that are reported are examined in terms of type of accident, severity of injury or damage, and possible contributing factors. Accidents are frequently attributed to numerous possible causal factors generally classified as those relating to (1) driver behavior; (2) vehicle condition or failure; (3) environmental (weather) factors; (4) sudden entrance to the roadway by other parties or vehicles; and (5) roadway conditions. The road conditions relate to both design features and the current-condition aspects of overall highway-system adequacy.

To further investigate the connection between highway improvements and the reduction in accidents on Pennsylvania highways between 1978 and 1981, table 6-3 shows the number of accidents in each of the four years for which one or more of the roadway conditions was reported as a possible causal factor. The number of roadway conditions cited rose dramatically from 1978 to 1979, then decreased again in 1980 (but not as low as the 1978

Table 6-3
Numbers of Accidents with Roadway Conditions as Possible Factors

Possible Factors	1978	1979	1980	1981
Broken, cracked, or bumpy pavement	974	1,238	851	884
Foreign substance on surface	425	564	542	529
Shoulder dropoff	562	994	1,399	1,571
Slippery road surface	14,344	18,953	15,487	18,938
Narrow roadway	167	183	169	169
Poor sight distance	206	287	305	252
Defective traffic-control devices	184	191	183	159
Obstructed traffic-control devices	55	61	45	35
Missing traffic-control devices	241	327	161	137
Poor or no pavement markings	13	26	23	13
Abrupt change in road alignment	199	829	814	1,718
Total: Roadway conditions	18,711	25,397	21,296	24,405
Total accidents	158,361	156,622	142,489	138,764

mark) and finally increased again in 1981. Thus although the total number of traffic accidents has gone down markedly from 1978 to 1981, the number of accidents for which road conditions have been listed as possible factors has generally increased.

That the number of instances where roadway conditions were cited—particularly slippery surfaces—decreased more than total accidents from 1979 to 1981 tends to support the notion that improvement in road conditions during that period contributed to the reduced accident rate, but this is by no means conclusive. It should be noted that the first few entries in table 6-3 relate to conditions included in the trained-observer survey. While the citations of "broken, cracked, or bumpy pavement" dropped substantially from 1979 to 1981 the numbers for "foreign substance" go down only slightly, and the instances of "shoulder dropoff" actually increase significantly. In light of the decreases in all the corresponding TOS reportable conditions, as presented in chapter 5, this would suggest that in the aggregate, or on a statewide basis, instances of these factors being involved in causing accidents may not be directly sensitive to reductions in TOS distress counts.

One problem is that multiple factors are often cited for accidents, but the data in table 6-3 do not distinguish between accidents with only one roadway condition cited, versus those with two or more cited or those with both roadway and nonroadway causal factors. Reformating the data so that the number of total accidents involving one or more roadway factors can be distinguished from those with no roadway factors would provide for clearer interpretation. Second, monitoring such trends over a longer period, five to ten years, for example, would also help to identify "off" years with extremely low or high accident levels and to discern real trends from less systematic year-to-year fluctuations.

Accident-Data Reliability and Validity

In general, the data collected by the Bureau of Accident Analysis are a reliable source for accident statistics. The assessment of the highway program's impact on accidents should not, however, be construed to be an evaluation of any one activity within the Department, for example, the Safety Investment Program. Aggregate impacts in terms of most of the effectiveness measures, of which the accident rate is one, relate to all activities of the Department. However, monitoring trends in total accidents and, in particular, the number of accidents involving roadway conditions as a possible factor, is essential if making progress toward the objective of safe transportation is taken seriously. At a minimum these data should be tracked in order to flag any precipitous increase in total accidents. Observed trends in accidents can be interpreted more realistically when travel volume and actual highway condition are also being monitored.

Several problems accompany the use of the Department's accident-statistics data base. The first problem is that the data base consists only of reportable accidents, that is, those that were reported to the police and that are, in turn, reported to the Department. In 1978 the definition of a "reportable" accident was changed. Now only those accidents in which a person has been injured or in which a tow-truck is required must be reported to the police. Moreover, an estimate of the cost of the accident is not included in the data base since the requirement for an on-site estimate of damages has been deleted. Average costs of a fatality, injury, or damage to property are available from a number of sources and could be factored in to impute estimated dollar costs, but these figures would have to be adjusted to be representative of costs in Pennsylvania and to account for inflation. Second, the identification of the possible factors is often a judgment call that can easily be misconstrued. For example, the incidence of "abrupt change in road alignment" as a possible factor increased by more than 800 percent from 1978 to 1981, an unlikely occurrence when total accidents are decreasing. Inquiry within the Department revealed that in response to criticism for apparently undercounting this factor in earlier years, coders are now including this item for any accident location in the approximate vicinity of a change in alignment. Such a reliability problem makes the indicator useless for any practical matter.

Standardization of the number of accidents per year by a measure of total vehicle miles presents yet another problem that, in fact, applies to all measures related to the total number of vehicle miles driven. This problem arises from the method used to determine the total vehicle miles driven in Pennsylvania per year. By multiplying total fuel consumption within the state (based on liquid-fuel-tax receipts) by a general consumption rate (usually 12.5 miles per gallon), a figure for vehicle miles driven is derived. Liquid-fuel-tax evasion and changes in fleet-mileage statistics and traffic mix tend to make the accuracy of a statistic derived by this method questionable. A possible alternative might be to compute the number of vehicle miles driven from inspection forms maintained by the Bureau of Traffic Safety. This will be discussed further under the topic of costs to users.

Project Evaluation

The direct effect of the Department's activities on the number of accidents can be measured by a variable that reflects the change in the number of accidents at potentially hazardous locations where corrective action has been undertaken. The data for the measure are provided by a before-and-after evaluation of the number of accidents at each completed safety-project site, and are aggregated for all sites over a one-year period. The Department's Traffic Operations Division currently reports this type of information to FHWA. Projects are monitored for three years and then dropped from the report. A significant decrease in this measure can be taken to indicate that the Department is succeeding in reducing the number of accidents at locations where it has attempted to eliminate a hazard.

For example, in 1977 the Department completed 141 projects under the safety-improvement program at a cost of $10.8 million. These projects varied diversely from those intended to better channel traffic, improve intersections, widen pavements and bridges, install guardrails, flatten grades, and straighten alignments, and so on. The great majority, however, involved skid-treatment overlays applied to highway sections with low skid resistance. Many of these kinds of improvements are known to reduce accidents in controlled situations.[3] Over the three years prior to these projects, these road sections collectively accounted for 4,906 accidents, with 1,826 involving fatalities or bodily injury. During the three years since project completion, they accounted for 2,447 accidents, with 1,634 involving fatalities or injury. This decrease represents a 50-percent drop in accidents on these particular roads. While not controlled experiments, before-and-after comparisons do indicate that the SIP was effective in reducing accidents at those sites. However, given an order of magnitude of 450,000 total accidents statewide over a three-year period, the accidents at these sites account for only 1 percent of the total.

User Costs

Measuring the costs of transportation services to users is more complex than measuring accident rates or service levels. The greatest difficulty is to decide what portion of total vehicle-operating costs can be attributed to factors that can be affected by the highway program. A partial solution is to include in a citizen survey a question about damage resulting from road conditions. Of course, the responses to this question will show some distortion caused by respondent's perceptions. The usefulness of such a survey is discussed in a later section of this chapter.

Inspection Records

Another source might be information from vehicle-inspection records, but such data would reflect the cost of all maintenance work done at the time of inspection, including that stemming from normal wear. It would not include work completed prior to or at any time after inspection. In the past the information obtained from inspection records has been very spotty and has not been reliable in terms of indicating the dollar amount spent on repairs, but the Bureau of Traffic Safety is contemplating changes in reporting requirements and data processing that will improve the quality of this information.

At present there appears to be little uniformity in reporting cost figures on the forms used by county-level officers to collect the data turned in by individual inspection stations and to report the information to the Department. Taxes on the fees may or may not be included, and the forms from some counties report maintenance work while others do not. Pending a decision whether or not to move from semi-annual inspections to annual inspections, PennDOT should be strengthening control over the whole inspection program—which is actually carried out by private service stations—and tightening up its reporting requirements. Presently the inspection data are not computerized, but when reporting quality is improved, it would probably be worthwhile to develop a computerized record, at least on a sample basis.

With reliable reporting and processing, this data base could be useful for a number of purposes. By collecting various kinds of information on the tenth or twentieth vehicle from each inspection report, a systematic sample could be used to estimate reliably the total number of vehicle miles driven, total repair costs at time of inspection, and the percentage of vehicles requiring alignment and/or suspension repairs as surrogate measures of user costs. The estimate of total vehicle miles driven per year does not relate directly to user costs, but it would provide a reliable indicator by which other measures could be standardized, for instance, number of accidents per 100,000 vehicle miles. It might also be combined with statewide fuel-tax data to produce average vehicle miles per gallon. This direct estimate of total vehicle miles in the state would be a significant improvement because presently the Department derives an estimate indirectly by applying an average fuel-consumption rate (such as 12.5 miles per gallon) to total fuel-consumption based on liquid-tax receipts.

An exploratory analysis of small sample data performed by the Department shows that of all vehicles inspected in January 1980, 36 percent required some maintenance work, and the average cost of repairs for these vehicles was $34. A year later, in January 1981, the percent requiring maintenance was virtually unchanged—37 percent—but the average cost of repairs had risen to $38. This increase in dollar costs to vehicle owners is likely to be due to higher charges at service stations, as it corresponds roughly to the general rate of inflation. Thus user costs in terms of repairs appear to have been static over the particular year in question. However, improving the quality of the data, enlarging the sample and focusing specifically on road-related repairs should provide better insight into program impacts on user costs.

Tort Claims

An additional indication of user costs could be obtained from records on tort claims pressed against the Commonwealth due to potholes or other dangerous highway conditions. This information would be especially critical because it reflects an assessment of excess costs borne by motorists due to negligence by the Department in maintaining the highway system. In 1978, Act 152 of the legislature waived the state's sovereign immunity for certain categories of liability, including the category for "dangerous conditions" in general and the category for potholes in particular.

Motorists can sue the state to recover costs of property damage and can receive compensation for bodily injury resulting from mishaps on the highways due to dangerous conditions other than potholes, the most common being slippery surfaces, excessive shoulder dropoff, and poor sighting as well as poor design. With respect to potholes, claims can be made for bodily injury only and when the Department has been given written notice of the specific pothole at least one week prior to the event.

Table 6–4 shows both the number of claims that have been made and

Table 6-4
Claims and Payments Due to Dangerous Conditions and Potholes

	Fiscal 1961-1979	Fiscal 1980	Fiscal 1981
Dangerous conditions			
Claims	622	759	510
Payments	$677,982	$365,075	$46,710
Potholes			
Claims	755	609	425
Payments	$25,532	$4,825	$1,728

the dollar value paid out to successful claimants for both dangerous conditions and potholes. The period from 1961 through 1979 is, for the most part, of historical interest, the relatively large payments representing a "catch-up" period the first year after the law was changed. Similarly, the relatively high numbers of claims and consequent large total payments in fiscal 1980 may well reflect a continuing backlog of cases moving through the system, with reduced claims and payments in fiscal 1981 reflecting an evening out of the caseload for a given year. Yet the significant drops in both claims and payments for both potholes and dangerous conditions may also represent an impact of the improved highway conditions as recorded by the trained-observer survey. While it is difficult to draw a firm conclusion of cause and effect during this initial period under the new law, it appears that the Department's success in reducing pothole counts and other dangerous conditions on the highways may also have been effective in reducing the bodily injuries and property damage that can result from these conditions. As time goes on, trends in these two indicators should have a clearer meaning; continued improvement in highway-system adequacy should further reduce the number of claims due to potholes and dangerous conditions. This is one aspect of user costs that is directly sensitive to highway conditions despite the possible additional influence of various external factors.

Level of Service

Measures of level of service should indicate whether travel times, comfort, and convenience are increasing or decreasing. Several alternatives are available for estimating point-to-point travel times, clearly the single most important indicator of level of service. One alternative would be to select several routes in urbanized areas as representative segments and to observe changes in commuting time through the use of time-and-distance surveys conducted by the Bureau of Advance Planning. The difficulty here is to ensure that the segments selected are truly representative of the state system, and with sufficiently large samples the fieldwork could be very costly. Moreover, there is a major question as to the sensitivity of such a measure. In a period when major new construction and reconstruction are necessarily de-emphasized, the Department's activities may have little impact on aggregate point-to-point travel times across the state. Before-and-after travel times through corridors that undergo major reconstruction or have capacity expanded in some other way might be worthwhile, although these improvements may have negligible impacts on a statewide basis.

Given the difficulty in collecting these data, along with the questionable significance of the measure, a more feasible approach might be to calculate the average time spent in transit between work and residence, based on responses to a survey of a random sample of highway users. A question of this type has been included in the proposed citizen survey discussed later. A second question, asking about distance to work, would be necessary in order to control for years in which increased travel time resulted solely from increases in commuting distance or when decreased commuting times result from people living nearer to their work places. Corollary questions on traffic congestion and perceived road conditions can also be included in a citizen survey.

Speed-Related Measures

An average-speed statistic would provide an indirect indication of point-to-point travel time, assuming the travel distance between points does not change. Average speed for state roads could be calculated from measuring speeds on a random sample of road segments similar to or the same as the sample used in the trained-observer system. Everything else equal, speed is directly related to elapsed travel time and is intuitively an appropriate indicator of effectiveness in light of the overall objective of providing fast, safe, and efficient transportation. While vehicle speed in a free-flow situation is largely a matter of driver choice, traffic conditions, and the posted speed limit, it is also affected by curvature, horizontal grades, condition, and rideability—factors over which the department should exert control.[4]

The Department has a very limited skeletal reporting system in place for monitoring speeds at eighty-seven stations around the state. However, the stations are all located along highway sections where free-flow traffic conditions exist and are useful mainly for monitoring compliance with the 55-miles-per-hour speed limit. This kind of data would be more useful if collected for a larger sample of roads that would not only provide statistical reliability but would also represent the diversity of roads and traffic conditions on the entire state system. Collecting speed data as part of the federal Highway Performance Monitoring System (HPMS) discussed in chapter 4 would be one alternative, but this is not incorporated by HPMS at present and could be quite costly to implement.

Of greater interest from a level-of-service standpoint is average vehicle speed under more restricted travel flow conditions where traffic volume and congestion tend to limit speeds to well under posted speed limits. For this purpose, a subsample of the road sections used by HPMS could be selected to include heavily traveled, primarily urban-area highways. The data could be collected mechanically and would be analyzed to monitor changes in the percentage of traffic forced to move at less than some specified "minimum desirable speed," for instance, 40 miles per hour. Technology exists for the mechanical collection of speed data, but it is not available at this time in the Department. It should be noted that contrary to the federal emphasis on speed in free-flow conditions,[5] in terms of level of service, travel time is the overriding criterion. For long distances over roads with free-flow conditions, point-to-point travel time is the most appropriate indicator; for short-distance trips in urban areas with congested traffic conditions, speed data provide an acceptable alternative.

As an alternative to speed statistics, volume-capacity ratios could be used as a surrogate measure of average speed for the same random sample of road segments. Volumes would be collected by using counters, and capacity could be calculated with some additional field data using a standard computer program maintained by the Department's Traffic Operations Division. The HPMS sample could most easily serve this purpose because the HPMS data base includes the design characteristics needed to compute capacity. It should be noted that according to the *Highway Capacity Manual,* changes in the volume/capacity (v/c) ratio are considered to be only a fair estimate of changes in average speed,[6] but the Urban Institute report suggests that using volume/capacity ratios—estimating the number and percentage of state-road miles, by class of road, with peak period v/c ratios greater than .75, 1.0, and 1.25, for example—may be a relatively inexpensive substitute for direct travel-speed indicators.[7]

Pothole Encounters

Chapter 5 presented results of the first three cycles of the trained-observer survey designed to track the condition of the highway system over time. The condition measures are indicators of system adequacy—the link between the Department's programs and their ultimate impacts—and as such are not direct indicators of program effectiveness. For example, the argument was made in chapter 2 that eliminating all the potholes, major cracking, and incidence of shoulder dropoff on a section of roadway that does not carry any traffic will really have no impact.

Yet condition indicators viewed in terms of the number of motorists or vehicles exposed to certain types of deterioration take on an element of service-level measurement because they represent both the availability and utilization of a public service. The condition measures reflect service provision, whereas ADT or VMT represents service consumption. Any indicator of highway condition that is of direct concern or utility to the motoring public provides additional insight into service levels when it is weighted by the amount of traffic it affects.

One such indicator can be defined as the number of "pothole encounters" there are on a given section of roadway, the number of potholes in that section multiplied by average daily travel (ADT). This represents the average number of times during a typical day that a vehicle encounters a pothole in that section. If a pothole-patching program targets primarily on sections with low ADTs at the expense of more heavily traveled roads that also are flawed by potholes, it is not as effective as the program would be if it targeted the high ADT roads first.

Table 6-5 shows estimates of total pothole encounters per mile developed for each MFC by multiplying the average ADT by the average count of all potholes per mile for that MFC. Overall it shows that service as defined in this manner improved dramatically during the period from fall 1979 to fall 1980, which is not surprising since the pothole count was cut in half while ADT and total mileage were quite stable over that time. However, it does cast a somewhat different light on comparisons among the five MFCs; although the mean pothole count for interstates is roughly one-sixth of that for local roads, for example, the average mile of interstate highway has nearly ten times as many pothole encounters per day as does the average mile of local road. Maintenance work targeted to free sections of interstates from potholes will therefore have much more impact on service than will

Table 6-5
Estimated Pothole Encounters per Mile

Maintenance Functional Class	Fall 1979, Cycle 1	Spring 1980, Cycle 2	Fall 1980, Cycle 3
Interstates	220,699	165,642	88,887
Principal arterials	280,134	230,034	135,298
Minor arterials	106,068	99,837	50,127
Collectors	45,742	44,442	25,188
Local roads	23,792	19,427	11,742

work aimed at getting rid of all the potholes on a section of local road, even though the interstate has far fewer potholes to begin with. Similar indicators can be developed for other TOS measures such as foreign objects on the roadway, shoulder dropoff, and missing signs and delineators.

Citizen Survey

In addition to point-to-point travel, statewide citizen surveys can be used to obtain information from the users' point of view regarding both user costs and their perceptions of average speeds on the highways they travel. The Urban Institute report cited earlier strongly recommends the use of such citizen surveys on a statewide basis for obtaining feedback on the whole range of state transportation programs. While this book is concerned only with monitoring the highway program, a citizen survey could solicit feedback on a range of DOT activities including mass transit, vehicle inspections, and driver licensing. Given top management's orientation toward providing service that is satisfactory to the public, familiarity with citizen's assessments of conditions, needs, and performance may be as useful to transportation administrators as the professional's "inside" perspective. Survey findings can also lend weight to top decision makers' policy stances or arguments concerning the need for more resources for transportation programs. For instance, a recent general-purpose statewide citizen survey in Pennsylvania, which found repair of state roads to be a "priority" of 86 percent of the residents, has been cited as evidence that increased expenditures on highway maintenance are warranted.[8]

While such multi-purpose citizen surveys are used in many states, they are limited in terms of how much information they can provide concerning transportation issues; specific transportation-focused surveys are not in use on a regular basis to provide state DOTs with feedback on service performance. Based in part on surveys that have been tested in North Carolina and Wisconsin, a citizen survey was developed and pretested for possible use by PennDOT.[9] The items pertain to both road condition and program effectiveness, and in general, these perceptual indicators complement the hard-data "factual" measures obtained from other sources. A sample size of 1,500 to 2,000 randomly selected citizens was proposed for the telephone-survey format. Considerations going into the development of this survey, as well as discussion of a version that was fielded and the responses it generated, are presented in chapter 8.

Two items in particular pertain to effectiveness indicators of the highway program in terms of service levels. The percent of all respondents saying that traffic congestion causes difficulties in commuting to work or other regular trips, and the percent indicating that the condition of the roads is better than in the past year, are two good indicators of service levels provided by the highway network from the citizen perspective. While the content of these two questions refers to road condition per se, the responses to these items represent how users perceive the transportation service provided to them. As this survey is intended to be repeated on a periodic basis, the real value of the feedback lies in the ability to monitor whether citizen perceptions improve or worsen over time.

A final note on interpretation of the effectiveness measures discussed in this chapter is necessary at this point. As with citizen-survey measures, the less subjective measures discussed earlier are all intended to reflect some outcome states or desired impact conditions that the highway program is supposed to influence. Yet these indicators are subject to numerous other influences, and the direct causal connections between program and impact may be weak. The difficulty therefore lies in interpreting the extent to which observed changes in impact conditions are the result of program activity.

The point needs to be emphasized, however, that these kinds of precise conclusions about cause and effect are less important in performance monitoring than in discrete, intensive program evaluation. In macro-level, comprehensive, but fairly superficial performance monitoring, the purpose is to track the operation of programs and to monitor relevant impact conditions without necessarily gauging each set of detailed cause/effect linkages controlling for all external influences. The potential effectiveness of the programs is known or else should be subjected to basic evaluation research. Performance monitoring, on the other hand, is aimed at addressing the question, "Do these programs appear to be effective?" The approach here is to observe trends in the relevant effectiveness indicators and to attempt to explain observed changes, either favorable or unfavorable, in terms of program operations and outputs in the context of shifting or static external factors. Where effectiveness is improving, the only plausible reason may indeed be the program itself, and where effectiveness is diminishing, the responsible program indicators or external factors may be equally clear. Frequently, this kind of general interpretation will be all that is needed, although sometimes effectiveness monitoring will generate results that are perplexing, in which case more sharply focused intensive evaluation may be appropriate.

Notes

1. For literature reviews and discussion of these relationships, see J.P. Janiewski, B.C. Butler, Jr., G. Cunningham, G.E. Elkins, and R. Machemehl, *Vehicle Operating Costs, Fuel Consumption and Pavement Type and Condition Factors,* Federal Highway Administration, June 1980.

2. W.F. McFarland, "Benefit Analysis for Pavement Design Systems," Texas Transportation Insitute, Texas A&M University, and the Center for Highway Research, The University of Texas at Austin, April 1972.

3. American Association of State Highway Transportation Officials, "A Manual on User Benefit Analysis of Highway and Bus-Transit Improvements," 1977; R.A. Lundy, "Effect of Traffic Volumes and Number of Lanes on Freeway Accident Rates," State of California, Division of Highways, July 1964; R.N. Smith, "Predictive Parameters for Accident Rates," State of California, Division of Highways, September 1973; and J.K. Kihlberg and J.K Tharp, "Accident Rates as Related to Design Elements of Rural Highways," Highway Research Board, National Cooperative Highway Research Program, Report 47, 1968.

4. M.A. Karan, R. Haas, and R. Kher, "Effects of Pavement Roughness on Vehicle Speeds," *Transportation Research Record* 602, NAS, Washington, D.C., 1976.

5. *Highway Performance Monitoring System: Field Implementation Manual,* U.S. Department of Transportation, Federal Highway Administration, Program Management Division, Washington, D.C., January 1979.

6. *Highway Capacity Manual,* Highway Research Board Special Report 87, Washington, D.C., 1965.

7. *Monitoring the Effectiveness of State Transportation Services* (Prepared for the U.S. Department of Transportation, DOT-TPI-10-77-23, Urban Institute, Washington, D.C., July 1977, pp. 36–37).

8. Dan E. Moore and Anne S. Ishler, *Pennsylvania: The Citizens' Viewpoint* (University Park, Pa.: Cooperative Extension Service, 1980).

9. See *Transportation Issues and Answers: A Survey of Public Opinion in Wisconsin, 1979,* Wisconsin Department of Transportation, 1979, and *North Carolina 1976 Transportation Effectiveness Survey,* North Carolina Department of Transportation, 1976. For the questionnaire proposed for Pennsylvania, see T.H. Poister, R.S. Huebner, G.L. Gittings, and K. Phillips, *Development of Performance Indicators for the Pennsylvania Department of Transportation* (University Park, Pa.: Pennsylvania Transportation Institute, 1980, PTI 8012, appendix B).

7

Transit-Program Monitoring

State government activity relating to urban mass transit has a much shorter history than in the highway area and has taken on an entirely different role. The states began to establish highway departments in the 1920s, and for the next four decades, highways were the only system of transportation in which states had more than regulatory interests. In the late 1960s and particularly in the 1970s, however, many of the more urbanized states followed the lead of the federal government in promoting revitalization of mass-transit systems in the nation's cities and began developing transit-assistance programs. State interests in aviation, railroads, and waterways also grew, and while some states still operate traditional highway departments, in the majority of states these have evolved into multimodal departments of transportation (DOTs) with a more balanced and integrated set of transportation programs.[1] Within this context, Pennsylvania was an early leader in converting to a DOT and taking a strong proactive stance toward urban mass transit.[2]

While state DOTs have direct responsibility for building and maintaining highways, they play a support role in urban mass transit. With the exception of the Maryland DOT, which operates the local transit system in Baltimore, states are not in the business of direct-transit-service provision. Transit systems are operated by local-transit authorities or other instruments of local government, and the states are involved through financial, planning, technical, and managerial assistance. Thus transit is typical of many programs administered through the intergovernmental system, being at least partially funded and controlled by higher levels of government but implemented at the local level.

The implication of this fundamentally different service-delivery arrangement for performance monitoring is that the indicators should reflect the systematic impact of the state programs as well as the performance of local-transit operations. Due in part to the recognized need for the states and federal government to monitor local-transit programs, considerable work has been done with respect to the development and use of indicators that measure various aspects of transit-system performance.[3] The data-collection systems that have been implemented serve different purposes, including detailed analysis of individual routes,[4] the management of a single local-transit system,[5] and the monitoring of local systems by higher levels of government for allocation and control purposes.[6] The kinds of information needed for these various uses are similar, differing primarily in terms of the amount of detail and the level of aggregation.

Penn-DOT's Transit Programs

Pennsylvania initiated its transit programs in response to the downward spiral of ridership and service—reflecting a national trend chiefly due to years of increasing suburbanization and automobile ownership—that threatened the continued existence of urban mass-transit systems. The general rationale underlying the state's initiative, as well as the federal program, was that transit is an essential source of mobility for the remaining "captive" riders. From a broader perspective, maintaining transit as a viable alternative to the private auto is in the public interest with respect to central-city economic, environmental, and energy concerns.

The first initiative was a capital-grants program, a state "buy-in" to the federal program that helped local operators purchase new vehicles and equipment. Soon afterward, Pennsylvania implemented an operating-assistance strategy that preceded the federal operating-assistance grants. The state's capital-grants program, currently funded at roughly $40 million per year, most recently has instituted a bus-pool purchase program aimed at speeding up delivery dates. The operating-assistance program is in the form of an annual "purchase-of-service" arrangement in which local operators must meet certain operating standards and guidelines prescribed by Penn-DOT in order to maintain eligibility. The level of effort for this program is currently around $138 million per year. PennDOT also administers a program in which local-transit agencies permit senior citizens to ride free of charge during offpeak hours. Local agencies are then reimbursed by the state for the foregone revenue. This senior-citizen "free-fare" program is funded by the state lottery in Pennsylvania and currently costs about $24 million per year. In addition to the financial-assistance programs, Penn-DOT carries on support activities such as sponsoring seminars and publishing manuals designed to help local managers improve the performance of their transit systems.

In general, PennDOT's role in this field is to promote mass transit in the state's urban areas, and to support local-transit agencies so as to assure their continued viability. Collectively, these three programs have been aimed at preserving transit service, expanding coverage where needed, and improving the quality and level of service provided in order to make it more attractive. The major objective has been to increase ridership inasmuch as ridership increases reflect gains in mobility and are seen as necessary for the secondary impacts to occur. More recently, given a more conservative political ethic in the face of continuing cost escalation, concern has focused on the objective of cost effectiveness and financial stability.

Local-Transit Systems Model

In monitoring the overall performance of local-transit systems that participate in the state's programs, PennDOT keeps track of the same kinds of variables that would be used in adjusting service levels in an individual system or evaluating the effect of a particular transit-improvement program.[7] Figure 7-1 presents a basic systems model of the logic underlying local-transit programs, whereby the use of resources is justified by anticipated impacts in terms of increased personal mobility, increased fuel efficiency, decreased congestion, improved central business district (CBD) parking, and increased downtown business. As usual, the resources can be measured in their natural measurement units, such as numbers of employees, pieces of equipment, or gallons of fuel, or they can be expressed in dollars.

The primary component is the operations component, which could be compared among local areas in terms of type of route configuration, peak-hour vehicles in use, frequency of trips, and so forth. The outputs are vehicle hours and vehicle miles operated, that is, measures of how much service is provided. The maintenance and marketing components are basically support components. The maintenance component consists of both preventive and unscheduled corrective maintenance, outputs being the numbers of preventive-maintenance inspections and unscheduled repairs, respectively. As the maintenance component is subordinate to the operations component, these activities are aimed at improving the *quality* of the vehicle hours and miles of service provided by improving the quality of the ride and guarding aginst vehicle breakdowns and service interruptions.

The direct effects of the program are measured in terms of ridership because the immediate objective is to afford trips that would not be made in the absence of public transportation, and to attract trips that would otherwise be made by private automobile. The linking variables between the operations component and adequate or increasing ridership levels are not shown in figure 7-1 but would represent the extent to which routes and schedules were perceived by potential riders as meeting their travel needs, along with the general perceived attractiveness and reliability of the system. The marketing component is made up of a variety of activities such as advertisements, information, promotions, and so forth, all of which are intended to attract new riders to the system.

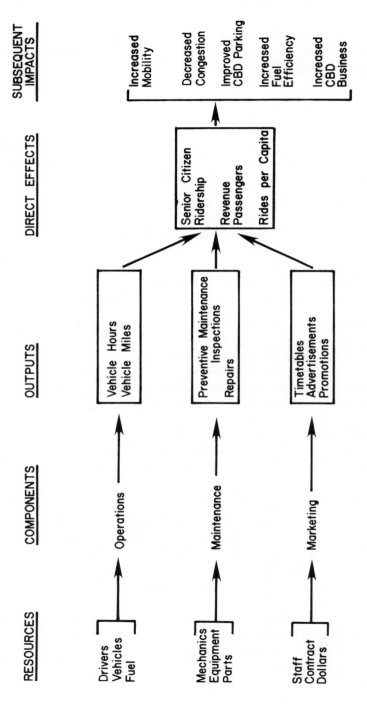

Figure 7-1. Local-Transit-System Logic

Performance Indicators

There are numerous measures that would be appropriate for tracking various aspects of transit-system performance as outlined previously,[8] and a substantial amount of research has been undertaken to analyze their usefulness and feasibility.[9] These measures vary considerably in terms of availability and reliability as well as what factors may influence or distort them. Moreover, the excessive detail that results from trying to incorporate all possible indicators can be more confusing than helpful when the purpose is to track progress for a number of transit systems. While an individual transit agency may need to track a much more extensive set of indicators, monitoring a limited set of key indicators, even on a disaggregate basis, is more suitable from a state perspective.

Table 7-1 presents selected transit-performance indicators that can be used to operationalize most major aspects of the overall systems model discussed earlier. The list is illustrative but certainly not totally inclusive of the kinds of indicators state DOTs might find useful for monitoring local-system performance. PennDOT collects these and similar kinds of data

Table 7-1
Selected Transit-Performance Indicators

Resources	*Utilization*
Total expense	Passengers per vehicle hour
Number of employees	Passengers per vehicle mile
Drivers, mechanics	Passenger miles per vehicle hour
Number of vehicles	Passenger miles per vehicle mile
Average age	
Marketing Expenditures	*Cost Effectiveness*
	Percent cost recovery
Outputs	Cost per passenger trip
Vehicle hours	Cost per passenger mile
Vehicle miles	Deficit
Percent on-time trips	
Number of breakdowns	*Environmental Variables*
	Service areas population
Effectiveness	Driver wage rate
Total passengers	Average speed
Revenue passengers	
Senior citizens	
Passenger miles	
Rides per capita	
Internal Operating Efficiency	
Cost per vehicle hour	
Cost per vehicle mile	
Vehicle miles per employee	
Maintenance employee per peak vehicle	

annually from each local-transit agency participating in state programs and then condenses and publishes the information in an annual statistical report.[10] The Department uses this information as a means of checking compliance with purchase-of-service standards and guidelines and as a basis for allocating operating-assistance funds. Penn-DOT supplements this principal mode of performance monitoring by reviewing annual-planning documents prepared for each local area, and through periodic site visits intended to answer questions and provide feedback on operations and performance.

The simplest indicator of resources consumed is total expense, but to understand variation in expense, it is useful to know how many employees, particularly drivers and mechanics, are on the local-transit agency's payroll. The number of vehicles operated by the agency, that is, the number of vehicles usually in service during peak periods, is another good indicator of the overall size of the system. Since most marketing is done by contract (printing costs, air-time rates, and so on), the amount of money spent on marketing is a relevant summary indicator of the level of effort of marketing activities. As mentioned earlier, vehicle hours and vehicle miles operated are the principal output measures representing the quantity of service provided. The percent of all trips that are "on time," for instance, within 3 minutes of scheduled departure or arrival time, and the number of vehicle breakdowns or service interruptions due to breakdowns provide some indication of the *quality* of this service.

The most direct measure of effectiveness is the total passenger trips made on the local-transit system, and it is useful to know the breakdown between fare-paying revenue passengers versus free-fare senior citizens in terms of assessing impact on different target populations. The number of passenger miles traveled by transit provides a more complete measure of the amount of service consumed, although these data tend to be less reliable than data on passenger trips. Overall impact is best measured in terms of the number of annual transit trips per capita, the best single indicator of the importance of mass transit to the local community.

There are many ways to measure internal operating efficiency, the most direct being total resources to output, namely, the cost per vehicle hour and the cost per vehicle mile. Since labor costs constitute a large portion of total costs, measures of labor productivity, such as vehicle miles per employee and the ratio of maintenance employees to vehicles in service during peak periods, are worth monitoring.

A second set of efficiency measures, referred to as "utilization measures" in table 7-1, are ratios of service consumed to service provided. Indicators such as passenger trips per vehicle hour, passenger trips per vehicle mile, passenger miles per vehicle hour, and passenger miles per vehicle mile relate some measure of utilization to an output measure. These indicators are important because they present a picture of the "fit" between the demand for transit service in an urban area and the amount of service being provided.

From both the state and local perspective, the "bottom line" in trying to determine how much service should be provided and to what extent the system should be subsidized should be cost effectiveness. These indicators relate resources consumed to direct effects; the lower the cost per passenger trip or cost per passenger mile, the more cost effective the transit system. As a summary indicator, the percent cost recovery—total revenue as a percent of total expense—is extremely significant because it represents the share of total costs that users of the service are willing to pay for directly. A complementary indicator is the deficit, that is, how much subsidy is required to fully pay for the service.

Local-Transit-System Performance

State funding agencies are interested in monitoring performance trends over time and comparing performance indicators among the local systems they assist. As mentioned earlier, PennDOT reviews annual data reflecting performance for all local-transit systems participating in the purchase-of-service program. Of principal interest are the transit systems serving the state's two large metropolitan areas, Philadelphia and Pittsburgh, and eleven "other urbanized areas" that are basically small- and medium-sized metropolitan areas. While data on the systems in smaller urban areas are included in PennDOT's statistical reports, their role is relatively minor and does not affect the statewide picture significantly.

In monitoring transit systems across local areas, cognizance must be taken of different environmental characteristics because such factors as population density, auto ownership, and traffic volumes may influence performance as much as the more controllable program variables or management practices. Table 7-2 shows the values of three environmental variables that have been found to be particularly relevant to transit-system performance,[11] for the two major metropolitan areas and eleven small- and medium-sized metropolitan areas in the state. The entries are ordered by service-area population, ranging from Philadelphia's nearly 6 million to Williamsport's 52,000. Population is important because mass transit tends to play a more important role in the overall transportation system of large metropolitan areas, where households have a greater propensity to generate transit trips.

Since labor costs are the major factor in most systems' operating expenses, some indication of wage rate is appropriate for stratifying local systems. As can be be seen in table 7-2, the transit systems' top wage rate is highest for Pittsburg and Philadelphia and tends to decrease with popula-

Table 7-2
Selected Environmental Characteristics

	Service Area Population	1979 Top Wage Rate	Average Speed
Philadelphia	5,819,926	8.58	12.4
Pittsburgh	1,829,233	9.01	12.4
Allentown	325,644	7.26	13.2
Harrisburg	293,654	7.30	11.7
Lancaster	254,491	7.00	15.6
Scranton	240,513	6.30	12.4
Wilkes-Barre	240,190	7.26	12.1
Erie	212,261	6.50	12.9
Reading	200,744	7.55	14.0
Johnstown	89,827	5.50	11.8
Altoona	74,396	5.64	11.0
York	65,334	4.80	11.8
Williamsport	52,524	4.72	17.4

tion size, reflecting the generally more competitive, and more highly union-ized labor markets in large urban areas. Average operating speed can be affected by transit management, but it is probably influenced more by street layout and traffic volumes. While this can be expected to influence driver and vehicle productivity, it is not systematically related to population size for the areas shown in table 7-2.

Resources and Outputs

Table 7-3 shows total operating expenses for the transit systems in the state's metropolitan areas for fiscal year 1976-1977 through fiscal year 1980-1981. As would be expected, total cost, the summary measure of resources going into these systems, has grown steadily in all thirteen areas. Expense increased by 11 percent between fiscal 1977 and 1978, by 8 percent in fiscal 1979, by 10 percent in fiscal 1980 and by 14 percent in fiscal 1981. However, these rates are roughly commensurate with the general inflation rate, and thus there is no indication of a net change in the real value of resources used by these systems.

The data on total operating expense show just how much the two major metropolitan areas dominate urban mass transit in the state. The Philadelphia system spends more than ten times as much as the eleven smaller sys-

Table 7-3
Operating Expense, by Transit System

Area-Transit System	1976–1977	1977–1978	1978–1979	1979–1980	1980–1981
Philadelphia	$235,232,424	$263,561,661	$284,181,544	$311,830,000	$354,487,561
Pittsburgh	74,292,858	80,953,655	90,791,305	100,322,000	116,787,570
Subtotal	309,525,282	344,515,316	374,972,849	412,152,000	471,275,131
Allentown	2,891,783	2,875,524	3,184,357	3,837,845	4,321,389
Erie	2,373,598	2,773,409	3,071,425	3,622,027	4,099,839
Harrisburg	2,939,467	2,908,252	3,049,140	3,611,783	4,208,174
Wilkes-Barre	2,258,724	2,477,774	2,735,166	3,147,795	3,710,898
Reading	2,113,161	2,175,176	2,523,386	3,181,376	3,739,240
Scranton	1,757,857	1,876,690	2,036,576	2,572,121	3,070,985
Lancaster	1,328,934	1,368,767	1,478,421	1,780,157	2,166,384
Johnstown	1,142,279	1,282,719	1,467,415	1,800,698	2,158,576
Altoona	918,480	1,060,214	1,023,391	1,286,558	1,353,097
Williamsport	661,225	713,471	782,576	927,290	1,096,587
York	—	664,469	719,413	1,078,048	1,130,842
Subtotal	18,385,508	20,176,465	22,071,266	26,845,868	31,056,011
Total	$327,910,790	$364,691,781	$397,044,115	$438,997,868	$502,331,142

tems combined, and Philadelphia and Pittsburgh together account for about 94 percent of the total expense. This pattern holds true for outputs and for most other aspects of the magnitude of transit operations.

Table 7–4 displays vehicle hours operated for all thirteen systems. In general, the level of output has been quite static over the period being considered, although it should be noted that vehicle hours decreased somewhat in the Philadelphia area over the most recent three years, while they increased very slightly among the eleven smaller systems. Vehicle miles operated follows a similar trend. Again the dominance of the two major metropolitan-area systems is overwhelming. It should be noted here that the Philadelphia system includes light-rail and heavy-rail commuter trains in addition to subways and buses. Although the rail service operates a relatively small share of the system's total vehicle hours, it accounts for a somewhat larger proportion of total vehicle miles due to the significantly faster operating speed on the rail systems. The rail service also accounts for a disproportionately high share of total operating expenses since it is so much more costly to operate.

Effectiveness Measures

Throughout most of the 1970s, the total number of passenger trips made on the smaller metropolitan-area transit systems was on the increase as these local agencies sought to revitalize service and attract new riders. While data on the major metropolitan systems for the first part of the decade are not reliable, table 7–5 shows clearly that from fiscal 1977 to fiscal 1980, the number of passenger trips on these systems was also increasing. Collectively, these thirteen urban-transit systems were showing greater effectiveness in meeting mobility needs and attracting new riders. In terms of ridership composition, however, the largest gains came in senior-citizen ridership rather than fare-paying revenue passengers.

Moreover, from fiscal 1980 to fiscal 1981, there was a very pronounced decrease in total passenger trips made on the major systems—a 13.6 percent drop in Philadelphia and a 4.8-percent decrease in Pittsburgh—while there was a 1.3 percent decrease among the eleven smaller systems. Whether this represents the beginning of a reversal from increasing to decreasing ridership remains to be seen; ridership could continue downward, level off, or even recover.

The big ridership decrease in the Philadelphia area was particularly due to strikes in fiscal 1980–1981 that shut down service for two weeks on one division and for six weeks on another. Yet the overall decrease is largely the combined effect of rising unemployment, coupled with the slight cutbacks

Table 7-4
Vehicle Hours Operated, by System

Transit System	1976–1977	1977–1978	1978–1979	1979–1980	1980–1981
Philadelphia	5,968,988	5,798,320	5,657,199	5,589,594	5,477,385
Pittsburgh	2,782,466	2,731,258	3,085,000	3,100,465	3,120,300
Total	8,751,454	8,529,571	8,742,199	8,690,059	8,597,685
Allentown	174,336	151,637	150,035	153,022	151,857
Erie	155,737	166,587	161,186	154,835	159,597
Harrisburg	160,503	142,924	142,826	145,320	150,098
Wilkes-Barre	152,624	147,554	147,350	147,143	147,031
Reading	116,459	118,729	128,009	134,840	131,241
Scranton	107,474	107,277	107,290	108,050	108,110
Lancaster	80,357	81,000	76,573	86,281	90,433
Johnstown	60,929	74,209	78,653	82,553	92,000
Altoona	64,840	63,656	47,192	52,676	49,017
Williamsport	44,300	44,300	44,100	44,100	44,100
York	—	29,568	36,550	36,350	44,163
Subtotal	1,117,559	1,127,441	1,119,764	1,145,170	1,167,647
Total	9,869,013	9,657,012	9,861,963	9,835,229	9,765,332

Table 7-5
Total Passenger Trips, by System

Transit System	1976–1977	1977–1978	1978–1979	1979–1980	1980–1981
Philadelphia	248,927,530	260,633,526	271,426,284	276,966,310	239,371,115
Pittsburgh	90,040,116	90,870,897	93,210,174	98,245,695	93,536,889
Subtotal	338,967,646	351,504,423	364,636,458	375,212,005	332,908,004
Allentown	4,435,955	4,331,415	4,632,289	5,028,097	4,738,644
Erie	5,454,692	6,329,512	6,514,934	6,120,256	6,011,676
Harrisburg	4,561,935	4,376,528	4,511,433	4,948,250	4,819,945
Wilkes-Barre	4,585,768	4,542,807	4,662,620	4,992,516	5,069,616
Reading	3,851,706	4,190,154	5,280,325	5,558,944	5,522,861
Scranton	3,426,704	3,486,716	3,552,198	3,819,987	3,706,234
Lancaster	1,536,520	1,672,678	1,701,721	2,188,583	2,222,576
Johnstown	1,502,763	1,492,250	1,646,713	1,843,813	1,866,479
Altoona	1,322,129	1,465,699	1,298,011	1,436,317	1,378,555
Williamsport	832,663	925,413	996,486	1,120,171	1,203,006
York	—	470,374	928,563	771,161	804,588
Subtotal	31,520,835	33,283,546	35,725,293	37,828,095	37,344,180
Total	370,488,481	384,787,969	400,361,751	413,040,100	370,252,184

Note: Figures include senior-citizen trips but not transfers.

in service noted earlier coming at the same time fares were being increased. Analysis of strike-adjusted data compiled by the Southeastern Pennsylvania Transit Authority (SEPTA) shows that ridership would have decreased by 9 percent even without these strikes. A drop in the primary effectiveness measure, such as the ridership decrease shown in table 7-5, definitely signals a problem that must be of concern to transit managers and should be watched for further developments.

The data on passenger miles traveled, as reported by the agencies, show a similar trend of increase and then decrease in fiscal 1981. Although this measure is less reliable because many systems do not accurately measure trip length, average trip length may be quite constant, and thus passenger miles would be expected to follow this pattern. The number of passenger trips per capita, which is on the order of forty in Pittsburgh, fifty in Philadelphia, and ranges from ten to thirty in the smaller metropolitan areas, can also be presumed to have decreased in fiscal 1981. Even though accurate population change data are not available on a yearly basis, this would appear to represent a decreased impact. Presumably, population size experienced much less of a decrease than did total ridership.

Internal Operating Efficiency

As shown in table 7-6, the unit cost of providing service have escalated dramatically from fiscal 1977 to fiscal 1981 on both the large and the smaller systems. It is interesting to note that both major metropolitan-transit systems have much higher costs per vehicle hour and vehicle mile than the eleven smaller systems. Not only do the major systems operate much more service, but their unit costs are much greater—in the case of Philadelphia more than double the unit costs of the smaller systems. This apparent diseconomy of scale is due to the higher wage rates prevailing in the major metropolitan areas, as mentioned earlier, and the fact that rail service costs more to operate per hour or per mile than does bus service.

The cost per vehicle hour went up by roughly 55 percent over the four-year period for the combined systems shown in table 7-6, and the cost per vehicle mile went up by 53 percent. This works out to an average annual rate of increase of about 11 percent and closely mirrors the increases in total operating expense discussed earlier. These increases reflect the general inflation rate during this period, particularly as it applies to drivers' and mechanics' wages, and the price of fuel which rose astronomically and totally out of proportion to other inputs.

While the data on cost per vehicle hour and vehicle mile show a dramatic decrease in cost efficiency from a financial perspective, due to the

Table 7-6
Unit-Cost Indicators, by System

Transit System	Cost per Vehicle Hour		Cost per Vehicle Mile	
	1976–1977	*1980–1981*	*1976–1977*	*1980–1981*
Philadelphia	$39.40	$64.71	$3.51	$5.29
Pittsburgh	26.70	37.42	1.95	3.13
Subtotal	$35.36	$54.81	2.95	$4.52
Allentown	$16.58	$28.45	$1.25	$2.15
Erie	15.24	25.68	1.29	2.14
Harrisburg	18.31	28.03	1.64	2.40
Wilkes-Barre	14.79	25.23	1.19	2.07
Reading	18.14	28.49	1.79	2.53
Scranton	16.35	28.40	1.32	2.34
Lancaster	16.53	23.95	1.15	1.60
Johnstown	18.74	23.46	1.47	1.82
Altoona	14.16	27.60	1.35	2.48
Williamsport	14.92	24.86	1.24	1.73
York	—	25.60	—	1.73
Subtotal	$16.45	$26.59	$1.37	$2.12
Total	$33.22	$51.44	$2.77	$4.23

effect of inflation, these indicators do not represent internal operating efficiency in terms of actual resource utilization. Table 7-7 shows the number of vehicle miles operated per employee for these local systems over the same period. Two points are worth noting: First, while the smaller systems operate more vehicle miles per employee, the disparity between them and the major systems is not as great as their disparity in costs per vehicle hour or vehicle mile. The major systems are indeed less efficient than the smaller systems in terms of the ratio of output to resources, but this disparity is widened because the larger systems pay their employees more than the smaller systems do. Second, the ratio of vehicle miles operated to the number of employees was remarkably stable over the period shown in table 7-7. It dropped by only 1.5 percent for the major systems and by less than half of a percent for the smaller systems. Thus internal operating efficiency has remained constant in a technological sence although it has deteriorated dramatically from a financial standpoint.

Table 7-7
Vehicle Miles Operated per Employee

Transit System	1976–1977	1977–1978	1978–1979	1979–1980	1980–1981
Philadelphia	7,846.93	7,874.09	8,339.83	7,942.32	7,817.54
Pittsburgh	13,168.88	13,362.77	13,229.01	12,519.62	12,657.84
Subtotal	9,192.69	9,170.99	9,591.70	9,107.61	9,055.50
Allentown	15,856.99	15,495.81	15,637.92	15,067.80	15,525.72
Erie	15,068.42	15,839.56	14,878.73	14,183.39	14,619.55
Harrisburg	12,099.40	12,499.52	12,152.90	12,302.43	12,975.11
Wilkes-Barre	16,761.14	16,254.64	15,435.29	15,186.17	15,172.52
Reading	14,033.24	13,140.89	13,879.68	14,433.87	13,774.77
Scranton	15,852.30	15,775.07	15,241.95	14,595.33	14,391.99
Lancaster	17,203.94	18,516.37	16,984.66	17,772.93	17,980.00
Johnstown	10,882.42	11,802.44	12,515.35	11,945.16	13,128.44
Altoona	13,013.33	12,111.35	9,674.57	10,702.12	10,469.06
Williamsport	15,142.86	16,698.14	17,265.42	17,384.58	17,508.42
York	—	13,522.00	11,666.70	13,183.88	15,120.40
Subtotal	14,565.43	14,716.57	14,255.04	14,203.68	14,497.00
Total	9,593.88	9,579.92	9,956.93	9,513.75	9,493.66

Service Utilization

Utilization measures, ratios of service consumption to service provision, are
the best indicators of the appropriateness of existing service levels in relation to the demand for mass transit. The higher the utilization, the higher
the load factors, and thus the more efficient the transit system is in trans-
porting passengers. Table 7–8 shows the number of passengers per vehicle
hour operated for all thirteen systems for fiscal 1976–1977 and fiscal 1980–
1981. Again there is a pronounced difference between the major systems
and the smaller operations, but it goes in the opposite direction from what
was noted in the previous analysis. While the two major systems operate
fewer vehicle miles per employee, meaning lower internal operating efficiency, they carry more passengers per vehicle hour—forty on average,
compared with an average of thirty passengers per vehicle hour for the
eleven smaller systems. Philadelphia is especially efficient on this indicator;
actually five of the smaller systems carry more passengers per vehicle hour
than does the Pittsburgh system.

More significant, however, is the finding that passengers per vehicle
hour decreased substantially on both of the major systems during the four-
year period covered by the data. By contrast, this utilization measure
showed increases on eight of the eleven smaller systems for the same period,
although for all eleven combined, there was virtually no change. In part,
this results from the addition of the York transit system to the data base
starting in fiscal 1980. While the major systems operated fewer vehicle
hours in fiscal 1981 than in fiscal 1977, their ridership decreased by a greater
margin. Collectively, ridership on the eleven smaller systems was almost
exactly the same in fiscal 1981 as in fiscal 1977 although it had been higher
in the intervening years. With a few exceptions, then, the smaller systems
appear to be maintaining a balance between service levels and ridership, but
on the larger systems that need greater utilization to offset higher costs,
there has been some attrition in this indicator.

Both the large and smaller systems appear to have been quite stable in
terms of passenger miles per vehicle operated, the ratio of total passenger
travel to vehicle travel. On the two major systems combined, passengers
traveled 17.1 miles for every vehicle mile operated in fiscal 1981, down just
slightly from 17.6 in fiscal 1977. On the eleven smaller systems combined,
the reported passenger miles per vehicle mile was 8.2 in fiscal 1977 and 8.6
in fiscal 1981. The data on passenger miles are not as reliable as the other
ridership data, however, for at best these figures are estimates derived from
multiplying the number of passenger trips by average trip lengths actually
recorded in boarding-and-alighting surveys conducted once or twice per
year. As ridership has fallen on the major systems, average trip length might
have increased, offsetting the loss in passenger miles. On the other hand,

Table 7-8
Passengers per Vehicle Hour, by System

Transit System	1976–1977	1980–1981	Percent Change
Philadelphia	55.8	45.8	− .17
Pittsburgh	36.1	29.8	− .17
Subtotal	49.6	40.0	− .19
Allentown	27.3	31.1	+ .13
Erie	36.9	26.9	− .27
Harrisburg	30.7	32.1	+ .04
Wilkes-Barre	31.8	34.6	+ .09
Reading	37.0	42.1	+ .14
Scranton	33.1	34.8	+ .05
Lancaster	19.8	22.8	+ .15
Johnstown	26.9	20.3	− .25
Altoona	21.3	28.1	+ .32
Williamsport	20.5	27.3	+ .33
York	—	18.2	—
Subtotal	30.1	30.4	+ .008
Total	47.3	38.9	− .17

Note: Based on total passengers including transfers.

the average-trip-length data may be flawed, masking actual decreases in passenger miles per vehicle mile.

Cost Effectiveness

As indicated earlier, aggregate service levels across the thirteen local-transit systems operating in the state's most heavily urbanized areas have been fairly constant over the five-year period under consideration. In addition, internal operating efficiency measured in terms of vehicle miles operated per employee has been quite stable. However, total expense, and thus cost per vehicle hour or vehicle mile, has gone up dramatically during the same period due to the inflated prices of factor inputs. The only way local operators can maintain financial viability under these circumstances is to try to generate commensurate revenue increases.

As shown in table 7-9, revenue did go up considerably on each of the thirteen systems over the period in question, up by 75 percent in four years

Table 7-9
Revenue and Percentage of Cost Recovery, by System

Transit System	Revenue		Percentage of Cost Recovery	
	1976–1977	*1980–1981*	*1976–1977*	*1980–1981*
Philadelphia	$101,518,946	$184,496,773	.43	.52
Pittsburgh	36,423,483	57,081,510	.49	.48
Subtotal	137,942,429	241,577,283	.44	.51
Allentown	1,378,414	2,032,608	.48	.47
Erie	1,474,588	2,093,546	.62	.51
Harrisburg	1,551,076	2,288,090	.53	.54
Wilkes-Barre	1,313,066	2,032,608	.58	.55
Reading	1,253,510	2,018,593	.59	.54
Scranton	1,038,371	1,202,025	.59	.39
Lancaster	583,924	1,080,996	.44	.50
Johnstown	707,190	1,039,095	.62	.48
Altoona	430,411	544,608	.47	.40
Williamsport	244,644	346,367	.37	.32
York	—	357,768	—	.32
Subtotal	9,975,194	15,036,304	.54	.48
Total	$147,917,623	$256,613,587	.45	.51

for Philadelphia and Pittsburgh combined, and by a little more than 50 percent for the eleven smaller systems taken together. Revenue increases on the major systems are due almost solely to fare increases; in Philadelphia ridership experienced a net drop from fiscal 1977 to fiscal 1981, while in Pittsburgh, overall ridership increased by less than 5 percent during a period when total revenue increased by well over 50 percent. Fare increases were also the primary reason for the growth in revenue on the smaller systems, where ridership increased by about 20 percent while revenues increased by more than 50 percent.

These figures take on added significance when viewed in relation to total expenses. Table 7-9 shows that the percent cost recovery—that is, revenue divided by expense, or the percent of total expense that is recovered through revenue—held constant for the Pittsburgh system and increased substantially, from 43 percent to 52 percent, for the Philadelphia system. Thus Pittsburgh continued to recover nearly half of all costs through its revenue, and Philadelphia improved its financial status to the point of recovering more than 50 percent of costs despite the loss of ridership noted earlier. Among the smaller operators, however, revenue gains were not commensurate with cost increases, the percent cost recovery decreasing in ten out of these eleven systems.

Two additional points concerning these data are worth noting. First, while the two major systems operate on a much larger scale than the others in terms of total expense, vehicle miles operated, total passengers and so forth, their percent-cost-recovery figures both fall within the range of 32 percent to 55 percent defined by the eleven smaller systems. Thus the overall rate of cost effectiveness is quite similar among the thirteen systems. Second, there appears to be a scale effect at work such that systems operating more vehicle hours and vehicle miles, for example, Allentown, Erie, Harrisburg, and Wilkes-Barre, have higher cost-recovery factors than the smallest systems such as Williamsport and York. In a few cases, particularly in Philadelphia and Pittsburgh, this is partially due to higher fare structures, but it also results from greater utilization of service on the large systems measured by passengers per vehicle hour (see table 7–8).

In one respect the percent cost recovery represents the "bottom line" in the management of mass-transit systems in that it shows how much money people pay to use the service in relation to what it actually costs to provide that service. If the revenue earned by these systems were a valid indicator of the benefit derived, then the costs would outweigh the benefits by a wide margin, and it would not be appropriate to support them. However, governmental subsidy of the remainder, the "percent not recovered," is generally justified on three counts: (1) There is consumer surplus involved,[12] as some passengers would be willing to pay more for the service than the fares they are charged; (2) transit is a necessary public service having a social benefit exceeding private benefit; and (3) equity considerations require the subsidization of public transportation as an aid to low-income families.

On the other hand, as the percent cost recovery decreases, it is more difficult politically to justify continued support, just as it is more difficult to fund the "unrecovered" cost, or deficit, as it grows larger. Table 7–10 shows the deficits for all these systems from fiscal 1977 through fiscal 1981. The amount of deficit is of concern to PennDOT because it indicates the need for state support; how much operating subsidy does the transit agency need to receive from federal, state, and local levels combined in order to continue providing service? As seen in table 7–10, deficits have increased in four years by slightly more than one-third for the two major systems combined and by nearly one-half for the eleven smaller systems, mainly due to costs increasing more than revenues. Given the conservative political ethic prevailing at present, this rapid increase in deficits, or in subsidy require-

Table 7-10
Operating Deficit, by System

Transit System	1976–1977	1977–1978	1978–1979	1979–1980	1980–1981
Philadelphia	$133,713,478	$126,804,519	$144,180,171	$162,247,000	$169,990,788
Pittsburgh	37,869,375	44,446,826	51,373,168	56,195,000	59,706,060
Subtotal	171,582,853	171,251,345	195,553,339	218,442,000	229,696,848
Allentown	1,513,369	1,547,335	1,767,081	2,198,188	2,288,781
Erie	899,010	1,073,362	1,325,511	2,111,578	2,006,293
Harrisburg	1,388,391	1,462,584	1,441,446	1,653,741	1,920,084
Wilkes-Barre	945,658	1,056,063	1,306,639	1,736,544	1,859,743
Reading	869,651	806,754	1,070,915	1,544,773	1,720,647
Scranton	719,486	929,177	1,052,144	1,570,803	1,868,960
Lancaster	745,010	735,637	840,000	1,009,015	1,085,388
Johnstown	435,089	539,737	717,610	843,852	1,119,481
Altoona	488,069	643,594	626,107	980,093	808,489
Williamsport	416,581	463,375	510,791	636,888	750,220
York	—	356,721	476,248	794,460	773,074
Subtotal	8,410,314	9,614,339	10,787,594	15,079,935	16,201,160
Total	$179,993,167	$180,865,684	$206,340,933	$233,521,935	$245,898,008

ments, is the most important factor threatening the continued viability of urban mass-transit systems in Pennsylvania and elsewhere.

State Program Impact

Since the general purpose of the state's transit programs is to support local-transit systems in order to assure continuation or upgrading of service levels, ridership, and financial viability, examining performance indicators for these local systems, individually and collectively, should be the primary focus of PennDOT's monitoring effort in the transit area. The main question is, "how well are these local systems performing?" Yet state funding agencies may also be concerned with particular aspects of the local delivery systems, which their financial-assistance programs are intended to impact on directly.

For example, having a sufficient number of vehicles in good operating condition has traditionally been a problem for many local systems. Penn-DOT's capital-assistance program is aimed at encouraging and helping local agencies to replace worn-out vehicles with new ones, and generally to update and improve the quality of their fleets. Thus the intended impact of this financial support is improved quantity or quality of a major resource going into local operating programs. One appropriate indicator here is the average age of the fleet, the objective being to maintain or reduce the average age of the vehicles operated by local agencies. The data reported by the local agencies show that for the two major metropolitan areas, the average age of the fleet was 15.0 years in fiscal 1977, decreasing by 14.6 by fiscal 1980, and to 13.1 by fiscal 1981, indicating that their fleets have been updated somewhat with the assistance of both federal and state funds. On the other hand, across the eleven smaller systems collectively the average age of the fleet increased from 7.0 in fiscal 1977 to 8.4 by fiscal 1981.

Another one of PennDOT's programs is aimed at encouraging senior citizens to make trips using mass transit by enabling them to ride free of charge from 9:30 a.m. to 3:00 p.m. This program has shown some continuing favorable impact, as the number of senior-citizen passengers increased by nearly 10 percent from fiscal 1977 to fiscal 1981 across the thirteen local systems in the aggregate. Table 7–11 shows these figures converted to a rate of senior-citizen passengers to the senior-citizen population base, although the data are not highly reliable in terms of sensitivity to changes in the size of this elderly target population. As with total passengers, the rate of senior-citizen tripmaking is greater in the major metropolitan areas, particularly Pittsburgh, as would be expected given the more concentrated service in these areas. More important, the rate of transit tripmaking by senior

Table 7–11
Senior-Citizen Passengers per Senior-Citizen Population

Transit System	1976–1977	1980–1981
Philadelphia	57.05	62.97
Pittsburgh	101.15	104.15
Subtotal	69.78	74.86
Allentown	36.15	40.47
Erie	28.83	35.31
Harrisburg	28.62	28.58
Wilkes-Barre	38.38	51.18
Reading	50.70	59.06
Scranton	38.36	49.50
Lancaster	20.44	24.97
Johnstown	38.23	53.92
Altoona	29.31	36.64
Williamsport	28.92	33.92
York	—	38.42
Subtotal	33.51	41.56
Total	60.18	66.05

citizens went up on all but one of the twelve local systems for which data
were available.

Purchase-of-Service Program

The most important outputs of PennDOT's transit programs are the operating-assistance funds paid out to the local operators under purchase-of-
service agreements. Table 7–12 shows the dollar amounts of these awards to
each local system from fiscal 1977 through fiscal 1981. For the two major
metropolitan systems combined, operating assistance increased by 52 percent, while for the smaller systems combined, the increase was on the order
of 130 percent in four years.

Subsidy outputs have been increasing at a rate commensurate with or
above the increases in total operating expenses examined earlier. For fiscal
1977, for example, the operating subsidies awarded to the Philadelphia and
Pittsburgh systems together accounted for 22.7 percent of their combined
expense; this figure remained stable, and for fiscal 1981 the operating subsidy was equivalent to 22.8 percent of their combined expense. For the

Table 7-12
State Operating-Subsidy Amounts, by System

Transit System	1976–1977	1977–1978	1978–1979	1979–1980	1980–1981
Philadelphia	$52,242,358	$52,787,166	$59,702,093	$71,418,000	$77,237,378
Pittsburgh	18,196,063	21,018,697	23,643,586	26,930,000	30,030,122
Subtotal	70,438,421	73,805,863	83,345,679	98,348,000	107,267,500
Allentown	315,863	408,715	454,233	509,890	582,972
Erie	143,863	160,729	216,488	343,381	442,796
Harrisburg	296,544	388,678	497,506	553,963	578,040
Wilkes-Barre	183,837	230,305	318,935	408,265	443,980
Reading	163,828	170,320	254,801	326,482	382,584
Scranton	137,424	200,367	280,316	453,589	365,876
Lancaster	167,632	177,377	210,333	250,759	250,005
Johnstown	61,334	116,878	178,878	190,944	270,726
Altoona	104,455	131,665	137,868	188,233	179,019
Williamsport	87,837	117,814	141,520	176,041	194,798
York	—	88,800	132,155	174,975	205,568
Subtotal	1,662,617	2,190,782	2,823,033	3,576,522	3,896,364
Total	$72,101,038	$75,996,645	$86,168,712	$101,924,522	$111,163,864

eleven smaller systems combined, the percent of total expense funded by
state subsidy has risen slowly but steadily, from 9 percent in fiscal 1977 to
12.5 percent for fiscal 1981. The higher percentages of costs covered for the
major systems reflect a PennDOT policy of compensating for the fact that
the formula for allocating federal operating assistance favors the smaller
systems. However, the increase in state subsidy per dollar of expense to the
smaller systems stems from the decreasing percent cost recovery by these
systems as opposed to the superior performance on this score by the two
major systems.

From the perspective of internal operating efficiency, it is worthwhile
to look at these subsidy amounts in relation to service outputs to examine
how much the state has been contributing to local systems per unit of service
provided. Again, there is a disparity between the larger versus the smaller
systems, but for both groups this figure has been increasing steadily. Thus
in order to maintain service delivery, PennDOT's subsidy per vehicle hour
for the major systems rose from $8.04 in fiscal 1977 to $12.48 in fiscal 1981,
while over the same period the state subsidy per vehicle hour on the smaller
systems increased from $1.49 to $3.34.

Table 7-13 shows these same operating-subsidy figures translated to a
per-passenger basis. In dollar terms the cost effectiveness of the state program has clearly declined, as the state cost per passenger roughly doubled
for both the major systems and the smaller systems from fiscal 1977 to fiscal
1981. However, this is primarily a result of the general rate of inflation
during this period and thus can be interpreted as a trend in cost effectiveness
only from a financial perspective.

Marketing Strategies

One of the underlying objectives permeating PennDOT's overall approach
to transit is to upgrade management practices employed by the local operat-

Table 7-13
State Operating Subsidy per Passenger, by System

Fiscal Year	Philadelphia at Pittsburgh	Other Urban Areas
1976–1977	$0.16	$0.05
1977–1978	0.17	0.06
1978–1979	0.17	0.07
1979–1980	0.24	0.09
1980–1981	0.31	0.11

ing agencies on the theory that this will translate into improved system performance. PennDOT pursues this objective through a variety of means including conferences, dissemination of written information, and site visits. To some extent, environmental factors notwithstanding, the performance trends observed earlier reflect the success or failure of local-transit managers to hold costs within reasonable limits, maintain service levels, and attract additional ridership.

One area that has been emphasized in recent years is improved marketing efforts aimed at selling transit service to a broader range of potential users. At the outset of this chapter, marketing was presented as a necessary support component in an overall local-transit program, and this is becoming all the more important as costs continue to escalate more sharply than revenues. Thus as a state agency committed to supporting urban mass transit, PennDOT is concerned about the extent to which the local systems have fleshed out a marketing component with a variety of activities aimed at increasing ridership.

Table 7–14 shows selected marketing strategies and whether they are employed by the individual local agencies under consideration. The most prevalent strategies are radio advertisements, complimentary tickets, monthly passes, promotional fares, and complaint forms, while the strategy utilized least is seasonal promotions. While a couple of systems utilize most of these strategies, others—especially the smallest systems—appear to employ very few. The data also show variation in the agency's marketing budget as a percent of total expense, with the major metropolitan area systems spending relatively less than the smaller systems on marketing. Presumably PennDOT would expect some of these local systems to upgrade their marketing efforts in the future, anticipating some connection between marketing efforts and ridership changes.

Summary

The purpose of this chapter has been to apply a systems model to mass-transit programs and to illustrate how a state agency could use the approach developed in this book to monitor the performance of its transit programs. The focus was necessarily different in this area than for the highway programs because the state role is to support local-transit systems rather than to operate them directly. The primary monitoring mode would be to track the performance of local systems participating in the state programs using the same kinds of indicators that would be useful to local managers in running their individual systems. In addition, a state funding agency like PennDOT might want to monitor some of the process measures such as average age of the fleet and the number of marketing strategies utilized in order to obtain

Table 7–14
Selected Marketing Strategies in Use by Local-Transit Agencies

Transit System	Written Marketing Program	System Map	Telephone Information Operator	Complaint Forms	Bus-Stop Shelters Systemwide	Schedule and Map Displays	Radio Advertisements	Monthly Passes	Complimentary Tickets	Promotional Fares	Seasonal Promotions	Prize Programs	Percent Marketing Budget
Philadelphia	X	X	X	X			X	X	X	X			1.0
Pittsburgh	X	X	X	X	X		X	X	X	X		X	1.0
Allentown	X	X	X	X			X	X	X	X			2.1
Erie			X		X	X	X			X			1.4
Harrisburg		X	X	X	X	X	X	X	X				1.1
Wilkes-Barre		X		X	X	X		X	X			X	1.4
Reading					X		X	X		X		X	2.0
Scranton				X			X	X		X	X		1.4
Lancaster	X	X	X			X	X	X	X			X	2.0
Johnstown			X		X		X		X			X	1.0
Altoona	X	X		X			X		X	X	X	X	1.5
Williamsport				X	X	X	X		X	X	X	X	2.1
York		X					X	X	X		X	X	0

Source: *Transit Marketing in Pennsylvania: A Handbook of Effective Transit Marketing Aids.* Pennsylvania Department of Transportation, 1981.

some idea of the impact of its own program initiatives on the way local-transit systems are managed.

Although many of the performance indicators of interest to PennDOT are the same as those useful to local managers, their frequency and level of detail may well differ. While PennDOT would monitor data for individual systems as a whole, local managers might want to see the same indicators disaggregated by route, and while PennDOT would monitor these indicators on an annual or perhaps semi-annual basis, local managers would want to have monthly or even weekly data available as a basis for making adjustments in their service plan. Finally, it is clear that it is difficult, if not impossible, with these aggregate data to sort out the impacts of the state programs from all other influencing factors, as would be desired in an intensive evaluation. Rather the intention of performance monitoring, as opposed to intensive evaluation, is to track the overall performance of local operators regardless of the specific impact of PennDOT's efforts. The assumption is that the local systems will continue to operate, for the most part, in a "steady state," and that if their performance falls below acceptable levels, this would trigger more detailed analysis of the sources of the problem and possible responses via the state program. The problem is further complicated by the fact that there may well be some conflicts among the state's objectives, especially in terms of maintaining service levels while holding the line on costs during an inflationary period. In large part, then, PennDOT's macro monitoring is geared to assess the continuing long-term performance of the local systems within their shifting environment as an aid to decision making and appropriate action at the state level.

Notes

1. See T.D. Larson, "Towards a More Effective State Role in Transportation," *Proceedings, 13th Annual Transportation Research Forum* 13, no. 1 (1972):257–269; D.R. Miller, "New Challenges, New Institutions," *Public Administration Review* 33 (May 1973):236–242; G.M. Smerk, "The States and New Mass Transit Aid," *State Government* 48, no. 2 (Spring 1975):73–78.

2. T.H. Poister and T.D. Larson, "Administering State Mass Transportation Programs in Pennsylvania," *Transportation Research Record* 603 (1976):1–7.

3. G.J. Fielding, R.E. Glauthier, and C.A. Lave, *Development of Performance Indicators for Transit* (Irvine, Calif.: Institute of Transportation Studies and School of Social Sciences, University of California, December 1977), Prepared for the U.S. Department of Transportation, Urban Mass Transportation Administration, NTIS:PB 278678; U.S. De-

partment of Transportation, Urban Mass Transportation Administration, *Proceedings of the First National Conference on Transit Performance,* Norfolk, Va., September 1977, UMTA-DC-06-0184-77-1; A.R. Tomazinis, *Productivity, Efficiency, and Quality in Urban Transportation Systems* (Lexington, Mass.: Lexington Books, D.C. Heath, 1975).

4. R.E. Glauthier and J.N. Feren, "Evaluating Individual Transit Route Performance" (Irvine, Calif.: Institute of Transportation Studies and School of Social Sciences, University of California, December 1977).

5. W.G. Allen, Jr., and L.G. Grimm, "Development and Application of Performance Measures for a Medium-Sized Transit System" (Prepared for presentation at the 59th Annual Meeting of the Transportation Research Board, Washington, D.C., January 1980).

6. J.H. Miller, "The Use of Performance-Based Methodologies for the Allocation of Transit Operating Funds," *Traffic Quarterly* 34, no. 4 (October 1980):555–585; G.J. Fielding and W.M. Lyons, "Performance Evaluation for Discretionary Grant Transit Programs," *TRR* 797 (1981):34–40; R.J. Zerrillo, C.A. Keck, and N.R. Schneider, "Analysis of Transit Performance Measures Used in New York State," *TRR* 797 (1981): 52–58; S.C. Anderson, "The Michigan Transit Performance Evaluation Process: Application to a U.S. Sample" (Irvine, Calif.: Institute of Transportation Studies and School of Social Sciences, University of California).

7. T.H. Poister, J.C. McDavid, and A.H. Magoun, *Applied Program Evaluation in Local Government* (Lexington, Mass.: Lexington Books, D.C. Heath, 1979), chaps. 6 and 7.

8. D.F. McCrosson, "Choosing Performance Indicators for Small Transit Systems," *Transportation Engineering,* March 1978, pp. 26–30.

9. Fielding, Glauthier, and Lave, *Development of Performance Indicators for Transit.*

10. *Pennsylvania Mass Transit Statistical Report 1978–1979* (Prepared by the Pennsylvania Department of Transportation, Bureau of Public Transit and Goods Movement Systems, 1981).

11. K.C. Sinha, D.P. Jukins, and O.M. Bevilacqua, "A Stratified Approach to Evaluate Urban Transit Performance" (Paper delivered to the Transportation Research Board Meeting, January 1980).

12. T.H. Poister, *Public Program Analysis: Applied Research Methods* (Baltimore: University Park Press, 1978), p. 399.

8

Citizen-Survey Pilot

As mentioned in chapter 6, part of the effort to develop performance indicators for PennDOT entailed designing and testing a citizen survey. The survey was intended as a possible source of effectiveness measures and other information that might contribute to the monitoring system or to other decision making in the Department. Survey research has been a staple part of general social-science-research methodology for decades, and public administrators have naturally turned to surveys for data for needs assessment and feedback on existing programs. Yet in recent years there has been considerable debate on the merit of using survey data for performance indicators. This stems from both the problem of reactive measurement and the sometimes volatile responses that are received.

Since most public programs are intended to impact directly on people at the individual or household level, citizen surveys provide a direct means of assessing program effectiveness and responsiveness.[1] If the "bottom line" is service to citizens or citizen satisfaction with these services, then citizen surveys seem appropriate at face value. Furthermore, surveys often provide complementary indicators to the more objective observational or "factual" data collected, and for some aspects of service delivery they may be the only practical way to measure performance. All of this clearly applies to transportation programs, impacts of which are measured in terms of service, safety, and user costs. In this context, citizen surveys can provide feedback on these programs from the perspective of those intended to benefit from them.

On the other hand, the indiscriminate use of citizen-survey data as performance indicators can potentially be misleading and harmful.[2] First, survey data can overstate concern with an issue or result in findings that reflect how the survey was taken and how the questions were presented rather than an accurate portrayal of citizens' perceptions and attitudes. In considering the use of a survey, it is well to remember that survey data are "created rather than simply collected."[3] Citizen perceptions may not be sensitive to variation in service levels, and citizens may not be informed enough about a particular policy or program area to make valid responses. Furthermore, the results, valid or not, may be dangerous politically. Survey data representing citizen preferences may tie administrators' hands, unduly restricting the options open to them. Moreover, surveys can produce results that are embarrassing in light of what they show about perceived program performance.

These concerns have prompted policy analysts and administrators to be more cautious in the design and use of citizen surveys. Methodologies for conducting surveys intended to feed into governmental decision making have been refined,[4] and such surveys now tend to focus on specific, tangible items and refrain from "fishing expeditions" having no clearly established direction. For the purposes of this book, suffice it to say that citizen surveys are a potentially attractive source of performance data, but they often come with attendant problems and must be devised and implemented carefully. However, it is worthwhile to note that such surveys may well be more appropriate to repetitive performance monitoring, where interest focuses on response trends over time, than to one-shot intensive program evaluations where the level of certain responses, not trends, is the primary concern.

Survey Design and Conduct

As indicated in chapter 6, an initial version of a citizen survey was developed and pretested in one county as part of the performance-indicator project. The pretest was a telephone survey that covered a variety of services provided by PennDOT, such as mass transit, and included fairly detailed questions on perceived highway conditions, particular kinds of deficiencies, and the identification of individual roads in need of repair. The results showed that a response rate in excess of 80 percent could be obtained in this manner, that citizens appeared to be knowledgeable about the items included in the survey, and that for the most part, they could distinguish between state highways and local roads.

The results of this pretest led the Transportation Advisory Committee, a group of senior individuals from government and the private sector who advise the secretary on policy, to recommend that PennDOT pilot a full-scale survey and consider the possibility of repeating it on an annual basis. Given the high costs of conducting thousands of interviews by telephone, it was recommended that the instrument be adapted to a mail-out survey format. Preliminary discussions of this proposal within the Department generated considerable interest, but reservations along the lines discussed earlier also surfaced. Thus it was arranged that the pilot study be conducted by university researchers and not formally sponsored by the Department.

To implement the pilot, a three-page questionnaire was distilled from the original, longer, instrument. It focused almost solely on the highway programs, and contained only simple and direct items, which were thought to be self-explanatory. The revised instrument is shown in appendix B, along with the cover letter enclosed in the mail-out to introduce the survey and to encourage recipients to fill it out. The sample was drawn from the computer file of all 7.2 million licensed drivers in Pennsylvania, a relevant target population for assessing highway-program performance. The sample was a disproportionally stratified random sample, purposefully oversampling in some counties that were of particular interest, and undersampling in others (such as Philadelphia and Allegheny counties), which would swamp the data set if proportional stratified sampling were used. Weight factors were subsequently developed to adjust for disproportional sampling, but the adjusted response patterns was almost identical to the unweighted data.

A total of 8,896 surveys with stamped return envelopes enclosed were mailed out at the end of November to the individuals in the sample. Of these, 8,310 apparently reached their intended recipients, the remaining 586 being undeliverable due to deaths, address changes, and so forth. Although a few surveys were returned but were discarded because they were incomplete or unintelligible, 3,777 valid, completed surveys were received. A response rate of 45 percent is impressive for mail-out surveys, especially when no follow-up postcards or telephone calls were used as reminders. This provides further evidence that citizens are interested in highway condition and PennDOT's service delivery and enhances the credibility of the results.

Respondent Characteristics

The citizen survey not only generated a high response rate overall but it also garnered completed questionnaires from a healthy cross-section of Pennsylvania licensed drivers. Table 8-1 shows that more completed survey forms were received from men than from women, 55 percent and 45 percent, respectively, and that there is a fairly even distribution across the three age groups between twenty and sixty-five years old who generally do the most driving. Only 2.5 percent of all the respondents are under twenty years old, and 12.3 percent are sixty-five or older. Among respondents under thirty-five years old, there is a fairly even split between men and women, but in the older age groups more men returned surveys than did women.

A problem that frequently arises with surveys of this nature is a disproportionately high response rate from people who are not working and therefore have more time at home. Thus elderly individuals who are retired and women not employed outside the home might be more likely to return a survey than men in the working-groups. Such a bias would be of concern with this particular survey because employed people, who tend to drive

Table 8-1
Survey Respondents and Licensed Drivers, by Age and Sex

Age	Males		Females		Total	
Survey Respondents						
Under 20	45	(1.2%)	46	(1.3%)	91	(2.5%)
20–34	655	(18.0%)	669	(18.4%)	1,324	(36.4%)
35–49	499	(13.7%)	397	(10.9%)	896	(24.7%)
50–64	499	(13.7%)	377	(10.4%)	876	(24.1%)
Over 65	299	(8.2%)	147	(4.0%)	446	(12.3%)
Total	1,997	(55%)	1,636	(45%)	3,633	
Pennsylvania Licensed Drivers						
Under 20	269,988	(3.7%)	223,262	(3.1%)	493,250	(6.8%)
20–34	1,313,532	(18.1%)	1,241,525	(17.1%)	2,555,057	(35.2%)
35–49	899,157	(12.4%)	817,885	(11.3%)	1,717,042	(23.7%)
50–64	894,149	(12.3%)	740,801	(10.2%)	1,634,950	(22.5%)
Over 65	521,391	(7.2%)	330,646	(4.6%)	852,037	(11.7%)
Total	3,898,217	(53.7%)	3,354,119	(46.2%)	7,252,471	

more regularly, would be underrepresented in the sample. However, this did not turn out to be a problem, probably because this was a mailed-out questionnaire that could be completed any time. Table 8-1 also shows the breakdown of the 7.2 million licensed drivers in the state by sex and similar age categories, and by comparison, the sample respondents are found to be remarkably representative. Although the youngest age group, those under twenty years old, is overrepresented in the sample, this group constitutes such a small proportion of the overall population of interest that the resulting bias is minimal. The fact that the resulting sample so closely reflects the population on these characteristics suggests that the inclination to respond to the survey was even across all categories of licensed drivers and thereby lends further credibility to the results.

Table 8-2 shows other respondent characteristics. The number of years the individual has been a licensed driver in Pennsylvania follows the age distribution, that is, nearly half the respondents have been licensed drivers for more than 20 years, and these basically would be people over forty years old. The survey shows that automobile ownership is high, at least among licensed drivers in the state. Almost none of the respondents reported zero automobiles, while 70 percent are from multiple-car households, including more than 20 percent reporting three or more vehicles. Furthermore, two-

Table 8-2
Selected Respondent Characteristics

Characteristic	N	Percent
Number of Automobiles in Household		
0	15	.4
1	1,082	29.0
2	1,776	47.6
3 or more	862	22.9
Employment Status		
Regularly employed	2,522	67.5
Not regularly employed	1,212	32.5
How Many Years a Licensed Driver		
Less than 2	82	2.2
2–10	902	24.0
11–20	939	25.0
More than 20	1,835	48.8

thirds of the respondents report being regularly employed outside the home at least twenty hours per week, while one-third do not. It should be noted that both employment and automobile-ownership figures would be expected to be higher among licensed drivers than the population at large.

Driving and Commuting Patterns

Table 8-3 shows a cross-tabulation between the estimated miles driven per year by the respondents and an estimate of how much of their total driving is within their home county. Nearly two-thirds of the respondents report driving 10,000 miles or less per year, which is perhaps somewhat surprising, while only 10 percent say they drive 20,000 miles or more. Nearly two-thirds report doing almost all their driving in their own county, while only 12 percent say that less than half or almost none of their driving is in their home county. There is a fairly strong association between these two indicators, as might be expected, such that those respondents who say they do little driving overall tend to do most of it close to home, while those who drive more total miles have less of a tendency to be confined to their own county.

Table 8-3 also shows the predominant mode of transportation used in commuting to work by those respondents who are regularly employed out-

Table 8-3
Driving and Commuting Patterns

Portion of Driving in Home County	Estimated Miles Driven per Year				Total	
	Less than 5,000 (Percent)	5,000 to 10,000 (Percent)	10,000 to 20,000 (Percent)	More than 20,000 (Percent)		
Almost all	86	69	48	21	2,363	(63%)
Half or more	11	24	38	33	928	(25%)
Less than half	2	6	13	31	354	(10%)
Almost none	1	1	1	15	94	(2%)
Total	1,090 (29%)	1,296 (35%)	962 (26%)	391 (10%)	3,739	

Gamma = .58   Sig. = .0001

Commuting Mode	N	Percent
Automobile	2,217	88.6
Transit	55	2.2
Walk	82	3.3
Other	155	6.2
Total	2,509	100.0

side the home. Nearly 90 percent use their automobile, while only 2.2 percent say they use transit, including bus, trains, or park-and-ride. Another 3.3 percent say they walk to work, and the remaining 6.2 percent use some other means of transportation. It should be noted that the overwhelming predominance of the automobile for commuting to work may be somewhat overstated for the population as a whole in that individuals who are not licensed drivers and who therefore may be more likely to use transit are not included in the sample. Nevertheless, it is the case that of all licensed drivers in the state who are regularly employed outside the home, an estimated nine out of ten use the automobile, alone or in carpools, to get to work. The condition of the roads is likely to be of concern to these people.

Road-Condition Rating

On a balanced scale of five responses ranging from "very good" to "very poor," respondents were asked, "How would you describe the present con-

Table 8–4
Road-Condition Ratings

Ratings of Present Road Condition	N	Percent
Very good	67	1.8
Good	805	21.5
Fair	1,594	42.5
Poor	881	23.5
Very poor	402	10.7

Road-Condition Change Over Two Years		Percent	Home-County Roads Compared with Other Counties	Percent
Better	693	18.6	466	12.5
Same	1,821	48.8	1,890	50.7
Worse	1,116	29.9	923	24.8
No basis	99	2.7	447	12.0

dition of state roads in your county?'' As shown in table 8–4, less than 25 percent rated the roads as good or very good compared with slightly more than one-third rating them as poor or very poor; 42.5 percent rated the roads as fair. While the overall pattern of responses to this item is not strongly positive, it represents a benchmark from which progress can be measured. If PennDOT is successful in making substantial improvements in the condition of the statewide highway system, it would expect to see this reflected in increasing percentages of respondents who give roads a good rating and, in particular, a reduction in the percent who rate the roads as poor or very poor.

Table 8–4 also shows responses to questions about road condition in a relative sense. When asked, ''During the past two years, do you think the condition of state roads in your county has become better, worse, or stayed the same,'' nearly half indicated they thought the condition was the same. More important, while 18.6 percent said the roads were in better condition than two years ago, almost 30 percent said the condition was worse now. Generally, the respondents do not indicate that they perceive substantial improvement in the condition of the state-highway system to date. In response to the question, ''How would you compare the condition of state roads in your home county with the condition of state roads in other Pennsylvania counties,'' half the respondents answered ''the same.'' Only 12.5 percent said the roads in their county were better than in other counties, while roughly twice that number thought roads in their county were worse than in other counties, and the remaining 12 percent said they had no basis for comparison. Thus substantial percentages of respondents feel that the roads have deteriorated over the past two years and that the roads in their counties are not as good as the roads in other counties.

In order to obtain a clearer idea of the pattern of responses to the present road condition item, table 8-5 shows these ratings broken down by several groupings of the respondents. The table shows a slight association between age and the condition-rating variable such that older respondents are more likely to rate the present road condition positively whereas younger respondents are somewhat more likely to give road condition a negative rating. This is probably nothing more than a respondent effect, with older people tending to be a little less critical in general than younger

Table 8-5
Response Comparisons to Road-Condition Question, "How Would You Describe the Present Condition of State Roads in Your County?"

	Very Good (Percent)	Good (Percent)	Fair (Percent)	Poor (Percent)	Very Poor (Percent)
Age					
Under 20	1.1	16.5	47.3	24.2	11.0
20–34	1.0	18.8	42.3	25.7	12.2
35–49	1.4	21.7	38.9	26.1	11.9
50–64	2.5	23.7	43.7	21.2	8.9
65 or Over	3.5	26.3	48.1	14.6	7.5
Sex					
Males	2.0	21.1	42.2	23.6	11.1
Females	1.5	22.2	43.0	23.1	10.2
District					
1	0.9	11.5	42.2	28.0	17.4
2	1.7	27.7	46.8	16.9	6.9
3	2.4	39.8	42.7	13.3	1.9
4	2.1	9.1	44.2	28.5	16.1
5	1.1	19.2	45.0	25.3	9.4
6	2.1	22.6	46.1	22.2	7.0
8	3.4	36.2	45.2	11.8	3.4
9	2.1	18.6	35.9	25.5	17.9
10	0.4	9.1	30.6	40.1	19.8
11	0.3	8.0	39.3	34.2	18.2
12	0.0	6.8	35.7	35.3	22.2

Table 8–5 continued

Age	Very Good (Percent)	Good (Percent)	Fair (Percent)	Poor (Percent)	Very Poor (Percent)
Number Automobiles					
1	2.8	21.1	42.6	23.0	10.4
2	1.7	22.7	42.9	22.7	10.0
3 or more	0.7	19.6	41.3	25.8	12.6
Miles Driven per Year					
Less than 5,000	2.2	23.7	42.0	22.6	9.4
5,000–10,000	1.5	21.3	43.2	23.5	10.5
10,000–20,000	2.0	19.3	43.0	23.6	12.1
More than 20,000	1.3	21.0	40.0	25.6	12.1
County Ranking: TOS Surface Index, Fall 1981					
Bottom quartile (worst)	0.6	11.3	43.1	29.7	15.3
Second quartile	1.5	15.9	39.4	28.5	14.8
Third quartile	1.7	22.9	48.1	20.4	6.9
Top quartile (best)	3.5	39.8	42.9	11.3	2.5
Gamma = .35	Tau C sig = .0001				

people. By contrast, there is virtually no association between road-condition ratings and sex; the response distribution is almost identical for males and females.

Clearly, there are notable associations between road-condition rating and the district in which the respondent lives. Responses, in percentages, that deviate substantially from statewide averages have been highlighted with boxes in table 8–5 to afford readability. As can be seen, considerably higher percentages of the respondents from Districts 3 and 8 rated the roads in their counties as good, while significantly higher percentages of respondents from Districts 1, 4, 10, 11, and 12 gave their roads poor ratings. In general, these findings conform with the perceptions of top management within PennDOT regarding relative road condition among counties and districts. Contrary to the expectation that people who drive more might tend to be more critical of the condition of the highways, table 8–5 shows that there is virtually no association between present-road-condition rating and either the number of automobiles owned by the respondent's household or the estimated miles the respondent drives per year. Response distributions are almost identical across all categories of these two variables.

However, there is an association between present-road-condition ranking and the actual condition of roads in the respondent's county as measured by the trained-observer survey. For this purpose, counties have been grouped into quartiles based on a composite index of the surface-condition indicators recorded in cycle 5 of the TOS, taken in the fall of 1981 just preceding the mail-out of the citizen survey. The comparisons show, for example, that while 45 percent of the survey respondents from the "worst" counties rated their roads negatively (poor or very poor), only 14 percent of the respondents from the "best" counties did so. Conversely, only 12 percent of the respondents from the "worst" counties rated their roads as good or very good, whereas 43 percent of the respondents from the "best" counties gave their roads these positive ratings. This is to say that to some degree citizen perceptions of the condition of roads in their county conform to the more objective indicators of road condition obtained from the trained-observer survey.

These ratings must be interpreted with some qualifications. The overall rating, somewhat more negative than positive, may well be an accurate representation of motorists' perceptions of road condition. Pennsylvania has had a notoriously poor highway system in recent years, as discussed in chapter 1, and these survey responses may be basically a reflection of this. It is possible that the negative responses are somewhat overstated in terms of extrapolating to the entire population because there may have been a greater tendency for those who are concerned with poor highway conditions to complete and return the survey, in conjunction with a lower response rate on the part of those who are less critical and/or less concerned with the condition of the highways. Furthermore, even in the "best" counties according to the TOS data, there are some respondents who rate the roads negatively, while in the "worst" counties some respondents give their roads positive ratings; to some extent this may reflect actual variability of road condition within counties (which is substantial), and to some degree it may result from individual respondents' having different standards for rating road condition. Finally, although the TOS data show that there has been a net improvement in highway condition on a statewide basis between cycles 1 and 5 (fall 1979 to fall 1981), more respondents said that the roads have gotten worse over that period than those who said they have improved. This apparent contradiction may indicate that while actual condition did improve in the aggregate, this improvement was the net effect of mixed changes in different indicators and in different districts that was not pronounced enough to be perceived consistently by survey respondents. There may also be a time lag between actual improvements in conditions and citizen perception of those conditions. These issues deserve more indepth analysis beyond the scope of this book.

Effectiveness Measures

As indicated in chapter 6, the citizen survey was a proposed source of effectiveness measures regarding vehicle-maintenance costs, commuting time, and problems with traffic congestion in addition to perceived road conditions. The questions concerning road-related vehicle-maintenance costs were included. In response to the question, "In the past year, have you had to make repairs to any of the cars in your household because of damage due to poor road condition," 51 percent answered yes, 40 percent answered no and 9 percent said they did not know. Table 8-6 shows the variation in the percentage indicating they made road-related vehicle repairs according to the number of automobiles in the household and the estimated miles driven per year by the respondent. As expected, the percentage indicating that such repairs were necessary varies positively with both variables in a very systematic overall pattern ranging from 37 percent for those respondents from one-car households driving less than 5,000 miles per year, to 71 percent for respondents from households with three or more automobiles and driving more than 20,000 miles per year. Given the possibility of a "halo effect" influencing the responses to all survey items relating to the condition of the highways, these figures may somewhat overstate the incidence of having to

Table 8-6
Percentage Indicating Necessary Auto Repairs Due to Poor Road Condition

Miles Driven Annually	1	2	3+	Total
Number of Automobiles				
Less than 5,000	37%	40%	48%	40%
5,000–10,000	45	49	55	49
10,000–20,000	53	60	68	61
More than 20,000	54	66	71	66
Total	44%	51%	60%	51%
Estimated Dollar Cost (For Those Reporting Necessary Road-Related Repairs)				
Less than 5,000	$129	$217	$188	$182
5,000–10,000	122	152	277	173
10,000–20,000	202	176	208	191
More than 20,000	173	227	366	270
Total	$148	$184	$254	$194

make such repairs. The magnitude of the response is nevertheless impressive; half of all the respondents report having had to make vehicle repairs during the past year because of poor road conditions.

Table 8-6 also shows the estimated dollar costs of such repairs to the respondent or other members of the household in the same one year period. The average estimated costs for all who responded that they had to make these repairs was $194. In general, the estimated cost varies positively with both miles driven and the number of automobiles, although this pattern of variation is not fully consistent. Extrapolated to the total number of respondents, including those who did not incur damage in the past year because of road conditions, this would mean that on the average, each household incurred nearly $100 in costs due to necessary road-related vehicle repairs. While both the percentage having to make such repairs and the dollar costs of these repairs may be overstated, it is clear that there is considerable room for improvement on these indicators. The real value of such a survey would be to establish trends in these kinds of indicators by repeating the survey on a periodic basis; hopefully the data would show that the highway-maintenance program is effective in reducing the incidence and dollar value of these costs to users.

As might be expected, there is a strong association between the rating of present condition of the highways and whether the respondent reported incurring necessary vehicle repairs due to poor road conditions. As shown in table 8-7, of those who said they did not have to make any road induced repairs, 42 percent rated the roads in their county as good or very good compared with only 10 percent of those who reported having to make such repairs. Conversely, of those not having to make such repairs, 14 percent

Table 8-7
Rating of Present Road Condition by Need for Road-Induced Vehicle Repairs

Rating of Condition of State Roads	No		Yes	
Very good	59	(4%)	7	(0.4%)
Good	563	(38.2%)	179	(9.4%
Fair	642	(43.6%)	766	(40.1%)
Poor	165	(11.2%)	632	(33.1%)
Very poor	44	(3.0%)	324	(17%)
Total	1,473	(39.6%)	1,908	(51.2%)
Gamma = .67 Sig = .0001				

rated the roads as poor or very poor, whereas 50 percent of those who had such repairs gave these negative ratings. Thus whether or not people have experienced, or at least remember having experienced the need to make auto repairs in the past year necessitated by poor road conditions serves as a good predictor of how they will rate present road condition.

With respect to service levels as perceived by citizens, the survey included an item that asked, "Do you ever have difficulty getting to work or other places you need to go because of transportation problems?" As shown in table 8-8, about 65 percent responded never or rarely, while 30 percent said sometimes and less than 5 percent said often. Those who responded sometimes or often were asked to indicate what these difficulties were by checking on a list of those problems that applied to them, or specifying whatever other kind of difficulties they faced in getting to work or other places. As shown in table 8-8, the most frequently cited problem was traffic congestion, followed by rough roads. Of those indicating they had difficulties getting to work sometimes or often, 61.4 percent cited traffic congestion and 44.1 percent said that rough roads were a problem. Since respondents could check off any or even all of these possible problems, many of the same respondents may have indicated both traffic congestion

Table 8-8
Transportation Problems Encountered in Going to Work or Other Places

Transportation Problems in Commuting	N	Percent
Never	991	27.5
Rarely	1,345	37.5
Sometimes	1,090	30.3
Often	173	4.8
Total	3,599	100.0

Problems Indicated	N	Percent	Percentage of Those Indicating Problems
Rough Roads	557	15.5	44.1
Traffic congestion	776	21.6	61.4
Traffic signals	233	6.5	18.4
Closed roads or bridges	315	8.8	24.9
Speed limits	150	4.2	11.9
Lack of public transportation	292	8.1	23.1
No convenient, direct route	212	5.9	16.8

and rough roads as difficulties they face. As a fraction of the total sample of respondents, about 21 percent cited traffic congestion and nearly 16 percent cited rough roads as problems. Almost 9 percent cited clcsed roads or bridges and almost 6 percent cited "no direct route." That 8 percent cited the lack of public transportation as a problem is significant since only licensed drivers were included in the sample and because so few of them indicated that they use public transportation for commuting to work. Probably the most important indicators with respect to the highway programs are the almost 22 percent who say that traffic congestion is a problem for them, the 15.5 percent citing rough roads, and the 8.8 percent citing closed roads or bridges. If subsequent surveys are conducted on a periodic basis, these indicators should be targeted by top management for improvement.

Commuting Speeds

One of the primary effectiveness indicators identified in chapter 6 is average commuting speed; improvements in carrying capacity, traffic control, and more direct routing should in theory serve to reduce travel times and thereby increase commuting speeds. Those respondents who indicated that they are regularly employed outside the home at least twenty hours per week were asked how far they commute to work one way in miles and how long this trip usually takes in minutes or hours. The results were used to compute an approximated commuting speed for each of these respondents, as shown in table 8-9 for employed people who commute by automobile only.

Roughly 55 percent of all these employed respondents have approximated commuting speeds somewhere between 20 and 40 mph; and another 15 percent have commuting speeds in the 40 and 50 mph range. Almost 3 percent show commuting speeds between 50 and 60 mph, while 1.5 percent have approximated speeds over 60 mph. At the low end of the spectrum, where the principal concern would lie, almost 25 percent have approximate commuting speeds of less than 20 miles per hour, and 5 percent actually have approximated speeds less than 10 mph.

Table 8-9 shows a breakdown of the average commuting speed of the respondents by the distance of their one-way trip. As expected, commuting speed, on the average, is lowest for those respondents who have relatively short one-way trips and increases steadily for longer and longer trips. Those who commute 4 miles or less have an average approximate speed of around 16 mph, while those who drive 20 miles or more have an average commuting speed of nearly 40 mph. Although it is questionable whether commuting speeds on an aggregate statewide basis are very sensitive to road condition and highway-system sufficiency, if the Department is serious about increasing capacity and reducing congestion, then the objective would be to in-

Table 8–9
Commuting Speeds

Approximate Commuting Speed	N	Percent
0–10 mph	103	5.1
10–20 mph	397	19.8
20–30 mph	582	29.0
30–40 mph	520	25.9
40–50 mph	311	15.5
50–60 mph	58	2.9
over 60 mph	30	1.5
Total	2,001	99.7

Miles Commuted	Average Commuting Speed (mph)	N
0–4	15.8	433
4–8	23.3	458
8–12	30.2	381
12–20	33.5	351
20 or over	39.6	386

crease these average commuting speeds, and particularly to reduce the percentage of commuters whose commuting speeds are less than 10 mph.

Responsiveness to Complaints

All respondents were asked whether they had ever contacted a PennDOT county or district office to complain about a road condition or other problem, and as shown in table 8–10, about 20 percent answered yes. When asked whether the problem had been resolved to their satisfaction, one-third said yes, while about 54 percent said no and the remaining 12 percent said they did not know whether it had been resolved. The 20 percent of all respondents who indicated they had made a complaint were also asked to indicate which, if any, of a few specified descriptive phrases applied to their experience. As shown in table 8–10, 15 percent indicated that the problem was corrected promptly, while 43 percent said the problem was never corrected, and 25 percent said thay had to keep pressuring to get results. Forty percent said that there was too much "run around" or "red tape." Finally,

Table –10
Responses Regarding Complaints Made to PennDOT

	N	Percent
Complaint Made?		
Yes	753	20.2
No	2,966	79.8
Problem Resolved to Satisfaction?		
Yes	242	33.3
No	394	54.3
Do not know	90	12.4
PennDOT's Response?		
Problem corrected promptly	114	15.3
Problem never corrected	324	43.4
Too much "red tape"	302	40.5
Had to keep pressuring	187	25.1
Personnel courteous	270	36.2
Personnel not courteous	68	9.1

36 percent said that the personnel involved were courteous and helpful, as opposed to 9 percent who said that they were not.

Safety Administration

Although this survey focused almost exclusively on the highway programs, given the sample selection from all licensed drivers in the state, it made sense to include questions about driver licensing and vehicle registration. These programs, which are the responsibility of PennDOT's Division of Safety Administration, are concerned directly with enhancing safety and minimizing accidents due to incompetent drivers and unsafe vehicles operating on the state's highways. While the ultimate effectiveness indicator here would be the number of accidents with driver or vehicle problems cited as contributing factors, measures of citizens' satisfaction with the process of licensing and registration provide an indication of how smoothly these programs are running.

In response to the question, "In the past two years, have you experienced any difficulty in obtaining your driver's license," less than 4 percent said yes, as shown in table 8–11. Most of these indicated that they received their license later than expected, and about half of them said that an error

Table 8–11
Responses Concerning Licenses and Registration

	Problems with Respect to Driver's Licenses						
					If Yes		
Response	*Difficulty in Obtaining*			*License Late?*		*Error by PennDOT?*	
Yes	135	(3.6%)	Yes	98	(72.6%)	69	(51.1%)
No	3,603	(96.4%)	No	21	(15.6%)	37	(27.4%)
Total	3,738		No response	16	(11.8%)	29	(21.5%)
			Total	135		135	

	Problems with Respect to Vehicle Registration						
					If Yes		
Response	*Difficulty in Obtaining*			*Registration Late?*		*Error by PennDOT?*	
Yes	338	(90%)	Yes	253	(74.9%)	177	(52.4%)
No	3,390	(91.0%)	NO	43	(12.7%)	84	(24.9%)
Total	3,728		No response	42	(12.4%)	77	(22.7%)
			Total	338		338	

had been made by PennDOT. Responses to a similar question regarding vehicle registration show that about 9 percent indicated they had had some problem, while 91 percent said they had no problem with vehicle registration in the past two years. Again most of these said that their registration was received later than expected, and slightly more than half said that an error was made by PennDOT. Thus the results show that the overwhelming majority of the respondents report no problem in obtaining either driver licenses or vehicle registration but that problems with registration are more prevalent than problems with drivers' licenses. While neither problem has a particularly high incidence, there is room for improvement. In subsequent years it would be worthwhile to look for changes, particularly a decrease in the percent of respondents who say that PennDOT made some error in processing their vehicle registrations.

Interest in Toll Roads

In addition to eliciting citizen feedback on program performance, such a survey conducted on an annual basis provides an opportunity to explore citizens' attitudes concerning other issues currently of interest to the agency.

For example, PennDOT has been considering the possibility of substantially upgrading a number of highways in high-volume transportation corridors that are heavily overcapacitated. Given funding constraints on new construction, one proposal is to rebuild many of these projects as limited-access toll roads on the model of the Pennsylvania Turnpike. To obtain some reaction to this idea, a set of questions concerning prospective usage of hypothetical toll roads was included in the survey, directed only to respondents who reported working regularly outside the home and commuting by automobile. These questions were designed to set a trade-off between anticipated travel-time savings and the maximum toll a respondent would be willing to pay if he or she would use the new facility.

The results, shown in table 8–12, indicate that if the travel-time savings from such a toll road were only five minutes, 75 percent of the respondents would *not* use the road and 25 percent would. As expected, the percent saying that they would not use the toll road decreases with greater time savings so that only 32 percent say they would not use it if the potential time savings were thirty minutes. The percentage indicating they would pay a certain toll drops off considerably with higher tolls so that a plausible demand curve could be approximated for each level of service. For example, for a set of commuters in a given area who would stand to save twenty minutes in making a trip, the data indicate that a total of 64 percent would be willing to pay at least 10¢ to do so, 53 percent would pay at least 25¢, 23 percent would pay at least 50¢, 7 percent would pay at least $1, and 1 percent would pay at least $2. While such responses are usually subject to the survey noncommitment bias, in which stated intentions overstate subsequent behavior, these findings at least provide some insight as to the maximum usage that such toll roads might generate.

Table 8–12
Percentages of Respondents Indicating a Willingness to Pay Various Tolls for Expected Travel-Time Reductions

Expected Reduction in Travel Time	Would Not Use (Percent)	Maximum Toll				
		10¢ (Percent)	25¢ (Percent)	50¢ (Percent)	$1 (Percent)	$2 (Percent)
5 minutes	75	19	5	1	—	—
10 minutes	59	23	15	3	—	—
15 minutes	42	22	24	10	1	—
20 minutes	36	11	30	16	6	1
30 minutes	32	6	20	24	13	4

Summary

The purpose of this pilot survey was to demonstrate the feasibility and usefulness of obtaining citizen feedback concerning transportation programs. The 45-percent response rate, relatively high for a one-shot mail-out survey, indicates that citizens are interested in having a chance to provide feedback concerning highway conditions and PennDOT's programs. Furthermore, the high degree of representativeness of the sample in terms of age and sex indicates that such a survey can obtain feedback from an unbiased cross-section of all licensed drivers. On a statewide basis, the total number of valid surveys allows for a fair degree of precision in estimates generalizing beyond the sample to the entire population. The level of response, given the overall strategy of sampling around 9,000 licensed drivers, permits some county comparisons, but not with a high level of statistical significance. More important for the purposes of a pilot study, internal-consistency checks showed that for the most part, individual respondents perceived the questions as intended and responded in a reasonable manner, whether positive or negative.

Results tend to indicate that from the citizen's perspective, there is considerable room for improvement in Pennsylvania's highway system. The overall road-condition ratings are not high, which makes sense given what other condition indicators show. In the same vein, significant percentages of respondents indicated that they had problems concerning traffic congestion and had incurred substantial dollar costs in making vehicle repairs necessitated by road condition. Far fewer respondents had complaints about driver licensing or vehicle registration. These data are by no means intended, however, to provide a summary assessment of PennDOT's performance. Their greatest utility would be to serve as a benchmark from which progress could be measured based on trend analysis of such data collected annually.

Notes

1. K. Webb and H.P. Hatry, *Obtaining Citizen Feedback: The Application of Citizen Survey to Local Governments* (Washington, D.C.: Urban Institute, 1973), chap. 2.

2. B. Stipak, "Using Clients to Evaluate Programs," *Computers, Environment, and Urban Systems* 5 (1980):137–154. See also B. Stipak, "Citizen Satisfaction with Urban Services: Potential Misuse as a Performance Indicator," *Public Administration Review* 39, no. 1 (January/February 1979):46–52; and B. Stipak, "Local Governments' Use of Citizen Surveys,"

Public Administration Review 40, no. 5 (September/October 1980):521–525.

3. E.R. Babbie, *Survey Research Methods* (Belmont, Calif.: Wadsworth, 1973), p. 144.

4. T.H. Poister, *Public Program Analysis: Applied Research Methods* (Baltimore: University Park Press, 1978); D.A. Dillman, *Mail and Telephone Surveys: The Total Design Method* (New York: Wiley, 1978).

9 Implementation

The notion of a monitoring *system* connotes integration in the processing and utilization of a wide variety of performance indicators and the development not only of a data component but analysis and action components as well. The objective of the research for PennDOT that forms the basis for most of this book was to identify, select, and develop a set of performance indicators rather than to come up with a grand design for implementing a formal monitoring system. However, since the development of particular indicators is keyed to specific management objectives and interests, they were not developed in an operational vacuum but with a sense of likely reporting frequencies and channels as well as potential utilization. Although a "system" design was not the objective in terms of a single computerized management-information system, as existing reporting procedures around the Department are modified and new data-collection efforts implemented, elements are falling into place and an overall monitoring system is evolving.

The key to the development of a performance-monitoring system, as opposed to an array of data, is the action component; beyond data collection and processing, the information must be utilized for the effort to be worthwhile. The kinds of indicators discussed in this book lend themselves to analysis of trends across time, and most also facilitate comparisons among organizational units. This kind of analysis serves to identify aggregate drops in performance and to flag uneven performance across districts and counties. The results then must be reported to the appropriate managerial levels and relevant organizational units on a timely basis so that they can evaluate activities and take action accordingly. The action component does not refer to the corrective action itself but to making useful information available to those in a position to take action when necessary.

Such an open-ended approach to the development of a performance-monitoring system may not be as haphazard as it first appears. Given the difficulties of implementing new management systems in general, in some cases it may be appropriate to concentrate initially on the data component, and later move on to develop the action component when real data are available to prove the worth of the system. This chapter begins by pointing out some difficulties in implementing a PMS, then moves to a more technical discussion of the development of each component, and concludes with some comments concerning overall implementation strategies.

185

Barriers to Performance Monitoring

Several kinds of barriers can impede efforts to implement a PMS. These include (1) problems with the availability and quality of data, (2) technological problems concerning data processing, (3) bureaucratic resistance to the introduction of a new system, and (4) costs. Dealing with data problems, and to a lesser extent with data-processing problems, has been the subject of much of this book, and these issues will come up again in this chapter. The point is that both of these problems are solvable by the analysts or technicians responsible for developing the data component. Internal organizational resistance and the problem of costs, however, cannot be disposed of so easily. They raise legitimate questions concerning the overall usefulness of performance monitoring, and thus should be taken into account in decisions about implementing a PMS.

Bureaucratic Resistance

The term "bureaucratic resistance" has a negative connotation, implying an automatic opposition to proposed changes based on the suboptimizing self-interest of entrenched organizational units. When a performance-monitoring system is being considered, it may draw this kind of reaction from organizational units whose performance is not strong and who therefore fear the results. This may inhibit cooperation in the early stages, but is by no means reason for not undertaking a monitoring effort; in fact, it further reinforces the need for a PMS.

However, bureaucratic resistance may also develop out of potentially valid criticism of monitoring efforts. The Urban Institute report on effectiveness monitoring for state transportation programs discusses several concerns about wasted resources and misuses of the data, which are legitimate but which usually can be alleviated by the way the system is designed and implemented.[1] The first concern is simply a question of whether performance indicators are really needed, and in some agencies or program areas where performance is established and understood, the answer may be no. However, when top management does not have a clear picture of performance by other means or when performance is known to be poor but efforts to revitalize programs are under way, or when a management system such as MBO of PPB requires performance targeting and tracking, then the answer is a resounding yes.

A related but somewhat different question is whether or not the data will actually be used. Many public agencies are already experiencing data overload and underutilization whereby large amounts of existing data do not appear to be used very frequently or very productively. Obviously, collecting data for the data's sake is not justified, and the concern over lack of utilization is appropriate. The point is that while a formal PMS might not be implemented all at once, the data collected should be oriented to specific management uses or decision processes. If the direct relevance of the indicators in terms of contributing to improved program performance is not clear at the outset, the effort should not be undertaken. Critics also claim that performance data are not useful because the indicators often have no immediate practical significance at the operating level. Performance monitoring is primarily a management tool for top executives, however, and it is therefore much more important that the data be useful at that level.

Performance monitoring often seems threatening to those at the operating level due to the perceived likelihood of misinterpretation or overinterpretation of the data, and the possibility that once available, the indicators will be put to uses for which they really are not suitable. One way to avoid misleading conclusions about what the data show and to help alleviate misgivings in the process is to provide for the participation of program managers and staff personnel in developing such interpretations and subsequent actions. Second, it should be made clear that the findings are the results of monitoring and not intensive evaluation, and thus conclusions about causal program/impact relationships should be approached carefully within these limitations. Third, top management should avoid injudicious use of the data in ways that really might be harmful. For example, performance data may be collected on a relatively small sample basis that is perfectly appropriate for aggregate monitoring purposes, but using the same data in performance appraisals of individuals may be highly unreliable and potentially damaging. In developing a PMS, the intended management uses should be identified and communicated to middle and operating level managers, but at the same time it may be helpful to identify potential abuses to be avoided.

Even from a top-management standpoint, there may be a built in wariness of performance-monitoring data because of the possibility they may make programs look ineffective. This is often a concern when data-collection instruments are used that are not traditional in a particular program area, and it is especially true of citizen surveys. On the one hand, top executives should want to have this information available to them, but on the other hand, they may find it prudent not to make it public. Since the PMS should be a fairly open process, with results disseminated for comment from the field, this may be difficult to control. In such circumstances, it may be preferable not to collect the data on those particular items in the first place. With potentially embarrassing indicators, the politically astute manager should probably be guided by the following decision rules: "If you don't want to know, don't ask," and "If you don't want others to know, don't ask."[2]

Costs

A final argument mounted by the skeptics is that the costs incurred in implementing a PMS outweigh the benefits it will produce. While it is simply not feasible to calculate benefit-cost ratios at this point, the question does merit attention. The costs include the direct costs of data collection, processing, and analysis, and the indirect costs of internal organizational strain and the potential for embarrassing results and the loss of external support. The previous section briefly discussed this latter category and pointed out ways to try to minimize such negative fallout. Nevertheless, top management will have to take these possibilities into account in deciding whether or not to initiate performance monitoring.

The direct costs of the PMS represent agency resources devoted to the monitoring effort that could be used for some other purpose. Some, or possibly all or most of this work may be absorbed by existing work units on top of their other responsibilities, but opportunity costs are incurred nevertheless. In a large-scale monitoring effort, additional individuals may be hired or transferred from other jobs to coordinate the data collection and processing and do the analysis.

When already-existing data sources serve the purpose, the additional cost for monitoring purposes may be marginal, but when new, stand-alone procedures are initiated, the costs can be substantial. Table 9–1 shows a cost itemization for one cycle of PennDOT's trained-observer survey, for example, and table 9–2 shows similar figures for the citizen-survey pilot discussed in chapter 8. One cycle of the TOS costs approximately $176,000; with 6,592 highway sections included in the data base, the unit cost is $26,70 per section. This efficiency level can be improved substantially by moving to a sample-within-a-section approach that could double or triple actual coverage. In the same vein, the estimated cost of conducting the citizen survey is $7,850. Given a total of 3,782 usable responses, the unit cost is $2.08 per respondent.

Whether these products are worth the cost can be debated. The objective should be to maximize the utility of a PMS per dollar of cost. The TOS, in particular, is expensive, but it must be assessed in terms of its usefulness in light of PennDOT's overall highway-maintenance budget of around $565 million. Top management has judged, in this case, that the TOS produces benefits greater than its costs in terms of its contribution to the improved performance of the program. Cost is one of the biggest barriers to implementing a PMS because management is always open to the claim that the money would be better spent directly on the program. Needless to say, if management does not conclude that the benefits outweigh the costs, or at least potentially do so, it should not implement a PMS. However, if a PMS is a good investment in the judgment of top management, then management

Table 9–1
Itemization of Costs: Trained-Observer Survey, Cycle 5

Salaries	$121,257
Expenses	9,475
Hotel accommodation	7,153
State car costs	35,668
Computer-system center	2,100
Total	$175,653

Table 9–2
Itemization of Costs: Citizen Survey, November 1981

Salaries		
Mailing preparation 200 hours @5.00	$1,000	
Sorting and coding returns 190 hours @5.00	950	
Keypunching 160 hours @5.00	800	$2,750
Supplies/printing		650
Mailing labels		500
Posting		
Out	$2,000	
Return	950	2,950
Computer processing		1,000
		$7,850

should move to implement the data-collection, analysis, and action components so as to maximize their payoffs in relation to their costs.

The Data Component

Data collection and processing is by far the most time-consuming and costly aspect of implementing a performance-monitoring system. Yet the data component is fundamentally the most important; if the data collection does not focus on appropriate indicators of performance, the subsequent analysis will not be worthwhile, and relevant action will not be forthcoming.

Conversely, including irrelevant indicators or extra data in the system will blow up costs out of proportion to usefulness. Thus the objective is to build a data component consisting of the most appropriate performance indicators without consuming more resources than necessary.

The preceding chapters show that there is a wide variety of data sources for measuring program effectiveness and efficiency, ranging from existing program-operation data to observational surveys and citizen surveys. It makes sense to key on the already-existing routine program data as much as is feasible in order to conserve costs. However, this kind of data tends to focus primarily on process measures and, therefore, will frequently need to be complemented by data from external sources to provide indicators of service quality and effectiveness.

Selecting Indicators

The nature of the indicators to be included is dictated by a substantive framework representing the program logic, as illustrated by the systems models developed in chapters 2 and 7. Candidate measures should then be assessed in terms of reliability and validity. With respect to routine program-operation data in particular, many of these data are collected and entered at lower operating levels and then aggregated at higher-level centralized offices. When large amounts of data are being reported up through the organization in this fashion, reliability is always a potential problem simply due to the amount of detail and the tediousness of the work.

This can be mitigated in two ways: (1) Editing checks can be built into the data-processing programs to look for internal inconsistencies and to flag items that fall outside normal tolerance limits based on previous experience, and (2) verification checks can be facilitated by indicating the specific source or identity of the detailed entries. For example, questionable data on highway-maintenance work completed can now be checked in the field because the physical location of the road section is reported with each entry of cost and output. In general, making such verification checks in the field when apparent problems arise—and the possibility of doing so on a purely random basis—will also help to keep the system "honest" by discouraging any purposeful underreporting or overreporting of indicators by decentralized field offices or organizational units.

Validity concerns the appropriateness of the indicators in terms of representing the conditions or characteristics that are supposed to be measured. In some cases, appropriate measures will be obvious at face value, while the validity of others may be apparent from previous experience or accumulated research findings. With respect to effectiveness measures, the degree of control over outcomes and the responsiveness of outcomes to programs often are less obvious to program managers. When such questions arise, candidate indicators should be subjected to sensitivity analysis—that is, identifying causal factors that seem to influence these measures and determining their relative importance.

Indicators should not be rejected simply because they are sensitive to influences beyond the control of program management; indeed, this accurately portrays the real world. Rather, it should be recognized that these indicators of impact conditions are affected by numerous factors and therefore do not necessarily represent direct program-to-impact cause and effect. Moreover, it may be helpful to include selected environmental variables identified by the sensitivity analysis in the overall set of performance indicators in that these can contribute to an understanding of program successes and failures.

Data-Base Scope and Structure

Choices also must be made concerning the amount of detail to be included in the data collection and the level of aggregation at which the data are to be stored. For example, highway-accident data are recorded by type of accident, amount of damage, contributing causal factors, and so forth and may be reported for individual counties or aggregated to the state level. For performance-monitoring purposes, it might be desirable to incorporate some of the detail to afford specific comparisons, or it might suffice to include only a few summarized statewide pieces of information. This depends on how the indicators are to be used and what kinds of decisions are contemplated in response to anticipated findings.

The overall system is more efficient if it can provide a common data base that can be assessed at different levels of aggregation by different organizational units. Since performance monitoring is principally a top-managerial tool, highly aggregated data are often the most appropriate, but the same kinds of data also may be of assistance at middle-management and operating levels. Just as routine program-operation data are often entered at dispersed sites and then aggregated up through the organization, data collected explicitly for monitoring purposes can usually be disaggregated to conform to regional or organizational units as well as aggregated to the organizational or statewide level. Assuming the data are to be computerized in a centralized common data base, it is totally feasible to read in the raw data and use the computer to aggregate cases as required for particular purposes. However, given the costs of computer processing, if the data are originally available in aggregate form, it makes no sense to disaggregate cases as long as there is no express use for such detailed information.

With respect to the range of information and the sheer number of indicators involved, it should go without saying that unnecessary items not be included. The problem here is the temptation to include everything that might have potential use, items that "might be interesting to look at" even though they have no explicit purpose in the overall decision framework. A primary objective in the development and testing of data-collection instruments then is to determine which items are of greatest significance.

One approach is to include items considered to have potential significance in order to demonstrate their utility. Again, given the high costs of data collection and processing, selectivity is important. During the system development and refinement stages, less useful indicators can be culled out while others may be modified or added. Overall the trend should be to emphasize the "important few" as opposed to the "trivial many" that are candidates for inclusion simply because the data are available. Especially during the early stages it is likely that data-collection instruments will be modified, and it should be kept in mind that one appropriate action in response to monitoring results is to alter the measures. With respect to PennDOT's monitoring effort, for example, the HMMS system for tracking the maintenance program (chapter 3) is being overhauled substantially to make it simpler, less expensive, and more reliable, and the trained-observer survey (chapters 4 and 5) is being modified to clarify various forms of surface cracking and joint deterioration and to eliminate a few items that top management has not found useful.

Implementing the data component also requires decisions about computerizing the data and maintaining data files. Some of the data may already be contained in computerized data bases so that for performance-monitoring purposes, the relevant information merely needs to be extracted in aggregate or semi-aggregate form and transferred to whatever formats are being used to report the monitoring results. Original data sets developed specifically for monitoring, however, will have to be computerized in order to distill results from the raw data. Small data sets could be hand tabulated, but the size of the data sets typically involved, along with the variety of computations that may be desired, almost make computerization mandatory. If the performance-monitoring system incorporates a number of different data sets, as with the systems discussed in this book, then decisions need to be made about integrating them. It may be useful to make these various data bases "conversational," for example, so that citizen-survey responses can be interpreted in light of more objective measures of service delivery and conditions.

Furthermore, it may be desirable to link performance-monitoring data to other, more fundamental data bases that document an agency's clients or programs. For instance, PennDOT may find it useful to attach trained-observer condition counts to the Department's road log, which contains basic descriptive information on all road sections in the state's highway system. However, to do so requires compatibility between the two data bases that might not occur automatically. The desirability of linking such data sets really depends on the intended use of the data beyond performance-monitoring purposes. If the need for such integration is not clear at the outset, it probably makes more sense to develop the monitoring data bases separately until the instruments are debugged, the monitoring activity stabilizes, and the need for data-base linkage becomes apparent.

Data-Collection Responsibilities

A final issue regarding implementation of the data component concerns the assignment of data-collection responsibilities. The routine internal operating data are usually reported by agency personnel working at the operating level, often in decentralized field offices. These data, concerning workloads and costs, and so on, are typically processed for payroll and other purposes, and it should not require too much additional effort to enter them into a monitoring data file if the amount of detail is not excessive. As discussed previously, reliability checks can be instituted to assure a reasonable level of accuracy.

A distinction should be noted here between data *entry* and data *collection.* Although the data may actually be entered into an MIS by numerous field personnel at dispersed locations, the central staff unit generally managing the PMS will have ultimate responsibility for developing data-collection procedures, coordinating data collection, and assuring the reliability and validity of the indicators.

With respect to new or original data sources initiated specifically for monitoring purposes, the choice of who should collect the data is not always so clear-cut. The three major alternatives are program personnel, central-agency staff, or outside consultants. Assigning new data-collection activities to the organizational divisions responsible for managing the programs is usually the least expensive alternative because the work can be at least partially absorbed by existing personnel. However, this may be the least objective approach, particularly with effectiveness measures that tend to be more difficult to verify at a later time. Apart from the possibility of individual or organizational unit self-interest creating reactive measurement problems, it would be difficult to assure consistency across organizational units. By contrast, assigning this reponsibility to a central-staff unit—a policy-analysis shop or an auditing unit, for instance—may greatly increase the likelihood of impartial and uniform data collection, although it would probably require the hiring of additional personnel and add other real costs such as travel to the budget.

With PennDOT's trained-observer survey, for example, it was feared that district or county personnel with line responsibilities could distort condition counts positively in order to enhance their own apparent effectiveness or negatively in order to lay a stronger claim for increased resource allocations. Therefore the TOS is conducted statewide by the Operations Review Group, a central-office staff unit with no vested interest in the outcome of the survey. Furthermore, the highway sections observed in any one cycle are sampled randomly and not made known ahead of time to field personnel. This prevents counties from focusing on or diverting attention from these roads so as to influence the results. The ORG personnel are trained together and then rotated around the state in different pairs. Intermittent reliability checks are conducted on the same sample road sections in an effort to maximize uniformity in the way the observers record deficient conditions.

In some cases, the agency will not have the requisite capability inhouse to conduct widespread surveys or for other reasons will prefer to contract the data collection to an outside party. The results of a citizen survey, for example, tend to gain credibility when published reports of the findings make it clear that the survey was conducted by an external and disinterested party. One attractive option is to contract responsibilities for conducting such surveys to an independent organization having stature as a neutral agency with a public service or a "good-government" orientation. For example, if PennDOT institutes a citizen survey on an annual basis, it has been recommended that it be conducted by the Pennsylvania Economy League, a business association concerned with improving state-government operations and the economic climate in the state.

The Analysis Component

The analysis component consists of manipulating the data base, aggregating cases and breaking them down into groups, performing computations and making comparisons, all of which are intended to convert raw data into meaningful information. The data sets built up in a performance-monitoring system are often large, sometimes massive by most researchers' standards. In the case of state transportation programs, for example, the data may be based on vehicle inspections reported by thousands of service stations, maintenance work completed by hundreds of work crews, pothole counts observed on thousands of road sections, and survey responses provided by thousands of citizens. The function of the analysis component is to make this mass of data interpretable and ultimately to develop a composite picture of what the data show that will be useful to top management.

The first order of business is data reduction, using descriptive statistics to summarize response patterns so as to make the job of examining the data manageable. The mean average dollar value of vehicle damage in accidents or the percentage of citizens responding that highway conditions are satisfactory can be readily absorbed, while the raw data from which these statistics are computed are usually incomprehensible. In some cases analysis goes no further than summarizing the data, particularly in early stages of performance monitoring when the main objective is to establish a baseline against which future progress will be measured.

Beyond this starting point, however, single summary statistics are not really meaningful in terms of assessing whether program performance is meeting expectations. To make this kind of interpretation requires some frame of reference, either on a relative or absolute basis. Thus in order to provide managers with information they can use to *evaluate* performance, the analysis should stress comparisons that highlight trends, variation among units, and actual performance in light of objectives.

Basic Comparisons

Current performance levels, as measured by a set of indicators, take on added significance when they are examined over time and compared across geographic regions or organizational units. As periodic cycles of data accumulate, trends can be examined to determine whether performance is improving, worsening or staying roughly the same. Indeed, this is the basic definition of performance monitoring given in chapter 1, that is, tracking programs' progress over time. Determining whether the mean count of major cracking per mile has gone down, whether the number of transit rides per capita has gone up, or whether the percentage of citizens who report no problems concerning their latest vehicle-registration renewal has increased is of primary importance to a transportation department. When target levels for these indicators have been set, the relative performance of the most recent periods compared with former periods is of major concern, particularly when reversals in trends occur.

Cross-sectional comparisons among regions or operating units are also worth looking at because they establish "average" performance levels for the agency as a whole and identify units with superior or inferior performance. This helps pinpoint where the problems are and identifies regions or organizational units that might serve as models for improving performance. Frequently analysis combining longitudinal and cross-sectional comparisons provides the most useful information; top managers can compare regions or units in terms of their performance trends over time. For example, top management in PennDOT is interested in seeing which districts and counties are improving road condition and which appear to be stagnating or retrogressing. Similarly, the transit performance indicators overviewed in chapter 7 show which local systems have improved their percent-cost-recovery factors and which have not.

In addition to looking at relative performance over time or across units, current performance levels can be compared against absolute values derived from plans and objectives. Simply looking at the level of effort, it is often worthwhile to compare actual costs of a program with budgeted amounts and to look at actual output levels against plan. Examining process measures in this way shows whether procedural objectives are being met, whether the program is being operated according to plan. Similarly, current efficiency levels can be compared with prespecified operating standards usually expressed as unit costs or hours per unit of output completed. Management may also set targets for effectiveness such as achieving a rate of highway accidents due to faulty road conditions at or below 1 per 100,000 vehicle miles, or helping all local-transit systems to reach a 50-percent cost-recovery factor. Actual performance levels can be measured against such impact targets as a straightforward indicator of success or failure. These kinds of comparisons—actual performance levels versus plan, standard, or target—can also be extended over time and broken down by organizational units to provide a fuller picture of program performance that can help management move from monitoring results to action.

Other Analysis

The analysis can be further fleshed out by making comparisons of performance levels or trends across relevant environmental characteristics. For example, the trained-observer road-condition data are most informative when broken down by maintenance functional class or pavement type in addition to districts and counties. Top management needs to know not only where the most severe problems occur but also on what type of roads. Along these same lines, it often helps to break citizen-survey data down by basic respondent characteristics, for example, in order to find out if dissatisfaction with transit service is spread out fairly evenly across age groups or heavily concentrated among senior citizens. One convenient way to display such comparisons is to use a format like the one shown in table 8–5 which presents the response patterns to a single key survey question for categories of respondents grouped by age, sex, county, and so on. A similar format could be used to communicate improvement in highway condition, for instance, with a table showing the change in the pothole count per mile for each functional class and then for each district. Alternatively, comparisons of means tables could be developed showing mean counts per district and by functional class.

One additional kind of analysis that may prove useful is to make comparisons across types of performance indicators. In particular, it is useful to examine changes in effectiveness levels in conjunction with changes in outputs or intermediate results in order to determine whether a lack of effectiveness is primarily due to program failure or theory failure. Tables can be constructed to show some outcome measures, that is, accident-rate reduction, broken down by district in one column, and in an adjacent column by the dollar value of completed safety projects in those same districts. While performance monitoring is not intended to isolate cause-effect relationships with fine precision, examining the extent to which these two measures are correlated would provide a general indication of whether or not the safety-improvement projects are producing real impact.

Analytical Capabilities

While the data may be collected by diverse sets of personnel, some central-staff unit should be designated the lead agency with responsibility for coordinating the collection and the analysis. In a large organization this may naturally fit in with the other missions of a policy analysis or research unit, a productivity-improvement program, a planning and evaluation unit, or program or financial-division staff who are concerned with management control. In some cases the analysis will be conducted internally by the central staff, but for those data bases used first and foremost for immediate programming and operating purposes, different organizational units may want to perform detailed analysis on their own. The role of the PMS unit in these cases would be to develop the analytical framework and reporting formats to be used for monitoring purposes.

Depending on how extensive the PMS and how much of the work is done inhouse, the analysis may occupy one individual or a small staff full or part time. Most of the analysis is descriptive and straightforward and does not usually require highly sophisticated techniques. In cases where data are collected on a sample basis, simple inferential statistics such as *t*-tests, chi-square and the like should be used to test for statistical significance. Thus the staff should have a moderate, but not necessarily advanced, statistical capability.

The assumption underlying this discussion is that in large organizations the performance-monitoring effort will be supported by a computer system. Packaged statistical programs such as the *Statistical Package for the Social Sciences* (SPSS) and the *Statistical Analysis System* (SAS) are available to facilitate the kind of analysis illustrated in this book.[3] Also the units responsible for MIS in large organizations usually can develop formats for computer output that are geared to the reporting formats (tables, charts, figures, and so on) designed for the PMS.

In smaller organizations, the lack of a computer system by no means precludes the possibility of developing a PMS. If the volume of data processing and analysis is large, the work can be contracted out to a private vendor. More important, the whole PMS in a small unit could be scaled down to the point where meaningful monitoring results can be produced by one individual who collects data from operating units and computes the relevant summary statistics with a desk calculator.

The Action Component

Too often larger governmental agencies invest substantial resources in data collection and analysis and then fail to profit in terms of improved program performance because results are not used intelligently. The action component consists of disseminating the results of the data analysis, soliciting reactions, and making assessments of what the results mean and then developing actions accordingly. Since the rationale of the system stems from the actions to be taken, information dissemination should be keyed to the question of who needs what kind of information in order to be in a better position to make recommendations or decisions concerning programs and their objectives. Thus implementing the action component is a matter of determining the most useful information flows, developing a process for coalescing interpretations of the monitoring results, and identifying the kinds of actions to be considered based on these findings. This is clearly the most critical component in terms of guaranteeing that the PMS will feed performance data into the decision-making process.

Disseminating the Results

Performance-monitoring results can be communicated in various reporting formats and to different organizational levels. Frequently it makes sense to supply the higher levels with highly aggregated summary reports and to provide more detail on their own operations to lower levels in conformance with the hierarchical data-base structure discussed earlier. Providing detailed data to regional offices or operating units shows them how well they are performing in light of established criteria and how their performance stacks up against other units, whereas a summarized version of the same results provides top executives with a composite view of relative performance among units and for the organization as a whole.

In PennDOT, for example, the *Management Objectives Report* discussed in chapter 3 is the central format for communicating much of the information the performance indicators are intended to convey. Much of the "process data" on construction and maintenance work accomplished, dollars spent, and efficiency fit the monthly format, as do some of the highway-status indicators such as the number of bridges that are weight restricted. With aggregate, statewide data on costs, activity levels, and efficiency measures, this report provides a basic means for top management to monitor the overall operations of the Department. Similar, but more detailed, data are reported on a disaggregated basis in the *County Management Objectives Report* so that district and county managers can monitor their own operations in the same way.

Data produced by discrete and less frequent data-collection efforts, such as the trained-observer and citizen surveys, should be disseminated in separate reports. A summary of aggregate data provided by the TOS should be prepared for the Department's top management, while Bureau of Maintenance staff would need very detailed information on individual deficiencies by road type for planning and programming purposes. District engineers should receive the summary reports plus detailed reports showing the same indicators for counties in their districts, and county managers should be given the results for their counties compared with district and statewide averages.

Similarly, an executive summary of results from the citizen survey should be prepared for the Secretary and assistant secretaries, while operating bureaus would receive more detailed reports on responses to specific items relating to their responsibilities and district engineers would be given complete reports on the findings from their districts.

The kinds of effectiveness measures discussed in this book often seem more elusive than process and road-condition indicators, and from a day-to-day operating perspective, they may appear to be less useful. Yet in the long run these are the measures that indicate current levels and trends in the characteristics of major concern. Ultimately, the Department's efforts should be aimed at reducing or holding the line on user costs, accident rates, and such service characteristics as congestion and travel time. If these conditions appear to be getting worse, whether or not they can be traced directly to faulty programs, the Department should seriously consider policy changes to combat the problem. Key effectiveness indicators should be updated on an annual or semi-annual basis and reported in the *Management Objectives Report.*

One difficulty lies with the lack of a clear operational response to indicators of decreasing effectiveness. Appropriate action is usually apparent in terms of efficiency measurement but less clear as we move to system-adequacy indicators and measures of effectiveness. Performance in terms of internal operating efficiency or improving road condition is more directly under the control of the Department, whereas impacts on accidents, user costs, and service levels are subject to a host of external factors that the Department cannot manipulate.

Yet is is still useful to know whether user costs and accidents are generally decreasing over time and whether service levels are improving. If not, the indicators should prompt investigation of whether the Department can alter programs and budgets in an attempt to improve the situation. Also, by including effectiveness measures in the system, the intended linkages can be examined over the long run. If construction and maintenance activities are becoming more efficient and if maintenance work is of higher quality, is there any correspondence in road condition as measured by the trained-observer survey? If road conditions are in fact improving, is there any noticeable change in accident rates, user costs, and travel time? Monitoring real effectiveness measures will allow some analysis of these assumed relationships and will keep top management apprised of the basic conditions the programs are supposed to impact.

In general, the frequency and timing of PMS reports should be geared to the substantive nature of the indicators and the intended uses of the information being disseminated. Aspects of performance that can be easily manipulated in the short run by managers should be reported out frequently, whereas those that are less sensitive to program changes in an immediate sense can be monitored less frequently. If the information is to feed into a specific decision process such as budget allocations, the timing of reports should be keyed to that schedule. For example, the transit system performance indicators discussed in chapter 7 are useful to local-transit managers for making short-term adjustments in operations as well as for longer-term planning purposes. Thus they find it useful to review these indicators for their own system on a monthly, if not weekly, basis. However, for macro-program monitoring purposes, short-term fluctuations are not important, and annual data suffice for noting overall trends across the state and relative performance levels among systems.

Generating Reactions

While the results should be disseminated in differing degrees of detail to various organizational levels, the most important client of a PMS is top management. Performance monitoring is primarily a tool to help executives maintain direction and control over programs, but if these executives do not make assessments of what the data show and what the implications are for continuing or improving performance, the PMS cannot serve its purpose.

Monitoring is not synonymous with evaluation; while the data are objective, managers must subjectively evaluate what the data mean. Sometimes top managers are fully capable of making such assessments in light of their own experience and judgment, and other times the patterns or trends across indicators are so consistent that an evaluation of success versus failure is obvious at face value. Frequently, however, it is beneficial to involve middle- and lower-level program managers in this process. Sometimes their reactions to the data will only confirm top management's conclusions, but in other cases, their input can provide significant insight as to why the performance indicators show what they do. In general, this kind of participation is advantageous to developing internal support for a PMS by making the monitoring effort a cooperative enterprise in conformity with the general division of responsibility for program management.

One approach to making use of input from program and line managers is to incorporate their comments in the routine performance-monitoring reports. As noted in chapter 3, for example, PennDOT's monthly *Management Objectives Report* identifies major variances between planned and actual performance levels, both favorable and unfavorable. This signals recognition of apparent superior performance in the first case, and flags apparent problems when unfavorable variances are found. The next step would be to provide an opportunity for managers to register reactions to these variances so that their comments can be included in the report that is actually published and distributed. Such an arrangement would give these managers a chance to clear up possible misperceptions or faulty interpretations of the performance data and at the same time provide top management with additional insight as to the significance of the results that could help them determine whether the matter should be pursued further or not.

In keeping with the spirit of management by exception, this approach keys selectively to those indicators that show performance to be substantially better or worse than expected; no further commentary is solicited regarding items showing actual performance to be within an acceptable tolerance of targeted values. Frequently the major variances will change from one indicator to another in successive reporting cycles, and thus the overall system will not become cumbersome. However, a more comprehensive approach might be advantageous with respect to the less frequent, specialized data bases developed especially for performance monitoring. When the data focus directly on effectiveness measures of program performance and thus tend more to be open to alternative explanations, it may be worthwhile to solicit reactions from division and program managers to the set of findings in general, on target or off target, favorable or unfavorable.

For example, the TOS data—or perhaps a synopsis of results along with management's interpretations—could be distributed to district engineers showing performance indicators for their districts as compared with targets and/or statewide averages. District engineers in turn would review similar data on a disaggregated basis with the county managers in their districts, soliciting reactions and explanations that would then be assimilated into their reports back to top management. Citizen-survey results could be communicated to district and county managers in the same fashion but would also be distributed to line managers in other program areas included in the survey, for example, driver licensing, vehicle inspection, and mass transit.

These managers would be asked to identify both problems and successes in their program areas, as indicated by the data, and to provide their own interpretations of why some programs seem to be performing satisfactorily while others are not. Furthermore, they should be asked for suggestions for alleviating problems and expanding on successes in the hope of providing further insights for action aimed at improving program performance and the agency's overall impact.[4]

Triggering Actions

As indicated in chapter 1, the kinds of actions taken by top management in response to PMS findings could be directed to (1) the objectives, (2) the program design, or (3) the monitoring and evaluation process itself. Hopefully, the most frequent response, especially with well-established programs, is to continue on the same course of action. This is not a nondecision or inaction but a very purposeful policy of not tampering with a program when positive feedback reinforces current operations. When the PMS shows that a program's performance is strong in light of its objectives or is at least acceptable with no major problems, it usually makes sense to continue as is. If performance levels are low but it is apparent that the major reason for this has been adverse environmental conditions, it still may make sense to continue on the same course *if* the environment is in a state of flux and it appears likely that these conditions will become more favorable in the future.

In other situations the monitoring systems may show that program performance has been consistently poor despite an apparently sound program design, suggesting that unmet program objectives may not really be feasible. Perhaps environmental conditions in the long run are not conducive to achieving the objectives, or perhaps constraints on available resources preclude a level of effort that is adequate to produce a noticeable impact. Alternatively, technological constraints may prevent the internal operation of the program from producing desired outputs. Somehow the evidence indicates that factors beyond management's control prohibit specific objectives from being accomplished. When this conclusion is reached, the relevant action centers on modifying the objectives—making them less ambitious or qualitatively altering their direction—in order to make them more realistic.

Decisions to modify objectives can also be prompted by PMS findings that show that some of a program's objectives are being met while others are not, or that some of an agency's programs are performing more effectively than others. When such a pattern emerges, it could lead to shifts in priorities among the objectives in one of two directions; one response would be to focus even more on those things the program can do well and deemphasize those areas where performance is weak, or alternatively, if the unmet objectives are still felt to be worthwhile and reasonably attainable, renewed efforts may be directed toward them.

Whether performance monitoring is being carried out in conjunction with MBO or some other formal management system, there is often a mutual adjustment process between performance targeting on the one hand and program design and operation on the other. In a rational decision-making process, programs should be modified to improve effectiveness in accomplishing objectives, but objectives may also be altered or reprioritized to better reflect realistic expectations. Frequently the direction and intent of a program's objectives are clear, but the amount of improvement that can be reasonably expected, or a realistic time frame for reaching objectives may be difficult to discern. As PMS data begin to accumulate, baseline conditions and trends emerge to provide the relevant frame of reference within which targets can be recalibrated more realistically.

The most frequent rational response to negative feedback from performance monitoring is to make changes in the program. When the results show that performance is poor, and the major interpretation holds that the objectives are both important and attainable, the conclusion usually is that the problem lies with the program configuration or management. Such problems of internal program operation may become apparent from examination of the relevant "process" measures included in the PMS, or may be suggested by middle- and operating-level managers in response to top management's requests for their interpretations of the overall pattern of results.

Action here focuses on the design or operation of program components and elements. A particular component of the program or piece of the underlying logic may be isolated as the source of the problem, or it may be apparent that the overall configuration of program elements is not working. If the process data indicate that output targets are being met, the problem is theory rather than program-implementation failure, and attention should center on alternative strategies or methods for moving toward the stated objectives. For example, PennDOT may determine that road condition cannot be further improved by the prevailing crisis approach to maintenance and may therefore move to a preventive-maintenance strategy. Conversely, if process monitoring indicates that output targets are not being met, then the problem concerns implementation and internal program operation. Depending on the specifics, the appropriate action here would involve changes in the resources going into the program, including personnel, the ways in which activities are conducted, and possibly the program managers.

In some instances when the monitoring data indicate that output is below planned amounts or that the desired impacts are not occurring, an assessment of the situation suggests that the indicators being reviewed are not valid measures of actual performance. Such questioning of the indicators themselves is most often prompted by reaction from the field to the effect that monitoring data are at odds with all other sources of information about the program based on first-hand experience and familiarity, past evaluations, field reports and site visits, and other objective measures. An investigation may reveal that there are serious reliability problems with the indicators in question, in which case data-collection procedures should be tightened up to correct these problems, or the indicators in question should be eliminated from the PMS. If, instead, the indicators are found not to be valid—not really measuring the appropriate outcomes—alternative indicators should be sought and the PMS modified accordingly. Analysis may find, however, that the indicators measure the appropriate outcomes but are overly influenced by environmental factors and not sensitive to marginal progress made by the program. In such cases, the indicators should not be abandoned, but poor effectiveness readings should *not* automatically be interpreted as evidence that the program is a failure.

Sometimes performance-monitoring data consistently suggest that a program is ineffective, but the reasons why—unrealistic objectives, program versus theory failure, or inappropriate indicators—are by no means clear. There may even be internal inconsistencies among different sets of indicators, and reactions from the responsible program managers may not produce a convincing, widely shared explanation of what the data mean and what the status of the program really is. Divergent views may be forthcoming, and the result may be further confusion rather than a single interpretation and recommended course of action. At this point the most rational action is to undertake a systematic intensive program evaluation to determine whether there is indeed a problem and, if so, what should be done to correct it. While program evaluation is certainly no panacea for improved program management, evaluations triggered by the results of prior monitoring are among those most likely to produce significant and useful findings.

Implementation Strategies

Since performance monitoring is primarily a top-management tool, the impetus and continuing support for developing a PMS usually must come from the top. Given the frequent perception at middle management and operating levels that monitoring entails considerable time and effort without commensurate benefits for them, there may be little incentive at these levels to cooperate unless it is clear that top management's full support is behind the idea.

The overall strategy for implementing a PMS will depend on the organizational and programatic contexts as well as the experience and style of the top executives. For example, if managerial control across the board is the principal concern, a comprehensive approach incorporating all of the agency's programs at the outset may be in order. However, if the main concern is to improve performance in a particular program or set of programs—as with the highway programs in PennDOT—then the initial effort may focus solely on those programs. The extent of initial commitment and the pace of implementation can also vary. Sometimes conditions facilitate a more holistic, one-shot design and implementation stage such as when the agency in question already has experience with information systems and a general performance orientation, or when there is a history of performance monitoring in agencies with similar programs that can be drawn on. In such circumstances, top management may commission a plan for implementing a PMS that includes not only a data component, but also fairly well defined provisions for dissemination and utilization of the results.

Incremental Approach

More often, however, it will be preferable to move incrementally, implementing some data-collection procedures, reviewing them and modifying them when necessary, adding other measures to the system, assessing their utility and eventually reaching a decision about their continuation. While performance monitoring clearly has potential, it is not equally appropriate in all settings. At the outset a number of factors are largely unknown—for example, whether the data will be plagued by serious validity and reliability problems, whether the indicators will be sensitive to program changes or reveal meaningful time trends, whether findings will be useful in terms of prompting corrective actions, what the total costs of the PMS will be, and so forth.

Given these uncertainties, the Urban Institute report cited earlier proposes a strategy for implementing a PMS in which a formal pilot project is conducted over a two- or three-year period to experiment with performance indicators and determine whether a PMS can be useful to the agency or not. This strategy would move through the following seven steps:[4]

1. Appoint a working group and a staff director to coordinate the pilot program.
2. Involve middle- and lower-level managers in the pilot program, possibly as a task force to monitor and advise on the effort (and at the same time to become familiar with the concept of effectiveness measurement).
3. Select a set of core measures addressing the areas of greatest concern.
4. Review existing data and measures to identify those that might be easily

incorportated into the measurement effort and explore the possibility of a citizen survey (including a multiservice survey involving several departments).

5. On the basis of the results of steps 3 and 4, select a pilot set of effectiveness measures that appears to be within the available budget, with the idea that these measures will be prepared regularly for a period of several years.

6. Undertake collection of the measures for at least a two-year period, revising the scope and procedures after the first year, as seems necessary.

7. Review the utility of the information obtained. If it is not sufficiently useful, and corrective adjustments of the effort do not seem feasible, the procedures probably should be dropped. If the information obtained proves to be of value, institutionalization of the procedures to provide for regular collection and reporting (without the need for special go-ahead decisions each year) should be undertaken.

This approach is attractive because it is pragmatic. The effort focuses first on existing data sets to provide the needed measures and then explores the possibility of developing additional data sources and revising the set of measures along the way. The two- or three-year time span facilitates going beyond the initial cycles of data collection to begin to look at time trends, to identify validity and reliability problems, improve data collection procedures, develop reporting formats, to get an idea of the costs of the system beyond first-year start-up costs, and ultimately to come to a conclusion about the utility of a PMS. While this proposal does not spell out plans for developing the action component, presumably such a pilot would in fact go beyond the data and analysis components and explore ways in which the results can be fed into the decision-making process.

The Developmental Process

The evolving nature of most performance-monitoring systems cannot be emphasized strongly enough. Performance-oriented managers may be philosophically receptive to the idea of monitoring but still be skeptical of the feasibility of developing performance indicators that are likely to have policy or operational significance for them on a practical level. Thus a pilot effort in which to experiment with the indicators or give the analytical staff an opportunity to demonstrate the utility of monitoring makes sense.

Starting with data sets that are already in place is attractive because it (1) provides for a quick start, (2) entails relatively little additional cost, and (3) focuses on indicators that tend to be familiar and accepted as relevant performance criteria within the agency. This establishes an initial data base that has a degree of consensual validity and is not likely to be threatening to middle- and operating-level managers. Incorporating new perhaps more specialized and less traditional, data sources at this point is more apt to be viewed as an extension of a very legitimate process. All of this goes through a developmental process in which performance indicators from both existing and new data sources are defined, tested, reviewed and modified in an attempt to provide valid measures of the relevant aspects for program performance.

Ultimately a PMS can only gain credibility through its proven validity and usefulness. Thus, although the incremental approach focuses on the data first, the selection of indicators cannot be guided primarily by the availability or feasibility of accessing different data sources. Rather, the development of a PMS must be keyed to an overall decision framework in order to become an effective management tool. To ensure this, it is important to begin with an understanding of the programs' design and underlying logic (illustrated by the systems models used in this book) as a substantive framework for developing and selecting indicators.

While there definitely should be an overriding design in terms of performance criteria and a decision framework—what kinds of decisions can be made relative to which aspects of performance—development of the nuts and bolts of a PMS will probably be incremental. In PennDOT, for example, the term "performance indicators" has definitely been a buzzword around the Department while "performance-monitoring system" has not. This reflects an awareness throughout the Department that top management is interested in tracking performance levels and implementing data-collection procedures to do so, even though no all-encompassing formal process has been instituted for reporting the results, soliciting reactions, and triggering action. Such processes are being developed now that the strengths and limitations of the data are becoming apparent.

In general, the early cycles of data collection may be marked by reliability and validity problems and information gaps. These data should be analyzed and disseminated on a limited basis and in trial reporting formats in order to begin involving managers in interpreting the results and exploring possible uses. When additional cycles are available, however, their significance should be greatly increased because trends over time will have begun to emerge. The PMS staff should prepare executive summaries for top management and begin to systematically request comments, explanations, and interpretations from the field aimed at identifying problems and suggesting solutions. As the PMS matures, the data bases are strengthened, interpretational problems are resolved, and the data acquire stability. At this point baseline conditions and initial trends have been identified, and management will have a clearer idea of absolute performance levels, variation among units, and rates of change. This may facilitate the targeting of objectives more precisely in terms of amounts of improvement anticipated and reasonable time frames. Top management then has a way of tightening up performance-monitoring acitvities and translating results into action.

A two- or three-year trial period should be adequate for determining not only whether the data are available, valid, and not too costly but also whether they have practical significance in terms of top management's decisions regarding policies and program operation. If top management concludes that the data are interesting but not really useful in any practical sense, it should decide to curtail the effort. However, if it appears that an action component is forthcoming and the costs are reasonable, top management should probably decide to institutionalize the PMS on a regular, continuing basis as an integrated part of its overall management system.

Conclusion

This book has discussed the logic of performance-monitoring systems and described procedures for designing monitoring tools for public-sector agencies. The major emphasis has been on models of program logic that identify various aspects of performance to be monitored and on the development of data sources and specific indicators to be incorporated in a monitoring effort. Implicit throughout has been the assumption that performance-monitoring systems are worthwhile undertakings in public-service agencies, supporting many other management functions and strengthening top executives' direction and control over programs. The original premise was that by giving top managers periodic snapshots of how well or how poorly programs are performing, monitoring can contribute to improved decision making and ultimately to improved service delivery.

While a homiletic argument can be made that performance monitoring should be included pro forma in any governmental unit's capacity-building efforts, more realistically it is not always clear that a PMS will pay for itself. This is primarily because of the tendency to implement performance-*measurement* tools, sometimes on a full-scale basis, without providing adequate mechanisms for using the data to actually *monitor* the results and feed the findings into the decision-making process.

Implementing a PMS is likely to incur both direct and indirect costs. Depending on the complexity of the measurement system and the availability of existing data, data collection can become quite expensive. To this may be added organizational strain emanating from additional work requirements imposed on personnel, as well as the possibility of adverse reaction to the perceived threat of generating negative assessments of performance. The benefits of a PMS will outweigh these costs *only* if the development of a monitoring system goes beyond the data-collection stage. Initial activities necessarily focus on development of the data component, but the whole effort will be of limited use if the analysis and action components are not subsequently implemented.

The likelihood of implementing a PMS, and more importantly the potential utility of a PMS to a particular organization, will depend on many factors. Management style, the general orientation toward service delivery and organizational maintenance, the range of discretionary decision making, the interplay of static and dynamic characteristics of major programs, as well as the relative importance of uncontrollable environmental factors and the more manipulable program factors in affecting final impact, will influence the degree to which monitoring might serve an agency's needs. Additionally, the general saliency of major programs in the political arena, along with interorganizational and even intergovernmental relations, can be expected to influence management's receptivity to monitoring.

The perspective taken in this book is that performance monitoring can be a very useful tool, but it is not necessarily appropriate for all organizations. Given the wide variety of implementation strategies in terms of full scale versus partial systems, detailed measurement versus more summary indicators, and incremental development as opposed to an initial "grand design," there will usually be a range of options in trying to tailor a PMS to meet a particular agency's requirements. More than any other single factor, however, is the need for top management's support at the outset and the eventual commitment to convert data into monitoring information and use this information as one basis for decisions and actions.

Notes

1. J.M Greiner, J.R. Hall, Jr., H.P. Hatry, and P.S. Schaenman, *Monitoring the Effectiveness of State Transportation Services* (Washington, D.C. Urban Institute, 1977).

2. B. Stipak, "Local Governments' Use of Citizen Surveys," *Public Administration Review* 40, no. 5 (September/October 1980):521–525.

3. N.H. Nie, C.H. Hull, J.G. Jenkins, K. Steinbrenner, and D.H. Bent, *Statistical Package for the Social Sciences* (New York: McGraw-Hill, 1975); J.T. Helwig and K.A. Council, eds., *SAS User's Guide 1979 Edition* (Cary, N.C.: SAS Institute, 1979).

4. J.M Greiner, J.R. Hall, Jr., H.P. Hatry, and P.S. Schaenman, *Monitoring the Effectiveness of State Transportation Services,* pp. 135–136.

5. Ibid., pp. 128–129.

Appendix A:
Reportable Conditions
for Trained Observers

Roadway

Unpaved Roads

Includes all roads with surfaces of earth or cinders or a mixture of earth and aggregate such as gravel, stone, slag, or red dog.

Surface Deterioration.

Dust Layer. Any 25-foot section of unpaved road surface that does not have the physical appearance of having a dust palliative—either chemical or bituminous—applied.

Unit count: Every 25 lineal feet.

Slope. Any unpaved surface with a slope of less than half-inch per foot fall from center to edge for a minimum distance of 6 lineal feet.

Note: On curve sections the surface can slope in the direction from outside to inside edge.

Unit count: Every 25 lineal feet.

Depression. Any depression hole or corrugation that is greater than a half-inch and less than 2 inches deep and at least 1 square foot in area.

Unit count: Every 25 lineal feet.

Surface Obstructions

Pothole. Any hole 2 inches or more in depth and at least 1 square foot in area.

Note: Any pothole or cluster of potholes over 1 square yard will count as a foundation failure (broken up) rather than an obstruction.

Unit count: Each pothole.

Foreign Object. Any objects over 6 inches in any dimension lying on the surface that would cause a vehicle operator to swerve either to avoid the object or after hitting the object.

Unit count: Each object.

Foundation Failure

Soft Spots. Any area at least 1 square yard that shows signs of mud, cracking, or softness or is rutted at least 2 inches deep for at least 10 feet.

Unit count: Every 25 lineal feet.

Broken Up. A pothole or cluster of potholes over 2 inches in depth and over 1 square yard in area.

Unit count: Every 25 lineal feet.

Flexible-Base Roads

Includes all highways with a base course other than reinforced or plain cement concrete and a wearing course of bituminous concrete, liquid bituminous and aggregate brick, or block.

Surface Deterioration

Depressions. Any depression hole or corrugation that is one-half to 2 inches deep and at least 1 square foot in area.

Unit count: Every 25 lineal feet.

Minor Cracking. The presence of irregular cracks, often referred to as "mapcracking," covering at least 1 square foot in area and indicating surface deterioration.

Unit count: Every 25 lineal feet.

Joints. Any single crack or a gap in a transverse or longitudinal paving seam, including the seam between roadway and shoulder, greater than one-quarter inch wide, at least 1 foot long, and 1 inch or deeper that needs to be filled.

Unit count: Every 25 lineal feet.

Surface Obstructions

Pothole. Any hole 2 inches or more in depth and at least 1 square foot in area.

Note: Any pothole or cluster of potholes over 1 square yard in area will count as a foundation failure (broken up) rather than an obstruction.

Unit count: Each pothole.

Foreign Object. Any objects over 6 inches in any dimension lying on the surface that would cause a vehicle operator to swerve either to avoid the object or after hitting the object.

Unit count: Each object.

Foundation Failure

Major Cracking: A severe cracking pattern, covering at least 2 square feet. These cracks are interconnected and usually accompanied by some degree of settlement or deformation of surface that indicates a base failure.

Unit count: Every 25 lineal feet.

Broken Up or Mud. Any area at least 1 square yard where the pavement has fractured. This condition is usually accompanied by chunks of the pavement missing or mud pumping up from the base. Also any depressions, pothole, or cluster of potholes 2 inches or more in depth and more than 1 square yard in area.

Unit count: Every 25 lineal feet.

Rigid Base Roads

Includes all highways with a base course of plain or reinforced-cement concrete and a wearing course of bituminous concrete, brick, or block.

Surface Deterioration

Depression. Any depression hole or corrugation that is greater than one-half inch and less than 2 inches deep and at least 1 square foot in area.

Unit count: Every 25 lineal feet.

Minor Cracking. The presence of irregular cracks, often referred to as "mapcracking," covering at least 1 square foot of area and indicating surface deterioration.

Unit count: Every 25 lineal feet.

Joints. Any single crack or a gap in a transverse or longitudinal joint, including the joint in between roadway and shoulder greater than one-fourth inch wide, at least 1 foot long, and 1 inch or deeper that needs to be filled.

Unit count: Every 25 lineal feet.

Surface Obstructions

Potholes. Any hole 2 inches or more in depth and at least 1 square foot in area.

Note: Any pothole or cluster of potholes over 1 square yard will count as a foundation failure (broken up) rather than an obstruction.

Unit count: Each pothole.

Foreign Object. Any tires, tree limbs, dead animals, other objects or rocks over 6 inches in any dimension lying on the surface that would cause a vehicle operator to swerve to avoid.

Unit count: Each object or cluster of objects.

Blow Up. Any transverse joint that has heaved at least 1 inch, for its full lane width. The presence of small spalls along the edge of the joint is a common occurrence.

Unit count: Each blow up.

Foundation Failures

Major Cracking: A severe cracking pattern, covering at least 2 square feet. These cracks are interconnected and usually accompanied by some degree of settlement or deformation of surface that indicates a base failure.

Unit count: Every 25 lineal feet.

Broken Up or Mud. Any area at least 1 square yard where the pavement has fractured. This condition is usually accompanied by chunks of the pavement missing or mud pumping up from the base. Also any depressions, pothole, or cluster of potholes greater than 2 inches in depth that extend over 1 square yard in area.

Unit count: Every 25 lineal feet.

Bituminous Patch. Any bituminous patch at least 1 square yard, which was properly installed but has deteriorated to the point at which it is depressed or severely cracked or broken up, and all bituminous patches that were not placed in accordance with Department standards and usually reflect a roadway failure. This includes patches less than or equal to 100 lineal feet.

Unit count: Every 25 lineal feet.

Rigid Pavement

Includes all highways with a surface of reinforced or plain cement concrete.

Surface Deterioration

Depressions. Any spalling of the concrete surface which is one-half to 2 inches deep and at least 1 square foot in area. This depression in *not* a slab settlement.

Unit count: Every 25 lineal feet.

Minor Cracking. Any cracking that intersects two or more transverse cracks or joints and indicates surface deterioration.

Unit count: Every 25 lineal feet.

Joints. Any single crack or a gap in a transverse or longitudinal joint, including the joint between roadway and shoulder, greater than one-forth inch wide, at least 1 foot long, and 1 inch or deeper that needs to be filled.

Unit count: Every 25 lineal feet.

Surface Obstructions

Potholes. Any hole 2 inches or more in depth and at least 1 square foot in area.

Note: Any pothole or cluster of potholes over 1 square yard will count as a foundation failure (broken up) rather than an obstruction.

Unit count: Each pothole.

Foreign Object. Any objects over 6 inches in any dimension lying on the surface that would cause a vehicle operator to swerve either to avoid the object or after hitting the object.

Unit count: Each object.

Blow Up. Any transverse joint that has heaved at least 1 inch for its full lane width. The presence of small spalls along the edge of the joint is a common occurrence.

Unit count: Each blow up.

Virginia Joints. Any pavement relief joint constructed of bituminous material that has pushed up at least 1 inch or more or has settled to 1 inch or more below grade or has cracks or depressions as listed in "major-cracking."

Unit count: Each Virginia joint.

Foundation Failure

Major Cracking. A severe cracking pattern, covering at least 2 square feet. These cracks are interconnected and usually accompanied by some degree of settlement or deformation of surface that indicates a base failure.

Unit count: Every 25 lineal feet.

Broken Up or Mud. Any area at least 1 square yard where the pavement has fractured. This condition is usually accompanied by chunks of the pavement missing or mud pumping up from the base. Also any depressions, pothole, or cluster of potholes 2 inches or more in depth and more than 1 square yard in area.

Unit count: Every 25 lineal feet.

Bituminous Patch. Any bituminous patch at least 1 square yard, which was properly installed but has deteriorated to the point at which it is depressed or severely cracked or broken up, and all bituminous patches that were not placed in accordance with Department standards and usually reflect a roadway failure. This includes mechanical patches less than or equal to 100 lineal feet.

Unit count: Every 25 lineal feet.

Shoulders

Unpaved Shoulders

Includes all shoulders composed of earth or cinders or a mixture of earth and aggregate such as gravel, stone, slag, or red dog. This item includes shoulders treated with dust palliative.

Surface Deterioration

Slope. Any unpaved shoulder with a slope of less than one-half inch per foot fall between the edge of pavement and edge of shoulder for a minimum of 6 feet measured along the edge of pavement. This deficiency would be corrected by grading, shaping, and compacting the existing shoulder. Incidental material may be added or removed.

Unit count: Every 25 lineal feet.

Depressions. Any depression or hole that is less than 2 inches deep and at least 1 square foot in area.

Note: Do *not* count a uniform dropoff of less than 2 inches at edge of pavement as a depression.

Unit Count: Every 25 lineal feet.

Buildup. Any earth or debris buildup along the guardrail, the edge of the shoulder, or on the shoulder for at least 25 feet. This buildup inhibits water runoff into a drainage channel or fill slope and is usually accompanied by the formation of a secondary ditch. This deficiency would be corrected by cutting, compacting, and hauling away excess shoulder material.

Unit count: Every 25 lineal feet.

Shoulder Obstruction

Pothole. Any potholes in the shoulder surface 2 inches or more in depth and at least 1 square foot in area.

Note: Any pothole or cluster of potholes over 1 square yard in area will count as a foundation failure (broken up). All potholes at private driveways or entrances and exits to business establishments will count as driveway obstructions.

Unit count: Each pothole.

Foreign Object. Any objects over 6 inches in any dimension lying on the surface that would cause a vehicle operator to swerve either to avoid the object or after hitting the object.

Unit count: Each object.

Bad Drives. Any private driveway or entrances and exits to business establishments that contain potholes, block or redirect water runoff, change shoulder slope, or allow water to run onto the traveled surface.

Unit count: Each bad drive.

Washouts and Slides. Any washout or slide on or from the side slopes that has encroached on the shoulder surface and is over 2 inches in depth and covers an area of 1 square foot. This item also includes any erosion due to water runoff of the shoulder surface over 2 inches deep and over 10 feet in length.

Unit count: Every 25 lineal feet.

Shoulder Failures

Rutted. Any shoulder with ruts at least 2 inches deep and 10 feet long that were caused by vehicles, including areas at mailboxes where rutting is caused by mail trucks.

Unit count: Every 25 lineal feet.

Broken Up. Any unpaved shoulder that has a pothole or cluster of potholes over 2 inches deep and over 1 square yard in area.

Unit count: Every 25 lineal feet.

Dropoffs

Edge of Pavement. 2 inches to 4 inches. Any dropoff along the edge of pavement of 2 inches but less than 4 inches and running at least 6 feet long. A pavement edge dropoff includes any potholes, washouts, or rutting at least 6 feet long and at the edge of pavement.

Edge of Pavement. 4 inches plus. Any dropoff along the edge of pavement greater than 4 inches and running at least 6 feet long. A pavement-edge dropoff includes any potholes, washouts, or rutting at least 6 feet long and at the edge of pavement.

Unit count: Every 100 lineal feet.

Edge of Shoulder. Any dropoff at the outside edge of a defined shoulder that is more than 4 inches deep and running at least 6 feet long. A drainage channel is included in this item.

Unit count: Every 100 lineal feet.

Paved Shoulders

Includes all shoulders with surfaces of bituminous concrete, oil and aggregate (surface treated), and reinforced or plain cement concrete.

Surface Deterioration

Slope. Any paved shoulder with a slope of less than one-half inch fall per foot between edge of pavement and edge of shoulder for a minimum of 6 lineal feet measured along the edge of pavement. Included in this category is shoulder heaving and any area greater than 6 feet in length and less than 2 inches deep, where water fails to drain properly from the shoulder and is forming a secondary ditch.

Note: Some paved shoulders were designed in the past with a positive slope on the high side of a curve and should *not* be considered as a reportable condition.

Unit count: Every 25 lineal feet.

Depressions. Any depression, hole, or spalling of concrete that is less than 2 inches deep and at least 1 square foot in area.

Note: Do not count a uniform dropoff of less than 2 inches at the edge of pavement as a reportable condition.

Unit count: Every 25 lineal feet.

Minor Cracking. Any bituminous concrete or surface-treated shoulders with the presence of irregular cracks, commonly called "mapcracking," at least 1 square foot in area or any cracking on concrete shoulders that intersect two or more transverse cracks or joints covering at least 1 square foot in area. This type of cracking would indicate a surface deterioration.

Unit count: Every 25 lineal feet.

Raveling. Any area of a surface-treated shoulder at least 2 square yards in area that has a progressive separation of aggregate particles from the surface downward or the edges inward.

Unit count: Every 25 lineal feet.

Buildup. Any earth or debris buildup along the guardrail, the edge of the shoulder or on the shoulder for at least 25 feet. Buildup indicates that excess material, which inhibits water runoff into a drainage channel or fill slope and usually forms a secondary ditch, must be hauled away.

Unit count: Every 25 lineal feet.

Shoulder Obstructions

Pothole. Any potholes in the shoulder surface 2 inches or more in depth at least 1 square foot in area. All potholes at private driveways or entrances and exits to business establishments will count as a driveway obstruction.

Note: Any pothole or cluster of potholes over 1 square yard in area will count as a foundation failure (broken up).

Unit count: Each pothole.

Foreign Object. Any tires, tree limbs, dead animals, other objects or rocks over 6 inches in any dimension lying on the surface that would cause a vehicle operator to swerve to avoid.

Unit count: Each object.

Washouts and Slides. Any washout or slide on or from the side slopes that has encroached upon the shoulder surface and is over 2 inches in depth and covers an area of 1 square foot. This item also includes any erosion due to water runoff of the shoulder surface over 2 inches deep and 10 foot in length.

Unit count: Each washout or slide.

Bad Drives. Any private driveway or entrances and exits to business establishments that contain potholes, block or redirect water runoff, change shoulder slope or allow water to run onto the traveled surface.

Unit count: Each bad drive.

Shoulder Failures

Major Cracking. Any surface-treated or bituminous concrete shoulder with "alligator-type" cracking covering at least 2 square feet indicating a base failure or any concrete shoulder with severe cracking covering at least 2 square feet indicating a base failure.

Unit count: Every 25 lineal feet.

Rutted. Any shoulder with ruts at least 2 inches deep and 10 feet long that were caused by vehicles.

Unit count: Every 25 lineal feet.

Broken Up. Any paved shoulder at least 1 square yard in area where the surface has fractured. This condition is usually accompanied by chunks of pavement missing or mud pumping up from the base. This item also includes a pothole or cluster of potholes over 2 inches deep and over 1 square yard in area.

Unit count: Every 25 lineal feet.

Dropoffs

Edge of Pavement. 2 inches to 4 inches. Any dropoff along the edge of pavement of 2 inches but less than 4 inches and running at least 6 feet long. A pavement-edge dropoff includes any potholes, washouts, or rutting at least 6 feet long and at the edge of pavement.

Edge of Pavement. 4 inches plus. Any dropoff along the edge of pavement greater than 4 inches and running at least 6 feet long. A pavement-edge dropoff includes any potholes, washouts, or rutting at least 6 feet long and at the edge of pavement.

Unit count: Every 100 lineal feet.

Edge of Shoulder. Any dropoff at the outside edge of a defined shoulder that is more than 4 inches deep and running at least 6 feet long. A drainage channel is included in this item.

Unit count: Every 100 lineal feet.

Drainage

Obstruction

Nonfunctional Ditch. Any section of ditch at least 6 feet long that is 50 percent or more filled with dirt, stones, or debris, contains standing water, or any condition that causes the ditch to be nonfunctional due to an inadequate slope of less than one-eighth inch fall per foot. This includes curbed areas where dirt, stones, or debris, at least 18 inches wide and 2 inches deep, is blocking the flowline at the curb.

Unit count: Every 100 lineal feet.

Nonfunctional Inlet. Any inlet or endwall that is full of dirt, stones, or debris to a height at least one-half of the pipe opening, any grate that is greater than 50 percent blocked or any condition that impedes the flow of water into the inlet.

Unit count: Each inlet.

Pipe Half-Full. Any cross-pipe or culvert, including bridges and boxes to a span of 20 feet, which is at least 50 percent filled at either end. Pipes and culverts more than 10 feet below the roadway are not included.

Unit count: Each pipe.

Pipe Count. Each cross-pipe or culvert shall be tallied in this category regardless of its condition.

Unit count: Each pipe.

Failures

Bad Pipe. Any pipe or culvert with the bottom missing or crushed.

Unit count: Each pipe.

Nonfunctional Endwalls. Any endwall that is tilted or broken and does not provide support to the slope at its back or any inlet that is severely cracked, spalled, collapsed or is missing a grate where one is required.

Unit count: Each endwall or inlet.

Appurtenances

Bad Striping. Any centerlines or edge lines that are no longer visible or almost invisible for at least 50 lineal feet. Do not count those roads on which lines have never been provided.

Unit count: Every 500 lineal feet.

Guardrail. Rotted posts. Any wooden post that is rotten and either fails to support its restraining element or is totally deteriorated at or near the ground level. Questionable posts may be tested via a firm shove or kick. Rotted posts may be tallied in curb areas where it has been determined that the posts are maintained by the Department.

Unit count: Every 100 lineal feet.

Guardrail. Nonfunctioning elements. Any restraining element that is missing, damaged, or mislocated to the point where it is nonfucntional. Where the entire fence is either too high or low because of improper shoulder grade or successive overlays—if the fence is otherwise satisfactory, this will not be counted as being nonfunctional. Examples of nonfunctional guardrail are a cable that is loose and out of place by 6 inches or greater; end-anchor not fastened and any panels disconnected at one end or crushed. Nonfunctioning elements may be tallied in curb areas where it has been determined that the guardrail system is maintained by the Department.

Unit count: Every 100 lineal feet.

Guardrail. Median barrier. Any restraining element such as a box or "w" section that is missing or damaged so as to render it nonfunctional.

Unit count: Every 100 lineal feet.

Signs

Regular Signs: Any sign that is missing; definite evidence of sign having been there, post in ground, sign laying down, or does not function properly day time or night time, 10 percent of message obliterated or 25 percent of reflective material missing. This item includes guide, directional, or warning signs.

Unit count: Each sign.

Delineators. Any delineator post whose reflective paint is badly deteriorated or any delineator that is missing or damaged or misaligned from its intended direction so as to render it nonfunctional. Misalignment in the horizontal direction may be no more than 20 degrees and no more than 10 degrees in the vertical.

Unit count: Each delineator.

L.R. or Station Markers. Any L.R., station marker, or mile marker that is missing, deteriorated to the point of being unreadable, or damaged so as to render it nonfunctional. Station markers should be at least each 1,000 feet. Mile markers are placed at intervals of either 200 feet or 0.1 mile.

Unit count: Each L.R. or station marker.

Litter. Two pieces of visible litter; cans, bottles, or paper, and so on, on or near the shoulder in any 25-linear-foot section.

Unit count: Every 25 lineal feet.

Appendix B:
Citizen-Survey
Cover Letter and
Questionnaire

THE PENNSYLVANIA STATE UNIVERSITY
COLLEGE OF THE LIBERAL ARTS
UNIVERSITY PARK, PENNSYLVANIA 16802

Institute of Public Administration
211 Burrowes Building

Area Code 814
865-2536

November 1981

Dear Pennsylvania Motorist,

You are one of a small number of people selected at random
from the 7 million licensed drivers in Pennsylvania to participate
in a statewide survey. This survey is being conducted in order to
obtain citizens' views on a variety of transportation-related
issues, including the condition of highways in Pennsylvania and
the performance of PennDOT in maintaining state roads. Results of
the study will be shared with PennDOT officials.

Your participation is voluntary and your answers will be kept
confidential. Your name will never be placed on the questionnaire.
Because it is important that the results reflect the opinions of a
representative cross-section of all Pennsylvanians, we urge you
to complete this survey and return it in the enclosed postage paid
envelope within one week. This is your chance to make your opinions
known!

Thank you for your help and cooperation.

Sincerely,

Ted Poister
Project Director

Enc.

PENNSYLVANIA ROAD USERS' SURVEY

1. How long have you been a licensed driver in Pennsylvania?

   (1) Less than 2 years _____   (3) 11-20 years   _____

   (2) 2-10 years   _____   (4) More than 20 years _____

2. Do you own or have regular access to a motor vehicle?

   (1) Yes _____   (0) No _____

3. About how many miles do you usually drive...

   <u>per week</u>   or   <u>per year</u>

   (1) Less than 100 miles _____   (1) Less than 5,000 miles   _____

   (2) 100-200 miles   _____   (2) 5,000-10,000 miles   _____

   (3) 200-400 miles   _____   (3) 10,000-20,000 miles   _____

   (4) More than 400 miles _____   (4) More than 20,000 miles _____

4. In an average week, about how much of your driving is within
   your home county?

   (1) Almost all of it   _____   (3) Less than half   _____

   (2) Half or more than half _____   (4) Almost none of it _____

5. How would you describe the present condition of state roads in
   your county?

   Very   Very
   (1) Good_____ (2) Good_____ (3) Fair_____ (4) Poor_____ (5) Poor_____

6. During the past two years, do you think the condition of state
   roads in your county has become better, worse, or stayed the same?

   (1) Better _____   (3) Stayed the same   _____

   (2) Worse _____   (4) No basis for comparison _____

7. How would you compare the condition of state roads in your home
   county with the condition of state roads in other Pennsylvania
   counties?

   (1) Better _____   (3) About the same   _____

   (2) Worse _____   (4) No basis for comparison _____

8. Are you regularly employed outside the home at least 20 hrs. per week?

   (1) Yes _____   (0) No _____   (If "no," go to question 12.)

9. How do you normally commute to work?   (1) Car_____   (2) Rail_____

   (3) Bus_____   (4) Walk_____   (5) Park and ride_____   (6) Carpool_____

   (7) Bicycle_____   (8) Other_____

10. How far do you commute <u>one way</u>?   _____miles

11. How long does it usually take you to get to work? _____min. or _____hrs.

12. Do you ever have difficulty getting to work or other places you
    need to go because of transportation problems?

    (1) Never_____ (2) Rarely_____ (3) Some of the time_____ (4) Often_____

    A. If "some of the time" or "often," why? (Check all that apply.)

    _____ Rough roads   _____ Speed limits too low

    _____ Traffic congestion   _____ Lack of adequate public
                                             transportation
    _____ Traffic signals don't work
          or are not located where   _____ No convenient direct route
          needed
                                       _____ Other (please specify):
    _____ Closed roads or bridges
                                       _____

13. (If you don't work outside the home or don't commute to work, go
    to question 14.)

    Suppose there were a toll road that would save you time in driving
    to work. Please circle the maximum toll you would be willing to
    pay for each of the time savings indicated below.

Reduction in Travel Time	Would Not Use	Maximum Toll You Would Be Willing To Pay				
5 min.	0	$.10	$.25	$.50	$1.00	$2.00
10 min.	0	$.10	$.25	$.50	$1.00	$2.00
15 min.	0	$.10	$.25	$.50	$1.00	$2.00
20 min.	0	$.10	$.25	$.50	$1.00	$2.00
30 min.	0	$.10	$.25	$.50	$1.00	$2.00

14. On a scale of 1 to 10, "1" representing an extremely rough, barely
    passable road, and "10" representing a road that is perfectly smooth,
    how would you rate the present overall riding condition of state roads
    in your county? (Circle the number that best represents your rating.)

        1   2   3   4   5   6   7   8   9   10
    Extremely   Perfectly
    Rough Ride   Smooth Ride

15. Recognizing that improving the condition of roads will cost more
    money, what level of riding condition do you think should be main-
    tained on state roads in your county? Again "1" on the scale
    represents an extremely rough road, and "10" represents a road that
    is perfectly smooth.

        1   2   3   4   5   6   7   8   9   10
    Extremely   Perfectly
    Rough Ride   Smooth Ride

16. How many licensed cars in operating condition are there in your
    household? _____ cars

17. In the past year, have you had to make repairs to any of the cars
    in your household because of damage due to poor road conditions?

        (1) Yes _____   (0) No _____   (2) Don't know _____

    If "yes,"
    A. How much would you estimate that repairs for damage due to
       poor road conditions cost you or members of your household
       in the past year? $_____

18. Have you ever contacted a PennDOT county or district office to
    complain about a road condition or other problem?

        (1) Yes _____   (0) No _____

    If "yes,"
    A. Was the problem resolved to your satisfaction?

        (1) Yes _____   (2) Still pending _____   (0) No _____

    B. How would you describe PennDOT's response? (Check all that apply.)

        _____ Personnel were courteous and helpful.

        _____ Problem was corrected promptly.

        _____ Problem was never corrected or not corrected satisfactorily.

        _____ Too much "run around" or "red tape."

        _____ Had to keep pressuring them to get results.

        _____ Personnel were not courteous.

        _____ Other (please specify): _____

19. In the past two years, have you experienced any difficulty in
    obtaining your driver's license?   (1) Yes _____   (0) No _____

    If "yes," A. Did you receive the license later than you expected?

                        (1) Yes _____   (0) No _____

               B. Was an error made by PennDOT?

                        (1) Yes _____   (0) No _____

20. In the past two years, have you experienced any difficulty in
    obtaining your vehicle registration?   (1) Yes _____   (0) No _____

    If "yes," A. Did you receive the registration later than you expected?

                        (1) Yes _____   (0) No _____

               B. Was an error made by PennDOT?

                        (1) Yes _____   (0) No _____

21. Age: (1) Under 20_____   (2) 20-34_____   (3) 35-49_____   (4) 50-64_____
          (5) Over 64 _____

22. Sex: (1) Male _____   (2) Female _____

Thank you for completing this survey.

                                            County Code _____

Index

About the Author

Theodore H. Poister is an associate professor of public administration at The Pennsylvania State University, where he divides his time between teaching and research in public-program and public-policy analysis. His principal interests are in applied-research methodology, urban management, and transportation policy. He is the author of *Public Program Analysis: Applied Research Methods* and coauthor of *Applied Program Evaluation in Local Government* (Lexington Books, 1979), and his articles have appeared in *Transportation Research Record* and *Traffic Quarterly* as well as *Public Administration Review, Journal of Criminal Justice, Public Productivity Review,* and *Evaluation Review.* Dr. Poister has also served as a consultant to several state and local agencies.